PRAISE F

BASIC TRAI

"Tim Kimmel instructs like a spiritual drill sergeant who knows how to get men across their daily battlefi̶e̶l̶d̶ ̶.̶ ̶.̶ ̶.̶ ̶i̶n̶ ̶o̶n̶e̶ ̶p̶i̶e̶c̶e̶.̶ ̶H̶i̶s̶ ̶b̶o̶o̶k̶ ̶r̶e̶a̶d̶s̶ like a riveting war novel while teach̶.̶.̶.̶ a strong leader, a moral businessma̶n̶ love most."

Congre̶.̶.̶.̶

"God's men have been at war for thousands of years. In *Basic Training*, Tim Kimmel provides timely humor and meaningful encouragement to those men who find themselves battle fatigued. I think you'll come away from *Basic Training* with a new resolve to fight the good fight."

Steve Farrar
Author of Point Man

"A new book by Tim Kimmel is a welcome announcement! I've learned to listen to and trust Tim's insights ever since I read *Little House on the Freeway* a decade ago. My prayer is that this new work will impact as many as his earlier ones."

Max Lucado
Author of In the Grip of Grace

"Across our great land, men are stepping forward to answer God's call for moral leadership. I'm consistently reading and finding tools that can help men fulfill that calling and keep their promises. *Basic Training* is a well-organized plan that can help equip you to lead, love, and serve courageously. Tim Kimmel will make you think, make you laugh, and inspire you to change into the kind of man God wants you to be."

Coach Bill McCartney
Founder and CEO of Promise Keepers

"Tim Kimmel's new book, *Basic Training*, is an original and thought-provoking work, filled with good advice for men who wish to improve their walk of faith."

Dan Quayle
44th Vice President of the United States

soldier knows it—good training is the making of the warrior. The more basic the better. And every good soldier knows the value of the field manual. A field manual provides the basic information necessary to equip the soldier to handle the variety of situations he will face in the field. Complex or simple, high or low, sublime or ridiculous, the field manual will tell you how to do it. The field manual is an instruction manual. It sticks to the basics. And it's for every soldier. Tim Kimmel has put together a solid basic training manual for every man wishing to win the battles facing him in this combative day and culture. Fall in, guys. It's a worthy mission!"

Stu Weber
Author of Tender Warrior

BASIC
TRAINING
FOR A FEW GOOD MEN

TIM KIMMEL

THOMAS NELSON PUBLISHERS
Nashville • Atlanta • London • Vancouver

Published in Nashville, Tennessee, by Thomas Nelson, Inc., Publishers, and distributed in Canada by Word Communications, Ltd., Richmond, British Columbia.

Unless otherwise noted, the Bible version used in this publication is the HOLY BIBLE, NEW INTERNATIONAL VERSION ®. Copyright © 1973, 1978, 1984 by International Bible Society. Used by permission of Zondervan Publishing House. All rights reserved. Scripture quotations noted NKJV are from THE NEW KING JAMES VERSION. Copyright © 1979, 1980, 1982, Thomas Nelson, Inc., Publishers. Scripture quotations marked NASB are taken from the NEW AMERICAN STANDARD BIBLE ®, © copyright The Lockman Foundation 1960, 1962, 1963, 1968, 1971, 1972, 1973, 1975, 1977. Used by permission. Scripture quotations noted KJV are from the King James Version of the Bible.

Library of Congress Cataloging-in-Publication Data

Kimmel, Tim.
   Basic training : for a few good men / Tim Kimmel.
     p.   c.m.
   Includes bibliographical references.
  ISBN 0-7852-8694-3
   1. Men—Religious life. 2. Christian life. I. Title.
BV4528.2.K56 1997
248.8'42—dc21   97–3884
                                            CIP

Printed in the United States of America.

3 4 5 6 — 02 01 00 99 98 97

THIS BOOK IS DEDICATED TO MY FATHER,
J. HOWARD KIMMEL,
WHO DIED WHILE I WAS WRITING IT.

HE WAS A GOOD MAN
WHO LOVINGLY PUT ME THROUGH
BASIC TRAINING.

CONTENTS

ACKNOWLEDGMENTS

Most authors don't slip away to a cabin in the mountains and come home a few days later with a completed manuscript on their hard drive. If it were that easy, everybody would publish. In most cases it takes several trips to the cabin, and a cast of dozens to the see the project turn from a passion in a writer's soul to a six-by-nine message on a shelf.

First of all, someone had to throw me the keys to their cabin. For that, I owe a huge thank you to Steve and Barbara Uhlmann.

Meanwhile, the lights stayed on at the office and the phone kept getting answered. Many thank yous to Holly Warnol, Tiffany Winkler, Shirley Foster, and Sharon Hustead for keeping the ongoing work at the Generation Ministries office running smoothly and for helping me in the long list of details that came with completing the project.

It's difficult for a book to rise above the standard of its publisher. I wanted to make sure that this message to men was entrusted to a team of people who had a reputation for excellence. I'm proud to have the Thomas Nelson logo on the spine of this book. A special thanks to five good men who played a key role in seeing this message move from an itch in my heart to the book you hold in your hands: Byron Williamson, Rolf Zettersten, Bruce Nygren, Victor Oliver, and Brian Hampton. These are men who have given their professional lives to multiplying messages of hope, help, and healing. I salute you.

I'm grateful for my literary representative, Steve Green. You have a quiet but thorough way of getting everyone on the same page and keeping us there.

When everything's said and done, the greatest joy of my life is when I go home at night. To my children: Karis, Cody, Shiloh, and Colt, thanks for your patience and encouragement during the writing process. And for the best reason I know of for why a man should marry, thank you, Darcy, for your tireless strength.

CHAPTER 1

GROUND POUNDERS

I couldn't stop shaking. My shoulders dug into the back wall of the Huey as it lifted out of the elephant grass and made its turn toward the river. Mortars kept exploding all around us, and bullets ripped across the clearing from the tree line. One buried itself in the fuselage just above the door opening and just inches from the starboard gunner's helmet. He screamed an expletive while leaning on his tether cable and maintaining a constant return of fire into the jungle. Hot casings from his .50 caliber machine gun sprayed back into the helicopter and stung my legs. *They're going to get us. We're going down.*

Someone swore at the pilot to hurry. He swore back while changing the pitch on the rotor blades and increasing the throttle. Another voice, up close, was crying out. He was only a few feet across the floor of the helicopter from me, but I still couldn't make out who he was. His legs kept jerking in violent spasms, and he fought the corpsman trying to shoot the morphine into his arm.

Off in the distance I could see an A-6 Intruder that had launched about fifteen minutes earlier from a carrier somewhere in the South China Sea. He was in a sharp bank to his left and lining up to drop his napalm over the hell we had just fought in. The starboard gunner stopped firing and yelled toward the enemy, "And the weather for the delta is clear skies, light breeze out of the southwest, AND 980 BOILING

DEGREES!" He laughed as he gave them one last burst of machine-gun fire. The bombs tumbled from the Intruder and turned the tree line into an inferno. All I could manage to do was hug my M16 close to my chest and shake uncontrollably.

The explosions rattled the windows next to my bed and brought my body from a deep sleep to a sitting position in a split second. "What the . . . ?" The third explosion brought me to my feet and out the door of my bedroom to the hallway. They had come from somewhere outside and toward the front of our house. I looked across the living room through our open front door. The screen door on the front porch was closed, but I could see through it enough to observe my mother standing in the front yard looking east toward the end of our street. Her hands were on her face, and her mouth was dropped open in a contorted look of shock.

Instantly, wearing nothing but my underwear, I was through the screen door. Mom fought me as I pushed her back into the house. She wanted to see what was going on. "Too bad, Mom, you've got to get in the house. You're in the line of fire." Two county police cars were parked sideways in front of our house while their occupants hid behind them with their guns drawn. I looked toward the end of our street. Our next-door neighbor's dogwood tree blocked part of my vision, but from the brief glance I got, I thought I saw my neighbor from two doors down and across the street standing with his deer rifle aimed at the cops. "What the . . . ?"

It was July 6, 1968. Saturday. My birthday. My *eighteenth* birthday.

As I headed for bed the night before, my father reminded me that when I got up in the morning, I had to get into town before noon to register for the draft. He said he wanted to ride in with me. When I told him I didn't think the Selective Service offices were open on Saturday, he simply said, "Yes, they are. I checked. Happy birthday!"

The year 1968 had been one that everyone was hoping to soon forget. Every village and hamlet of America was caught in a cross fire of divergent convictions and conflicting ideals. The war in Vietnam had polarized the people. The old school, World War II vets and the generation before them, maintained a choke hold on the belief that any conflict America chose to get involved in must be worthy of our support. Members of the longhaired, dope-sucking generation who were supposed to fight that war for them had other ideas. They had asked some simple questions such as *why* and hadn't been satisfied with the answers they had received. The land of the free and home of the brave was under siege, and I found myself center stage in that drama wearing nothing but my underwear while trying to keep my mother from getting her head blown off.

BORN IN THE USA

The morning I woke up out of one nightmare to face the other one in my front yard would burn in my brain as a metaphor—a little slow-motion parenthesis at the pinnacle of my youth. It illustrated the contradictory world in which I lived.

Let's back up for a second and get some context. First of all, I wasn't a dope-sucking hippie during my teenage years. I was a predictably conservative thinker born and raised in a church-going Republican family. I did have a drug problem. I was drug to Sunday school, drug to church, and drug to prayer meeting. I never took illegal drugs. My father would have killed me. I didn't even try them.

I didn't grow up on the wrong side of the tracks. I grew up on the tracks. I was reared in a family that teetered on the thin line that separates barely having enough and having all you need. My neighborhood was a quiet resort community just south of Annapolis, Maryland. That's what made the rifle fire so frightening. Up to that point, things like that just had not happened.

I was the third son of Howard and Winefred Kimmel, living in the third house on the left at the end of a dead-end street. But I didn't have a dead-end life. I had been loved, I was taught right from wrong, I had a sense of respect drilled into me, and I had a strong love for my country stirring deep down inside me. I teared up when soldiers passed by in parades (still do), and I believed that God had indeed shed his grace on America.

But the 1960s had taken their toll on everyone. And 1968 had been the year when everything seemed to hit critical mass.

The Tet offensive started in January. Martin Luther King, Jr., had met a sniper's bullet that spring. The dirt was still fresh on Bobby Kennedy's grave over in Arlington Cemetery.

We as a nation were paying a heavy price to stop the onslaught of communism in Southeast Asia but at the same time had embraced one of its fundamental presuppositions: "the end justifies the means." In order to live out the philosophy of the end justifies the means, you have to eliminate a clearly stated set of absolute standards. We did that. As a nation we decided that God really gave Moses the Ten Suggestions when he hiked up Mt. Sinai. He came down with them written on a couple of Etch-A-Sketches.

It went downhill from there. When a nation decides there are no true points on the moral compass—no absolute north of right and wrong—it makes way for the contamination of leadership. Leadership's job, among others, is to give the people who follow a sense of vision. But we were adrift, and the people who were supposed to be leading us were not certain where they were trying to take us.

What caused me some fitful nights of sleep as I counted down to my eighteenth birthday was not that I might have to go into the service or even that I might have to stand in harm's way, but that I might have to do all of that when the people sending me had lost sight of the moral horizon, and the people for whom I was fighting could care less that I went.

And for thousands of good men and women who served, there was a void waiting for them when they got home. It was a sense of having done their duty, but they were now being punished for doing it. One of the overwhelming signs that a nation or a group of people has lost all sight of purpose is turning the tables on the innocent and righteous. The past thirty-five years of our nation's history have been an ongoing legacy of protecting the guilty at the expense of the innocent, of financing the irresponsible with money from the pockets of the conscientious, of bending over backward to give the unrighteous the benefit of the doubt while vilifying the righteous when they dare stand for the truth.

THE PRICE TAG

In the area of politics, we mortgaged our grandchildren's future by strapping them with a national debt that defies the imagination. We got Watergate, the Iranian hostage crisis of the seventies, the Iran-contra affair, the check-kiting scandal, the S & L nightmare, Whitewater, Travelgate, Filegate, and Hwang Gate. Leaders who tried to stand up for right and wrong had their heads ripped off and handed back to them. Vice President Dan Quayle found out just how vicious amoral thinkers can be when he dared to criticize the standards of a fictitious character on a television sitcom. He was tarred and feathered. And then he was stalked and hounded by his detractors for the rest of his term. It was irrelevant to the press that reams of statistics and case studies could be stacked up that would validate his stand. Quayle took a bold position based on the core convictions of his heart as well as what he believed were the best interests of a nation. And for his honesty and courage, they pounded him.

In the area of academics, we mortgaged our minds. We turned our public school system into a bully pulpit for godless presuppositions. Its commitment to atheistic teaching complicated its simultaneous commitment to value-neutral education. Value neutral *always* becomes value hostile. The commitment to fairness and equality at the academic level was solved not by bringing low achievers up but by bringing high achievers down. Poor test results were solved by making tests easier rather than pushing students to learn the material more thoroughly.

This reality came home to me this past year when a friend told me of a parent-teacher forum he attended at his son's junior high. The parents were invited to the school to meet and talk with teachers in the math department and learn about the areas of mathematics that were going to be covered that year. The teachers had put some samples of the algebra, geometry, and beginner calculus up on the white board for the parents to see. Unfortunately, one problem had a wrong answer. My friend, a scientist, had sat there doing each problem in his head. He assumed they put the wrong answer to the problem there deliberately so that they could demonstrate how the kids would be taught to find the correct answer. When the evening started to come to a close and they still had not mentioned anything about the problem, my friend, Michael, spoke up.

MICHAEL: The third problem you list there on the board, were you going to demonstrate for us how the kids would learn to correct it?

TEACHER: Correct it? What do you mean?

MICHAEL: The answer that is on the board is incorrect. The correct answer would be _____ (and he gave the correct answer).

TEACHER: No it's not. The answer on the board is correct.

At that point Michael calculated the problem out loud for her and arrived at the answer he had given. The teacher got a big smile on her face and shifted the direction of the conversation.

TEACHER: This is a great example of what we're trying to teach the kids this year. You see, it's not as important that they get the correct answer as it is that they learn to cooperate in study groups to try to solve the problem together.

MICHAEL: But we're talking about math here. There is an equals sign in that problem. When there is an equals sign in a math problem, there is only one answer that is supposed to go to the right of it—the correct answer.

TEACHER: We're more concerned that they learn to think collectively.

MICHAEL: But I want my son to learn how to do algebra and to arrive at the correct answer.

The dialogue quickly became a debate among all of the parents as different moms and dads chimed in with their input. To Michael's surprise, the majority of the crowd sided with the teacher. They thought it was great that their children's grade was going to be determined by how much they worked with others on finding the solutions to problems. Getting the answer right was not as big an issue. Finally, the teacher came back at Michael with a question.

TEACHER: Did you see the movie *Apollo 13*?
MICHAEL: Yes.
TEACHER: Do you remember that scene where they took a half dozen scientists into a room and dumped a bunch of materials on a table and said, "Make me a filter"?
MICHAEL: Yes.
TEACHER: That's what we're trying to teach the students this year, how to work together to solve problems.
MICHAEL: Since you referred to *Apollo 13*, do you remember the scenes where scientists were sitting at their workstations running calculations over and over again on their slide rules? And ultimately, they figured out that the degree of entry the space capsule was on had to be corrected or it would bounce off the earth's atmosphere and there would be no way they could get it back to the earth. If those scientists had taken math from you, we would have lost three astronauts.

Boom! The crowd went to the teacher's defense and turned on Michael. The consensus was that the teacher's feelings were more important than whether or not the kids got correct answers.

I'll admit that Michael's words might have felt about the same as a blunt instrument to the temple. But if that was not the time to deal with the issue, then when? And if not Michael, then who? It was a good example of not only our crisis in academics, but also the cultural shift toward feeling good as opposed to being right.

In the area of law, we mortgaged our ability to protect ourselves from injustice and to punish evil. We have turned our juries into twelve people who decide which side has the best lawyer(s). And we have removed the concept of accidents from our legal vocabulary too. No one simply trips and falls anymore. It has to be the fault of the company that made the person's tennis shoes, the company that poured the concrete for the sidewalk, the city that didn't provide enough light for the jogging path, the sprinkler company that watered the grass that the man cut across before he got on the jogging trail, which in turn gave him slippery footing, or the hat company that put inferior elastic in the hat the guy was wearing down low over his eyes, and so on and so on.

In the area of entertainment, we mortgaged our leisure time and idle thoughts. Prime-time television is no longer questionable; it's dangerous. I don't think there is a dad in the country who would step aside and let people in protective suits march into his house carrying toxic waste and then proceed to let these people dump the poison all over his kids. But dads by the millions sit idly by while immoral television shows, movies, and CDs dump sexual and violent sewage all over their kids.

In the area of our families, we mortgaged our legacies. We have taken the hope out of our future by removing the moral infrastructure from our families' hearts. Too many families would be hard-pressed to define the core values upon which they are building their future. Millions of our country's children face their biggest challenge just getting out of the mother's womb alive. And then, once they're born, they are too often required to compete with their parents' busy agenda, a schedule filled with distractions, sound-bite religion, and too many dads missing in action.

THANK GOD, THERE IS A REMNANT

Despite all of this, I couldn't be more optimistic about the future for two reasons: (1) God has kept a remnant of people who have not bowed their knees to public opinion, and (2) God is recruiting large numbers of new soldiers for his army.

In all that we have been through, there has been a faithful army of believers who have not forgotten who they are fighting for and what they are fighting for. They have maintained their posts, they have followed their marching orders, and they have refused to aid and abet the enemy. We have had a legion of righteous people who have served valiantly in the political arena, the academic arena, the legal arena, the entertainment and sports arena, and have stood vigilant on the home front. They're battle weary. But they have refused to flinch.

And God is bringing in fresh troops. Men by the hundreds of thousands are signing up for active duty in the cause of Christ. There is a stirring of the soul, not just in America, but throughout the world. And God is once again asking men to swear their allegiance, take the oath of service, don their uniforms, pick up their gear, and follow him to the front lines.

But we need to be trained. Lack of training causes disillusionment among soldiers on the lines. Cracks in the lines cause defeat.

ENOUGH IS ENOUGH

I don't know about you, but I'm tired of constantly getting my tail kicked in by culture. I'm tired of seeing our streets being ruled by thugs and punks, our kids' minds being manipulated by smug elitists, the marketplace being dominated by cunning and deceit, and our families being stolen out from under us.

We need to tighten our ranks.

Ours is too good a country to lose over a couple of bad decades. Our wives and children are too precious to be left undefended. The future is too important to those coming after. It's time to take our stand.

I DIDN'T HAVE TO GO

My eighteenth birthday was a real wake-up call for me. My neighbor ended up having a very bad day. He was letting off some dangerous steam as a result of some frustrations in his family. Fortunately, no one got hurt physically. But it was painful to watch the strain it added to his family. Unfortunately, it would be just one of hundreds of such episodes I've had to personally watch in my career.

And as far as Vietnam goes, I didn't have to go. Uncle Sam told me that if I wanted to be a chaplain, I would have to go to college and have a few years of seminary. I went on to college, and while I was there, they decided to put all our birthdays in a hat and draw them out. Mine was #327. When I finally finished college, they said they didn't need me. We were pulling out of Vietnam and downsizing our armed services. But Vietnam still left its mark on my heart. It did through my friend Carl Dean and the fifty-six thousand others whose names are etched on a wall near the Lincoln Memorial. It did through the 8.7 million faithful who went and served and stood their posts, but never got their parade when they returned home. They are examples of everything good about our nation, and their treatment on their return is an example of our problem. They are overdue for the recognition they deserve for the sacrifice they were willing to make. It probably won't come in their lifetimes, and the ones I know aren't checking the mailbox every day for word of some parade planned in their honor.

But I feel certain that when the generations of the future take a stick and sift through the ashes of the Vietnam era, they will find among the antiwar posters, the protesters, and the ambivalent political leaders true nuggets of gold—the precious handfuls of faithful men and women who donned their uniforms, moved to the front, and did not flinch.

Now we all need to lock arms, get in step, and pick up the cadence for the challenge before us. We're at war again. We're up against an old enemy, but the issues are fresh, new, and real. And the spoils of this war are your wife and your kids. Don't worry about the outcome. I peeked at the last chapter of the Book. Our side wins. But in the meantime, we need to stand up, stand together, and stand strong in the power of the Lord Jesus Christ—ground pounders for God. Many individuals stand to lose if we don't. Some of them look like you. They have your chin line, your shuffle, and your mannerisms. Or maybe it's that woman you gave a ring to a while back. They're all counting on you.

You, too, will personally lose if you are not prepared to fight the battle that is raging all around you. You're going to either stand and fight or go down. There isn't any middle ground in this conflict. Since you have to fight, you might as well go into battle prepared. In the pages that follow, we're going to go through "basic" together. Join me in this spiritual boot camp. The recruiter's office is open.

STUDY AND DISCUSSION QUESTIONS

UP FRONT AND PERSONAL

1. I think this chapter is about
   a) the author's early years.
   b) the Vietnam War.
   c) taking a stand on moral issues.

2. Are you surrounded by people with clear moral compasses? What effect (good or bad) do those people have on you? Do you have your own standards of absolute right and wrong based on biblical principles?

3. What kinds of situations tempt you to modify your sense of right or wrong? Why?

4. Can you recall one time in the last thirty days you expressed a moral stand at work or home, or with friends, on an issue you felt strongly about? Would you do it again? Why or why not?

FOR THE GROUP TO DISCUSS

1. Describe an amoral thinker.

2. Do you agree or disagree with the statement "Value neutral becomes value hostile"? Explain your answer.

3. If you were Michael and faced with the stressful situation described in the visit to his child's math class, would you have handled it differently? If so, how?

4. Discuss any alternatives that might have been available to Michael.

5. Is it possible that the "tolerance" and "liberalism" some men profess are really just covers for their reluctance to state their position on important moral issues?

APPLYING GOD'S WORD

1. Read Matthew 15:14 followed by 1 Timothy 6:12–14. Apply the meaning of these passages to the concept of taking a stand in chapter 1 of *Basic Training*.

2. Pray for each other, so you might gain in strength and wisdom when it is your turn to take a stand.

CHAPTER 2

ACCIDENTAL SOLDIERS

*The only thing necessary for the triumph of evil
is for good men to do nothing.*
—Edmund Burke

Fresh barley. Its smell floated on the easy breezes coming through the barn door. The new crop was making its way through the good earth that rolled off in the distance. He loved this time of the evening.

It was almost dark as he put the finishing touches on a long day. The animals huddled quietly in the corner of the stall while he pitched a forkful of hay into their feeding trough and checked their water. They weren't hungry. They had grazed all day. But they would be by tomorrow morning. "Just in case I sleep in," he said out loud. "Consider this my idea of breakfast in bed for you guys." He laughed at his joke as he picked up the lantern and fetched his coat from the peg next to the door. It had been a long day—a long week. He could use some time off.

But there was a war on, and his three older brothers had been sent to the front lines of the conflict. There were four brothers left at home. But for some reason, he got stuck with the bulk of the sheep-keeping responsibilities. Like it or not, he was *it* until they came home. Dad was too old to be of much help.

He was the baby of the family. The dreamer. The aesthetic.

There was usually a poem sifting around in his head or some new melody that he would be humming. He had read every book in the house several times, and he loved to design mansions in his head when he worked. He should have been studying at the conservatory by now, but his brothers' call to duty left him holding down the fort until they got back—if they got back.

The word from the front was that things weren't going well. They had been in a standoff for some time. Morale was low. Rumor had it that the enemy was getting the psychological edge in a battle of wits. His dad feared that there could be a bloodbath when the enemy soldiers finally made their move. And to make matters worse, the mail between the front lines and the home front had dwindled down to nothing. His dad feared the worst. At breakfast, he had mentioned that if he didn't receive something in the mail from the boys today, he was going to have to do something desperate.

That's how David, the accidental soldier, found himself on the front lines. He didn't go looking for a fight; he went looking for his brothers. But once he got there and realized how serious the situation was, he didn't hesitate to move from the safety of the bunker to stand toe-to-toe with Goliath.

You know the story. It's classic Sunday school stuff. It's so much a part of the backdrop of world literature that even the biggest skeptics of the faith refer to their most imposing challenges of life as their "Goliaths." But I believe the incident actually took place. I feel confident that if we could slip through a time warp and go back to a certain date and a certain location, we would see David, the accidental soldier, knock Goliath's lights out.

David is a good example of the kind of soldier God has called each of us to be. We don't have to go around looking for a conflict, but when one comes our way, we don't hesitate to take our stand. It's the least we can do or should do. All may seem quiet on the home front, but if you listen closely, you can pick up the shifting gears and moaning engines of the enemy's forces as they move within artillery range of the people you love. You may not see them now, but they're out there.

YOU'RE IN THE ARMY NOW

When David slapped Goliath upside his head with that rock, he was surrounded by an army of soldiers who had found themselves on the battlefield for at least three reasons.

1. SOME ENLISTED

Like all wars from the beginning of time, a call was sent out across the land for volunteers. There was a threat to the people's welfare. The enemy army was forming on the borders. The people they loved had something to lose if they didn't go and something to gain if they did. Standing on the hill, up behind David, were many men who had answered the call. His brothers might have been among them.

2. SOME WERE DRAFTED

In David's day, this was most likely how men found themselves on the front lines. A king could simply order them into battle. In peacetime, a volunteer army is usually adequate to maintain a political and civil status quo. But when a conflict is brewing, wise governments anticipate their need and start drafting soldiers. When you have the enemy breathing down your neck, there is often a scramble to fill the ranks. Getting the soldiers trained and equipped in such a short time becomes a problem. That's why a lot of countries maintain an ongoing Selective Service program.

3. SOME WERE SOLDIERS BY DEFAULT

David is the only person we know of there at the battle scene who wasn't a soldier. But that doesn't mean he was the only one. If his father, Jesse, sent a civilian to the front lines, it's safe to assume that other parents did the same thing. Some enemies have less compassion than others. When they invade, they kill everything in their path. In those situations, a civilian has to do what he has to do to survive.

In fact, civilians play a key role in the success of any army. Civilians form part of the crucial lifeline to the soldier's physical, emotional, and spiritual needs. David had searched out his brothers so that he could check on their welfare, deliver personal supplies, encourage them, and take their greetings back to his father. It just so happened that while he was there,

Goliath made the mistake of showing up and speaking out. That was when David felt compelled to shut him up.

David actually brought an advantage to the battlefield that the soldiers there didn't have. For these very same reasons our military maintains a constant flow of civilian advisers. Sometimes an outsider can see things that people up close can't.

I've heard the story of David and Goliath since I was a little kid. Most of the times I've heard it developed by a Bible teacher, a lot of effort has been put into painting the Israelite army as a bunch of cowards. I don't think they were, at least not at the outset of the battle. They had simply learned hopelessness by the time David got there.

When Goliath first came out to make his challenge, I believe it is fair to assume that there was a genuine desire among the leaders to deal with his threat. The problem was that he was challenging them individually, but they had been trained to think like an army. The scenario hadn't been dealt with in their strategy classes back at the academy. Taking Goliath on, on his terms, created a host of headaches for the leaders besides the obvious one of his shish kebabbing the guy who ultimately went out to face him. Who should go? Should it be an officer or a noncom? Should we take him on at the morning threat, when we have all day to fight the rest of the Philistines, or should we wait until his evening threat in case we lose (1 Sam. 17:16)? If we just ignore his individual threat and send a platoon out after him, what does that say about us as an army or as individuals? What if we send a guy, and he loses? Do we really have to become slaves?

Regardless, after hearing a nine-and-a-half-foot man challenge them, call them cowards, and insult their God eighty times in a row, they had lost their courage. David had the luxury of hearing him only one time. And he came from a context of a daily musing on the Word of God, a daily singing of praises, and a daily maintenance of work disciplines. Those practices, along with his confidence in the power of Jehovah over any enemy, sent him out to meet the giant.

His work as a shepherd had done two things that came in handy at that point in his life. First, it had made him strong. If you think walking around in the hills leading a bunch of sheep all day is wimpy work, you haven't done it lately. You have to be in good shape. You have to take on the elements. The extreme hots and colds as well as the storms that rumble over the hills make you tough. Second, he had been forced to become accurate with a slingshot. His years of practice and his strength merged with his courage and confidence to make him a lean, mean fighting machine.

When Goliath made the challenge, David took it personally. He saw Goliath as a threat against his own welfare and everything he held near and dear. All of those factors converged to draw him into the battle by default.

At some point you joined the army of the Lord Jesus Christ. Maybe you walked down an aisle at your church, prayed with a friend, or opened your heart to Jesus in some quiet, private moment. Maybe the exact time is murky in your mind or as clear as the nose on your face. Regardless, you ended up in the army of the Lord Jesus Christ.

This is where the rub occurs for a lot of men. They have a small misconception about their conversion to Christ that causes them to spend the bulk of their Christian life in either mediocrity or defeat. They don't realize they are being inducted into an *army*. They see their conversion more like joining a fraternity.

KAPPA GAMMA WHATEVER . . .

Fraternity row at the average university is a long way and a far cry from the barracks at the army base. In a fraternity, you are "brothers." You live together in harmony and understanding. You sit together at football games and do your special fraternity cheer. You wear your fraternity sweaters to class and try to look superior when a guy wearing a sweater from another fraternity walks by. You keep a close relationship with a sorority and have beer busts with the members on Saturday night. You stay up late working on the float for the homecoming parade and sleep through your classes the next day.

You keep to yourselves and discourage new freshman guys you meet from joining other fraternities. And if you meet a freshman who wants to be in your fraternity, but doesn't meet your self-imposed standards, you blackball him. Occasionally, you put on dark clothes and pull a good old fraternity prank such as putting a cow in the girls' dormitory or some student's car in the library. Then you sit up the rest of the night talking about how brave you were stealing that cow or how clever you were thinking of the library prank before some other fraternity thought of it. And should a foreign enemy happen to invade your campus, you would probably scream like frightened children and be the first ones to bolt and run.

You see, fraternities aren't designed to fight battles. They're into fellowship, camaraderie, and convenient civic projects. They don't recruit men to give up their rights, deny their urges, train in pain, or shed their blood. No one would want to join. Too many Christian men are playing out their Christian experience in comfortable frat houses with steeples on the roof.

Men, we're at war! An enemy is out there. He is working from a strategy. He has got a hit list. Your name—and the name of everyone you love—is on it.

He wants your daughter—the girl who thankfully looks like your wife and has all those guys calling. He has got plans for her—big plans—in the backseat of some yahoo's car. He is whispering in her ear every time she looks in the mirror, telling her lies such as she's not pretty, she's too fat, she's too flat, she's stupid, no one really likes her, no guy will ever want her—setting her up for the kill.

He wants your son—the boy who stands in front of an open refrigerator for five minutes and manages to ingest half its contents. He has plans for him too. He has some profanity to teach him and some pornography to show him. He has some lies he wants to get him to believe and some fears he wants to embed in his heart. He wants to teach him to take shortcuts in life— that what he wants is best attained through the easiest method available.

He wants your baby—the cute little thing who lights up when you come in the door. He wants to wipe that excitement off his little face. He wants to teach him that there is no hope. He wants your child raised without boundaries. He wants you to meet his physical needs, misunderstand his emotional needs, and neglect his spiritual needs. That way the enemy can turn him into a selfish adult with a chip on his shoulder.

He wants your wife—the special woman you once promised everything. He wants her feeling as if she's unappreciated. He tells her she is getting old and is no longer beautiful. He tells her you don't care about her much anymore. He is constantly trying to get her to think that her house is inadequate, her friends have more fun, she is wasting her life, and she could find what's missing in her life in the arms of some other man.

He wants you. He knows that if he can just get you, he can get your daughter, your son, your baby, and your wife. And the main way he wants to get you is to get you to think that the Christian life is some holy huddle with matching sweaters and genuine leather Bibles. He wants you preoccupied with noble goals that don't ultimately make much difference. He wants you to treat your baby like a doorstop, to treat your son like an extension of your ego, to sleepwalk through your daughter's teenage years, and to starve your wife of your affection, affirmation, attention, and sense of partnership. And then after he has used you to nail them, he wants to finish you off.

I repeat, you're in the army. If you've given your heart to Jesus Christ, you're in a battle for your family, your community, your country, and the essence of your very own life.

But you don't have to show up for duty in God's army. You can live comfortably in your little Christian fraternity house. Circle up in your men's group at Denny's and give your occasional nod to God. And if you do, there is one thing you can be sure of—you're going down, you and your family.

ENLISTMENT LINES ARE OPEN

Or you can join the millions of men who are tired of fraternity cheers and bonfires with the sorority sisters and sign up to wear the uniform of a soldier of the Cross. We're not talking about a bunch of spiritual Rambos or religious soldiers of fortune. We're talking about balanced men who fear God and love their families; good men who don't just want to spend their lives sucking up air and taking up space; brave men who believe in the cause and have counted the cost. God wants *you!*

Many men have joined. But somewhere between the enlistment office and the induction center, they got sidetracked. Others have burned their orders. They have turned their backs on their marriage vows, they have traded in the wives of their youth for younger models, they have sold out to the company store, they have sat benignly by and let their kids play in the middle of a cultural freeway, and they have refused to stand their posts and make sure everyone in the family is getting in before dark.

YOU'RE 1-A

If you have given your life to Jesus Christ and you'd rather not sign up for active duty in his army, you need to know something. You really don't have a choice. Every man in the Christian movement is classified 1-A. If you were born in the U.S. after they discontinued the draft, let me bring you up to speed on what I mean by 1-A. When you turned eighteen years old, you were required to report to the Selective Service office in the town nearest you and register. At that point, the recruiters went through a process to determine your classification.

4-F. The first thing they did was to give you a physical. If you had extremely poor vision, some kind of disability, major emotional or intellectual shortcomings, breathing problems, and so on, you were classified as 4-F, meaning that it would be difficult, if not impossible, for you to be able to fulfill your duties as a soldier, and you were therefore exempt from the draft. I played football with two all-state running backs who were given a 4-F deferment for flat feet. They could run like the wind, but the army said they had flat feet. For some reason flat feet work great if you're carrying a football, but apparently fall short if you're carrying a rucksack and an M16.

2-S. This meant you were heading for, or were currently in, college. Apparently, some congressmen had convinced a lot of other congressmen to provide a deferment for people going to college from having to be drafted. Most officers back then were college graduates. The way they said it to me was that smart guys didn't always make good foot soldiers because they thought too much. In other words, conventional wisdom assumed that smart guys didn't follow orders. I found that thinking amazing since all my young life, I had been taught that it was the dumb guys who didn't follow orders.

4-D. This was a divinity deferment. It meant that you were either training for or involved in the ministry. Uncle Sam felt we needed people working with the hearts of the folks on the home front. Unfortunately, there were some men who claimed this deferment who didn't deserve it. I knew a couple of guys in the sixties who were conveniently "called" to the ministry until the war in Vietnam was finally over. I personally refused this deferment.

CO. This stood for "conscientious objector." A person might feel—for moral or religious reasons—that there was no way he could, in good conscience, carry a weapon and possibly kill another human being. The government made an allowance for him.

1-A. If none of these deferment classifications applied to you, you were given a draft card with 1-A printed on it. If Uncle Sam said he needed you, you had to go. To refuse was punishable by fines and jail terms. One of the more pitiful sights of the 1960s was the image of young men defying the government by burning their draft cards. Others chose to flee the country in order to avoid service.

Guess what? There are no deferments in the cause of Christ. We're all classified 1-A.

You say, "But, Lord, I'm not capable of standing in the gap for my family. I'm not real bright. I'm not real stable. I'm not real healthy. I have flat feet." God says, "Tell it to Oprah and report for duty."

You say, "I need to spend more time in Bible study and discipleship before I can be effective as a soldier for you, Lord." God says, "This is an army, not some spiritual think tank. I'm not after your mind. I'm after your heart. Report for duty."

You say, "Lord, I'm in training to be an officer. I'm going to Bible college or seminary. This frontline commitment would keep me from my Hebrew homework and homiletics class." God says, "Trust me. All that stuff will make a lot more sense when you're studying it in uniform. Report for duty."

You say, "But I'm a tender heart . . . a gentle soul. I'm not into violence and warfare." God says, "Buy a vowel for crying out loud. Turn it around. Figure this puzzle out. It's not that tough. We're not shooting anyone. We're not killing anything. This is a peacemaking mission. We're protecting people. Get a clue. Report for duty."

WARRIORS BY DEFAULT

Or you may be like David, minding your own business, playing the position God has assigned you in life when, Boom! the war will suddenly explode all around you. That's why you need to maintain ongoing training. You're like the reserves. One way or the other, though, there is no escaping the battle—not if you want to have a thread of a chance. Your odds skyrocket when you know the basic strategies of the enemy. Later on, I'll take you through those strategies so that you'll never get caught off guard.

> *You cannot choose your battlefield,*
> *God does that for you;*
> *But you can plant a standard*
> *Where a standard never flew.*
> —Stephen Crane, "The Colors"

STUDY AND DISCUSSION QUESTIONS

UP FRONT AND PERSONAL

1. When the Goliath of your conflicts steps forward to challenge you, do you have the attitude of a volunteer or a conscript? Explain.

2. Was David's confidence in victory over Goliath just an example of the arrogance of youth? Read 1 Samuel 17:34–37 and relate its message to dispatching your personal Goliath.

3. Have you ever thought of yourself as a soldier in the army of God? If you are part of a spiritual army, can you identify the enemy?

4. If you have said, "Yes, I am in the army of God!" have you asked for a deferment? Are you a noncombatant? What does the author say about your spiritual draft classification?

FOR THE GROUP TO DISCUSS

1. Do you agree or disagree with the author's contention that when we accept Jesus Christ as our Savior, we join God's spiritual army? Why?

2. Fill in the blank: "So far, I would classify my actions as being those of _____."
   a) an enthusiastic enlistee
   b) a draftee
   c) an accidental soldier
   d) a draft dodger
   Explain your answer.

3. Read the account of David versus Goliath in 1 Samuel 17. Does it sound as if David's victory was a fortunate fluke, or could he have been better prepared to face Goliath than anyone thought?

4. Why did David volunteer for what appeared to be a suicide mission? Discuss the possibilities, then read aloud 1 Samuel 17:46.

5. Were the concerns of "management" justified? Was God considered in those concerns? See 1 Samuel 17:11.

Applying God's Word

1. Read aloud and memorize 2 Timothy 2:3–4, that your place in God's army will be fortified.

2. Include in your daily prayers the officers in God's army. They are your pastors, deacons, and elders; ask that God will strengthen them to defeat our modern-day Goliaths.

CHAPTER 3

"YES, DRILL SERGEANT"

Hi there, my name is Jer—"

"Smackhead, do you think anyone around here cares what your first name is?"

"But I was just trying to introduce myse—"

"Shut up, post over here, straighten up your back, put your feet together, drop that bag, don't look, blink, scratch, or think unless I tell you to. Do you understand?"

"Uh, yeah, I guess so—"

"What did you say?"

"I mean, yes, sir!"

"You don't call me sir! I'm a drill sergeant. I work for a living!"

"Yes, Drill Sergeant!"

And so it goes. They meet you at the induction depot. They're starched, straight, shined, and polished. There is no glad-handing, no showing you pictures of their kids, no exchanging of recipes. They're stern, fierce, and imposing with their campaign hats resting on top of their shaved heads. And each drill sergeant has his or her own way of making you think that you have just made the dumbest decision of your life. It's crucial if they want to build you into a soldier. It's vital to the interest of the unit. It might even save your life.

The wake-up call new recruits get when they climb off the bus and walk into the depot is a carefully crafted part of breaking them down in order to build them back up into something much better. But when it's happening, you think you just died and went to the narthex of hell!

I have a friend named Don who enlisted in the marines on his eighteenth birthday. The year was 1966. Uncle Sam sent him a bus ticket to San Diego. When he got there, he followed his instructions to meet up with the other men who were arriving about the same time. Once they met, one of them volunteered to call the Marine Corps Induction Depot to let them know they had arrived. Don said that he watched the guy walk into the phone booth, make the call, say something into the phone, then suddenly stand straight up at attention! Whoever was on the other end of the line was yelling very specific orders to him.

He came out and informed the group that the guy on the phone said that they were to go to a certain spot on the sidewalk outside the bus station and stand at ease until someone arrived to pick them up. When they got out there, one of the guys asked what "at ease" meant. The guy who had made the phone call said that he thought it meant you stand with your feet comfortably apart and your hands behind your back. At that point Don informed the group that he wasn't going to stand in front of the bus station in that position looking like a fool. He barely had the words out of his mouth when an olive green truck with a Marine Corps emblem on the door pulled up to the curb. A couple of sergeants jumped out and literally threw them and their gear into the back of the truck. When they arrived at the camp, they were dropped off at a place that had seventy-five sets of footprints painted in gold on the concrete. They had to stand with their feet on those footprints until all seventy-five were filled. He stood there for almost three hours until seventy-five guys arrived to form their unit.

The initial encounter serves a profound purpose in showing the soldier how things are going to operate in the armed services. The Bible has many examples of these initial encounters with the Savior.

Consider the calloused fishermen fixing their nets by the lake. They're preoccupied because of being skunked the night before. *No fish means no money. No money, no food. The boat payment is due, and we're three months behind on our slip fee at the marina. A couple more nights like this, and we're toast.*

Enter Jesus with a crowd. "Do you mind if I sit on the edge of your boat and talk to the folks? They'd be able to see and hear me better."

"Yeah, whatever," one says, but his mind is elsewhere. He doesn't realize that Jesus isn't there to teach a crowd. He is there recruiting officers for a mighty army he is assembling.

A while later Jesus says, "Put out into deep water, and let down your nets for a catch." He is pulling a drill sergeant on them. He is telling them to do something they don't want to do. They'll question his authority. He'll repeat his command. They'll submit because of his imposing presence at that moment. Sure enough, he'll be right and they'll be wrong. And in the process, they'll learn some mighty lessons, such as, maybe I'm not as smart as I thought I was, maybe he isn't as naive as I thought he was, maybe teaming up with him isn't such a bad idea after all.

Here's how it reads:

> [Jesus said,] **"Put out into deep water, and let down the nets for a catch." Simon answered, "Master, we've worked hard all night and haven't caught anything. But** *because you say so,* **I will let down the nets." When they had done so, they caught such a large number of fish that their nets began to break. So they signaled their partners in the other boat to come and help them, and they came and filled both boats so full that they began to sink. When Simon Peter saw this, he fell at Jesus' knees and said, "Go away from me, Lord; I am a sinful man!" For he and all his companions were astonished at the catch of fish they had taken, and so were James and John, the sons of Zebedee, Simon's partners. Then Jesus said to Simon, "Don't be afraid; from now on you will catch men." So they pulled their boats up on shore,** *left everything* **and followed him.** (Luke 5:4–11, emphasis added)

Peter's words have a strange ring to them. He just got the biggest catch of his career on a tip from a Galilean carpenter, and he suddenly feels self-conscious about his private life. He put two and two together: *If this guy can make the fish jump in our nets this afternoon, then he's probably the same one who told them to avoid our nets last night. And if he can control the swimming patterns of fish, he probably knows a lot more about me than I'd prefer him to. He is not only looking at me, he's looking through me.*

They are also expected to do what every other soldier is expected to do when he starts basic training—leave personal stuff behind. He commanded them to follow him (Matt. 4:19). With him taking off across the land, it was obvious that they couldn't follow in their boats. If they were going to follow him, it would have to be on his terms. You might show up at the induction depot in Bermuda shorts and a ponytail, but you won't have them by the end of the day. Your hair will be "high and tight" by noon, and you'll be in a uniform by dinner. It's not a divesting that Jesus is after here; it's an emptying—a detaching—that is crucial to the unencumbered, focused life of a soldier.

A soldier wanna-be bumped into Jesus on his way out of the country club. He stood in sharp contrast to the blue-collar fishermen who made up Jesus' initial recruits. The guy had manicured fingernails, soft skin, and styled hair. He wore a Hart, Schaffner, and Marx robe and smelled of expensive cologne. He wanted to know what it took to inherit eternal life. He had already inherited more money than he knew what to do with. We know he inherited it because he was young (Matt. 19:20). Young men back then didn't go out and suddenly get rich. In the first place, it was a heavily taxed economy, so it would take a while to accumulate a fortune. And we know that it was an economy based on influence. There wasn't a level playing field economically. A few people controlled the bulk of the wealth. So the kid didn't have to work for the money he had, and he didn't want to work for eternal life. He wanted to *inherit* it too.

Jesus knew what he was up against. The guy wanted to march in the parades but not have to fight any battles. He wanted to hang out at the Officers Club and sleep through reveille. Jesus started by sharing with him the Code of the Corps. He said, "Don't mess with women who aren't your wife, don't kill people, don't take things that belong to someone else, and be sure to take care of your parents." The young man's smug remark was, "Been there, done that" (Luke 18:21). Then Jesus brought up the "emptying of self, detaching of personal agenda" issue that he shared with Peter. He said, "You still lack one thing. Sell everything you have and give to the poor, and you will have treasure in heaven. Then come, follow me" (Luke 18:22). The Scripture said that when he heard this, "he became very sad, because he was a man of great wealth" (v. 23).

Jesus eliminated the guy at the induction depot. Jesus knew he wasn't fit to be a soldier because he wasn't up for the sacrifice. He wasn't ready to identify with the corps and swear his allegiance to it.

Look at Paul the apostle's induction into the army of the Lord Jesus Christ. He had been a war protester, burned his draft card, and spit on veterans. He was the least likely candidate to enlist. He was on his way to Damascus to capture Christians and bring them back to Jerusalem to stand trial and face execution. Jesus held a giant light in his face, knocked him to the ground, and said, "Saul, Saul, why are you persecuting Me?" (Acts 9:1–4 NKJV). Sound familiar? "Hey, Smackhead, what do you think you're doing?"

When Saul (later named Paul) asked what was going on, Jesus didn't explain. He just gave him orders: "Now get up and go into the city, and you will be *told* what you must do" (Acts 9:6, emphasis added).

SHOOT THE RECRUITER

You can't count the number of enlistees who have wished they could go AWOL from boot camp long enough to go back to their hometowns and slap their recruiters silly. All of the pride, nobility, and romance that the recruiter talked about is hard to imagine when you're hip deep in some swamp, wearing fifty pounds on your back, and only halfway through a fifteen-mile hike. It's the up-front price a soldier must pay in order to march in the graduation parade. It's also necessary to ensure that he has the right stuff when the bullets start flying.

The first few days in basic set the stage and the cadence for a successful career as a soldier. A handful of crucial elements make up the first few days that have a direct parallel to our role as soldiers for the cross of Jesus Christ. Let's look and learn together.

1. ORIENTATION

I'm a native of Annapolis, Maryland. When people put the word *Annapolis* in a sentence, I'm not sure whether they are referring to the town or the United States Naval Academy. One is a synonym for the other.

The Naval Academy is special to me because of a lot of great memories attached to it while I was living in the area and attending Annapolis High School. I also have one extremely bad memory that centered on a boxing match I had in the ring at Dahlgren Hall with a second classman who put my lights out—but that's another story.

My wife's stepfather graduated from the Naval Academy in 1941 and headed out to the South Pacific to spend the war on an attack submarine. He retired from the navy as a captain after a long and extremely productive career. My closest friend's son just completed his plebe year there, and I know several other midshipmen, past and present, who have given four years of their lives to study within its walls.

But it's not just the picturesque stone buildings along the Severn River or the traditions, color, and pageantry of academy life that draw me through its gates when I'm home. It's what it represents. It's America's best, given the best that America has to offer, to preserve the best things about us—our freedom, our matchless Constitution, and our rich heritage. Sure, America has had some dark chapters in its history. And the Naval Academy has received its share of black eyes along the way too. But in an imperfect world, our country and its military academies still rank at the top of the list of shining historical achievements.

When my family and I vacation in Annapolis, I like to get up early in the morning, drive downtown, park near McGarvey's, and take a morning jog. A good part of my three-mile run is through the campus (known as "the yard") of the Naval Academy. Even if I'm slipping through the gate at 6:00 A.M., the midshipmen are not only up, but they have already scratched several items off their "to do" lists. Most of the young men and women running around the yard in the summertime are the plebes—fresh meat for the upperclassmen who are there to train them in the nuances of academy life.

The initial six weeks of training are a major part of their orientation to navy life. The intense training will put every ounce of their physical, intellectual, emotional, and spiritual dimensions to the test. The transformation takes place quickly. On induction day they walk onto the campus looking like a thousand individuals from every point on the compass. By the end of that day, the only thing that distinguishes one from the other is the nameplate on each person's chest. Their first few hours as a plebe are carefully designed to remove any trappings of individuality or personal agenda. By the end of that day, they stand side by side looking like one single unit. They are dressed alike, stand alike, walk in step, and answer questions shouted at them the same way.

The upperclassmen are in the faces of these brand-new plebes, verbally drilling into them a whole new way of thinking. I look at these young men and women, fresh from graduation from high school, with their clean haircuts, clean uniforms, and the shocked look of a deer caught in the headlights, and I have to chuckle. This sure isn't what the brochure made it look like. But after a month and a half of physical and emotional torture, it finally settles down for them to a nice ten months of hell. That first year at the academy plays a key purpose in what follows. The demands placed on them will pay off in spades when they find themselves in command in later years.

Orientation to military life includes getting their hair removed, storing their civilian clothes and being issued a series of uniforms, being issued a weapon, being assigned to a room, a team, a squad, a platoon, a company, a battalion, which—along with the other battalions—makes up the brigade of midshipmen. They're hustled from one part of the yard to the other. They are taught that there is a navy way to do everything: "This is the navy way to store your gear. This is the navy way to put your supplies in your medicine cabinet. This is the navy way to walk, sit, eat (sit at attention, buttocks resting on the front half of your chair, back straight, both feet flat on the floor, don't look around, keep eyes on the top rim of your plate, take only small bites of food, and after putting the bite in your mouth, put the fork on your plate and your hands in your lap, then begin chewing), and answer questions. On and on it goes.

Your spiritual orientation includes similar issues:

You're in God's army.

> **And I saw heaven opened, and behold a white horse; and he that sat upon him was called Faithful and True, and in righteousness he doth judge and make war. His eyes were as a flame of fire, and on his head were many crowns; and he had a name written, that no man knew, but he himself. And he was clothed with a vesture dipped in blood: and his name is called The Word of God. And the armies which were in heaven followed him upon white horses, clothed in fine linen, white and clean. And out of his mouth goeth a sharp sword, that with it he should smite the nations: and he shall rule them with a rod of iron: and he treadeth the winepress of the fierceness and wrath of Almighty God. And he hath on his vesture and on his thigh a name written, KING OF KINGS, AND LORD OF LORDS.** (Rev. 19:11–16 KJV)

Who is in charge?

> **And He [Jesus Christ] is the head of the body, the church, who is the beginning, the firstborn from the dead, that in all things He may have the preeminence.** (Col. 1:18 NKJV)

What's your uniform?

> **But put ye on the Lord Jesus Christ, and make not provision for the flesh, to fulfil the lusts thereof.** (Rom. 13:14 KJV)

What about your personal agenda?

> **I have been crucified with Christ and I no longer live, but Christ lives in me. The life I live in the body, I live by faith in the Son of God, who loved me and gave himself for me.** (Gal. 2:20)

> **Anyone who loves his father or mother more than me is not worthy of me; anyone who loves his son or daughter more than**

me is not worthy of me; and anyone who does not take his cross and follow me is not worthy of me. (Matt. 10:37–38)

Then Jesus said to his disciples, "If anyone would come after me, he must deny himself and take up his cross and follow me." (Matt. 16:24)

Can you reconsider?

Jesus replied, "No one who puts his hand to the plow and looks back is fit for service in the kingdom of God." (Luke 9:62)

So what do you eat?

I am the bread of life. Your forefathers ate the manna in the desert, yet they died. But here is the bread that comes down from heaven, which a man may eat and not die. (John 6:48–50)

2. CONDITIONING

One of the most demanding parts of basic training is the physical training required of a soldier. Soldiers have to be tough, strong, and able to endure extraordinary demands on their bodies.

Endure hardship with us like a good soldier of Christ Jesus. No one serving as a soldier gets involved in civilian affairs—he wants to please his commanding officer. (2 Tim. 2:3–4)

For physical training is of some value, but godliness has value for all things, holding promise for both the present life and the life to come. (1 Tim. 4:8)

Do you not know that in a race all the runners run, but only one gets the prize? Run in such a way as to get the prize. Everyone who competes in the games goes into strict training. They do it to get a crown that will not last; but we do it to get a crown that will last forever. Therefore I do not run like a man running aimlessly; I do not fight like a man beating the air. No, I beat my body and make it my slave so that after I have preached to others, I myself will not be disqualified for the prize. (1 Cor. 9:24–27)

3. MILITARY PROTOCOL

I stopped by the Pentagon a couple of years ago to have lunch with a friend. In the course of the day, I happened to be escorted from one place to another first by a lieutenant and last by a major. The first spent a lot of time snapping his hand up to his forehead and saluting the higher ranking officers who passed by. He was low man on the totem pole. In basic, you learn what the different rankings are, not just in your own branch of the service, but in every branch of the service. There is protocol in the military, and one of the most important things you have to learn is the chain of command. In God's army, he has a chain of command, but it's quite different from other branches of service.

Jesus called them together and said, "You know that the rulers of the Gentiles lord it over them, and their high officials exercise authority over them. Not so with you. Instead, whoever wants to become great among you must be your servant, and whoever wants to be first must be your slave—just as the Son of Man did not come to be served, but to serve, and to give his life as a ransom for many." (Matt. 20:25–28)

The greatest among you will be your servant. For whoever exalts himself will be humbled, and whoever humbles himself will be exalted. (Matt. 23:11–12)

Then make my joy complete by being like-minded, having the same love, being one in spirit and purpose. Do nothing out of selfish ambition or vain conceit, but in humility consider others better than yourselves. Each of you should look not only to your own interests, but also to the interests of others. Your attitude should be the same as that of Christ Jesus:

Who, being in very nature God,
    did not consider equality with God something to be
    grasped,
but made himself nothing,
    taking the very nature of a servant,
    being made in human likeness.
And being found in appearance as a man,
    he humbled himself
    and became obedient to death—
    even death on a cross! (Phil. 2:2–8)

You may have been through basic training for a branch of the service. Maybe it was at Parris Island or Camp Pendleton so that you could earn the privilege of wearing the marine uniform. Maybe you went to Ranger School at Fort Benning and learned how to jump out of perfectly good airplanes. Or maybe you went to the standard grunt camp for the army. Regardless, you went through a process of being broken down in order to be built into something better.

God wants to do the same with us. It's amazing how induction into his army parallels many of the rites, rituals, and regimens found in most military boot camps. But as you can see, being soldiers in the army of the Lord Jesus Christ calls to a challenge far higher and a reward far greater than anything we could ever have hoped to achieve in an earthly army. In the next chapter it's time to fall in for inspection. We're going to open up our lockerboxes, check out our uniforms, and see how well we can shoot our weapons in anticipation of the battle before us.

STUDY AND DISCUSSION QUESTIONS

UP FRONT AND PERSONAL

1. Have you had a problem (or problems) because you question authority?

   Was that authority   ____ a parent? (Eph. 6:1–3)
     ____ a boss? (1 Peter 2:18–23)
     ____ a police officer? (Rom. 13:1–7;
     1 Tim. 2:1–4; 1 Peter 2:13–17)
     ____ God? (Dan. 9:5, 9)
     ____ other?

2. "Being completely honest, on a scale of 1 to 5 (with 1 being totally willing and 5 being totally unwilling), I would rank myself (*circle one*) 1 2 3 4 5 on my willingness to obey authority."

3. Complete this sentence: "I could submit to God's authority if only _____."

FOR THE GROUP TO DISCUSS

1. How many of you agree with the military method of breaking a person down so he can be built back up into something better?

2. Does God do this? How do you know?

3. Who is the commander in chief of God's army? See Colossians 1:18.

4. List at least three ways to condition yourself for spiritual battles.

5. Read aloud Matthew 20:25–28. Does this mean the chain of command among God's followers is the opposite of a real military chain of command?

APPLYING GOD'S WORD

1. Matthew 10:37–38 declares, "He who loves father or mother more than Me is not worthy of Me. And he who loves son or daughter more than Me is not worthy of Me. And he who does not take his cross and follow after Me is not worthy of Me" (NKJV). What does this mean in regard to the love you have for your family?

2. Renew your personal commitment to being a soldier in God's army, and memorize 1 Timothy 4:8: "For physical training is of some value, but godliness has value for all things, holding promise for both the present life and the life to come."

CHAPTER 4

FALL IN FOR INSPECTION!

Except for the muted lights near the "head" and the burnt orange glow of EXIT signs over the doors, the barracks is pitch dark. Heavy breathing and light snoring fill the holes in the otherwise silent night. It's still an hour until reveille and an hour and a half before dawn. It's also a perfect time for an inspection.

The sergeant and his staff like to time it so that the overhead lights, the banging lid on the galvanized trash can, and the series of barked orders happen instantly and simultaneously. Soldiers deep in their sleep suddenly find themselves standing at blocked attention at the foot of their bunks in their boxer shorts. And somewhere in all the commotion they hear that they have six minutes to be ready for a uniform, bunk, locker-box, and weapon inspection.

The guys who moan the loudest are the ones who know that six minutes won't give them enough time to be ready. Their gear isn't stowed properly, and their weapons are dirty. For them, a gigantic ball starts to form in the stomach as they envision the verbal humiliation they're going to have to endure when the sergeant sees just how inept they are.

Other men, however, feel fairly confident about what is about to come down because their lockerboxes are in order and their weapons are clean for inspection. All they have to do is make their beds properly and get dressed in clean uniforms. They should have seconds to spare.

Your wife calls you at work to inform you that she needs to talk with you that evening after the kids go to bed. It seems she needed to print off a paper for a class she is taking at the university and the home PC was throwing a fit. She got your notebook computer out of the bottom of your closet and hooked it up to the printer. When the screen came up, she started to give the commands to download her file from her floppy into the program. But an unusual icon caught her eye, and she double-clicked on it to see what it was. She wants to discuss with you why you have pornography on your computer.

Your son is talking on the phone and telling a friend about Jesus. He is excited about the response on the other end. He has been using his Bible, reading verses to his friend, when he suddenly covers the mouthpiece and says, "Dad, where's that verse that says that salvation is a gift and not a result of our good works?" All you can do is look back at him with a confused look on your face.

You're teaching a Sunday school class. National elections are two days away. You suddenly digress from your lesson plan and go into a monologue about how you feel the only legitimate candidate that a Christian can vote for is candidate so-and-so. About two-thirds of the way into your spiel a couple introduced earlier in the class as guests get up and walk out.

Surprise inspections. They happen all the time to soldiers of the Cross. In the three instances listed above, the soldier's lockerbox was a mess, his weapon was dirty, and he was out of uniform. They are all scenarios I have either observed or been told about in my travels. And in each one, the soldier felt overwhelming embarrassment and shame. That can be the nature of surprise inspections if we're not prepared.

There are two basic types of inspections: scheduled and surprise. They coincide with the two basic types of encounters with the enemy. The Iraqi army pulled off a surprise invasion of Kuwait. The neighboring country was caught completely unprepared for Saddam Hussein's troops. But when the United States and the other allies of Kuwait came to its aid with retaliation, there was no surprise at all. Iraq knew we were coming, we told them we were coming, CNN showed them our forces assembling on their border, and they prepared their troops for our assault. The actual moment of the invasion might have been a surprise, but the invasion wasn't.

God maintains ongoing inspections—both scheduled and surprise—in your life too. If you're struggling with a drinking problem and find out the Sunday school class is stopping by after dinner for some dessert, you'd probably hide the liquor. But when your ten-year-old son, who is having a hard time sleeping, walks out onto the back patio in the middle of the night to find you plastered, you've just flunked a surprise inspection. The purpose of scheduled inspections is to train you how you are to be at all times so that a surprise inspection doesn't catch you off guard.

ATTENHUT!

Let's consider this a surprise inspection. I'm not going to give it to you. You are going to give it to yourself. My role is to point out standards and expectations of a well-prepared soldier in the army of the Lord Jesus, and your role is to see how you measure up. The purpose here is to see where you are doing well and where you need to concentrate more effort.

YOUR UNIFORM

Each branch of the military has a uniform that distinguishes it from other branches and then several types of uniforms within that branch to be worn for different functions. You don't want to be out of uniform or in the wrong one at the wrong time.

Let's talk about being in uniform first. In Romans 13:13–14, Paul urged, "Let us behave decently, as in the daytime, not in orgies and drunkenness, not in sexual immorality and debauchery, not in dissension and jealousy. Rather, clothe yourselves with the Lord Jesus Christ, and do not think about how to gratify the desires of the sinful nature."

A military uniform serves two purposes besides the functional one of providing clothing. First, it identifies the wearer with a branch of the military. When I see a man walking down the middle of an airport terminal wearing the uniform and patches of the Eighty-second Airborne, I am duly impressed.

That uniform, and the patch on the sleeve that designates him as a member of the Eighty-second Airborne, tells me a lot about the man inside it. It tells me about his commitment to sacrifice, his tenacity, his loyalty, and his courage.

Second, a uniform communicates to others the standard of behavior we can expect from the person wearing it. If later on I see that same soldier insult a ticket agent because his flight was overbooked and chew her out because he happened to lose his seat, I would not find that behavior in line with the uniform he wears. His uniform tells me that I can expect him to behave in a calm and gentlemanly manner regardless of the inconvenience he might encounter. He has been taught to honor and respect people who are trying to serve his needs and not to punish the innocent. I can expect that of him. The uniform says so.

If I happen to see him even later standing inside one of the airport bars with his coat off, his tie loose, his collar open, and his body swaying in inebriation, I would definitely be disappointed. If he happened to be discovered in that state by a fellow member of the Eighty-second Airborne, an officer, or an MP, he would also be big-time disappointed. The soldier could be court-martialed for being drunk while in uniform. Fellow soldiers don't appreciate one of their own shaming the uniform that all of them wear.

The apostle Paul used a similar parallel. Maybe he had seen too many movies or was in downtown Philippi when the troops were on leave. Soldiers do have a reputation of dropping their guard when they have a weekend pass in their pockets. Tons of movies have made a stereotype out of off-duty soldiers heading to town and getting carried away with their drinking, brawling, and carousing. It's true for some. A lot of decent guys behave themselves when they're off duty, but they get a bad rap because of the vocal few who don't. No doubt being a soldier, with all of its regimentation, can cause a guy to let his "high and tight" hair down when he gets away from his company commander—especially in a war zone. But the commanding officer still expects him to behave in a manner that does not bring shame to his outfit. Paul leaned on that imagery.

He said, in verse 13, to "behave decently, *as in the daytime.*"

His point was, "You know the standard of character that is expected of you when you are on duty? Maintain it when you're off duty too." A soldier who is supposed to be standing his post or carrying out some order, but happens to be discovered engaging in a sexual activity, doing something unbecoming of a soldier, getting intoxicated, arguing with a fellow soldier, or spreading lies or rumors about another soldier, is in serious trouble. Behavior like that weakens the lines and makes the entire unit vulnerable.

How often have you heard someone say, "I understand that so-and-so goes to that church; if he is a sampling of that church's brand of religion, count me out"? He is referring to someone who was caught out of uniform. We are to wear the Lord Jesus Christ. When people watch us in action, something about how we behave should set us apart as members of Christ's Corps.

I said that one of the purposes of a uniform is to identify you with a branch of service. Therefore, you are to portray to people that you are identified with Christ. What does that mean? Entire books have been written on this subject, and I have only a few lines to summarize it. If you want to study it in depth, I recommend you spend some time poring over Romans 6–8. It's one of the best passages in the Scripture for understanding our identification in Christ. But let me quote a few verses from it that especially capsulize it:

> Therefore, there is now no condemnation for those who are in Christ Jesus, because through Christ Jesus the law of the Spirit of life set me free from the law of sin and death. For what the law was powerless to do in that it was weakened by the sinful nature, God did by sending his own Son in the likeness of sinful man to be a sin offering. And so he condemned sin in sinful man, in order that the righteous requirements of the law might be fully met in us, who do not live according to the sinful nature but according to the Spirit. (8:1–4)

> You, however, are controlled not by the sinful nature but by the Spirit, if the Spirit of God lives in you. And if anyone does not have the Spirit of Christ, he does not belong to Christ. (8:9)

What, then, shall we say in response to this? If God is for us, who can be against us? (8:31)

For I am convinced that neither death nor life, neither angels nor demons, neither the present nor the future, nor any powers, neither height nor depth, nor anything else in all creation, will be able to separate us from the love of God that is in Christ Jesus our Lord. (8:38–39)

If you are in Christ, you have transferred from darkness to light and from death to life. You have all of the power of God living *in* you. You have power over sin, over your urges, over fear, and over death through the fact that you have been bought and paid for on the cross of Calvary. You have the Holy Spirit living in you.

One way that people should spot the uniform of the Lord Jesus on you is your outward display of the fruit of the Holy Spirit. Paul wrote, "But the fruit of the Spirit is love, joy, peace, patience, kindness, goodness, faithfulness, gentleness and self-control" (Gal. 5:22–23). Compare these characteristics to the ones he told us not to be known for in Romans 13:13. They're opposites.

Let me show you another characteristic that demonstrates to others that you are wearing the uniform of the Lord Jesus Christ. It's found in 1 Peter 5:5–6, "All of you, clothe yourselves with humility toward one another, because, 'God opposes the proud but gives grace to the humble.' Humble yourselves, therefore, under God's mighty hand, that he may lift you up in due time."

On several occasions various branches of the armed services have invited me to address their spiritual needs. I have noticed that the higher the rank, the more humble the officer behaves around me. Often these are men and women who lead thousands of the fiercest fighting machines who have ever worn combat boots. Yet they serve with a tempered pride—pride tempered by humility.

STUDYING A SOLDIER'S LEFT SLEEVE

You can learn a lot about a soldier by studying the patches at the top of his left sleeve. They tell his outfit and maybe a specialty within that outfit. We, too, as Christian soldiers wear identifying patches. A patch might say "First Baptist Church" or "Church of the Nazarene." We might have a special marker that identifies us with a group within the larger group, such as "Campus Crusade for Christ," "Focus on the Family," or "Promise Keepers." That's great. We just want to make sure that we don't do anything to shame the reputation of these specialty ministries or that we get so identified with the specialty ministry that we forget that we wear the uniform of the Lord Jesus Christ, which represents his entire body.

Subtle Ways to Be Out of Uniform

Let me mention another way to be out of uniform that ultimately brings shame to it. It's by attaching anything to the uniform that adds to or takes away from its stated essence. One Christmas, I took my family to one of the largest churches in the Phoenix area to enjoy the Christmas pageant. This church is famous for its spectacular musical. We always leave it overwhelmed by the profound power of the Christmas story.

I had dropped Darcy off close to the church so she could get the younger kids checked into the nursery while I parked the car. I walked through the entrance where we were supposed to rendezvous and was waiting for Darcy when a handsome and friendly middle-aged man approached me. He welcomed me to the church and to the pageant. I figured he was a greeter. He asked me the usual stuff, such as whether I was a visitor, how long I had lived in the valley, and so on. Then he asked me if I owned my home or rented. "What?" I said. He clearly caught me off guard. Then he proceeded to hand me his real estate card and go into his sales pitch. He interspersed his advertisement with verses of Scripture and spiritual platitudes. Then he named a bunch of prominent Christians' homes he had either bought or listed. The whole time he was talking, I kept looking for one of the church "bouncers"—a deacon or an elder who could put the guy in his place. When I couldn't find anyone, I did it myself. He was out of uniform by using the blood of Jesus Christ to make real estate commissions.

One time I was serving Communion in my church. I attend a large church. Usually, sixteen to twenty people serve the

Communion elements at the same time. Once we've finished passing out the bread, we meet in the narthex and then go back down to the front of the church to pick up the juice to be passed out next. In the brief moment that I was standing in the narthex waiting for the others, a man who was involved in local politics approached me to tell me how I should vote on a proposition on the upcoming ballot that would curtail cigarette smoking. That action had absolutely no place in the church—especially in the middle of a Communion service.

Picture what would happen if a drill sergeant stepped up to examine a soldier's uniform and suddenly focused on a button that had the peace symbol on it. Too many people use their faith to push their economic agendas, ego needs, or political preferences. Please don't misunderstand me. If you are a Christian and also an American, you have every right to hold political convictions. These political convictions (such as your stand on the abortion issue) might be forged from deep within your relationship with Christ. You even have a right to convey your political and moral beliefs to others. But you don't want to make the mistake of using Christ to uphold an "American," but necessarily Christian, agenda. On these issues, deal with them as an American who happens to be a Christian.

God has shed his grace on the United States. Our nation was founded by some devout followers of Christ. We have enjoyed a rich Christian heritage. But we are not a Christian nation. We never have been. We have always had diversity, and the Christians who played such a crucial role in founding our nation were careful to protect others' different religious beliefs. It was the best way to protect their own freedom to follow Christ.

We must always work to protect that freedom. Very clear philosophies and forces are trying to sway our country away from its moral and religious underpinnings. We have every right—I dare say responsibility and obligation—to oppose them and their thinking. But we must do it in a way that does not confuse or bring harm to the bigger agenda of Christ in the world.

Much harm has been done to the cause of Christ by portraying Jesus as a right-wing conservative who votes Republican. I might be a right-wing conservative who tends to vote

Republican. But Jesus is God. He isn't an American. He isn't a Republican. Anytime we confuse Jesus with American, `olitical issues, we're out of uniform.

In other words, it's okay to be a biker for Jesus. It isn't okay to say that Jesus would have driven only a Harley! We need to keep personal issues and preferences personal. Sunday school class isn't to be a bully pulpit for your favorite candidate, and prayer meeting isn't where you go to pick up business leads.

You're in the Wrong Uniform

One final thought on the uniform. A soldier doesn't wear his dress uniform on a ten-mile hike. He doesn't wear his combat gear when he goes to a reception at the general's house. Within the cause of Christ there is a time to suit up a certain way.

Here's the problem: some Christians are always wearing their combat uniforms. They are committed to fighting some major threat to our faith or our safety as a people, but they fight it *all the time*, even when the threat isn't there.

An example that comes to mind is the abortion issue. A couple in our church felt called into the front lines of the fight to protect the unborn. They became a liability to the fight simply because they failed to keep it in context. If our pastor didn't bring up the issue in every pastoral prayer and make some point about it in his sermon, they nailed him. They wanted it mentioned during the worship time. They expected our pastor to get arrested to show how passionately he was against abortion. When he didn't oblige them, he was tagged as a "sellout" to the pro-choicers.

Hey, I'm absolutely against abortion. I speak out about it, write articles about it, and take on the issue in radio interviews. But when it's time to worship, I worship. When it's time to pray for the pastor, I pray for the pastor. When it's time to have fellowship, I have fellowship. As wise King Solomon said in Ecclesiastes (and his words were later popularized by the Byrds),

> **There is a time for everything,**
> **and a season for every activity under heaven:** . . .
> **a time to tear down and a time to build,** . . .
> **a time to embrace and a time to refrain,** . . .

a time to be silent and a time to speak, . . .
a time for war and a time for peace. (Eccl. 3:1–8)

You get the point.

Other Christians want to wear only the parade uniform. They want the worship, the praise, the pomp, and the pageantry. But you can't get them to park cars or work in the nursery. They show up for all the fun but have other plans when it's time to sweat. The fact is that a soldier seldom gets to wear his parade uniform. When I'm at a military installation, most of the time the uniform of the day from the general on down is work fatigues.

Now, it's time to look over your uniform. Give yourself a fitness report by answering the following questions.

TWENTY QUESTIONS
FOR UNIFORM INSPECTION

1. If someone asked your neighbors about you, would your belief in Christ be toward the front of their description of you?
2. Do you put fish symbols on your business cards?
3. Do you ever catch yourself talking politics in church?
4. Have you ever used Christ's name to help close a sale?
5. Do you laugh at racist jokes?
6. Have you ever been intoxicated in public (it's bad enough in private)?
7. Have you ever caught yourself demeaning another denomination?
8. Do you occasionally peek at pornographic magazines when you are in airports a long way from home?
9. Do you ever catch yourself thinking, *There's no way I can resist this temptation*?
10. When you've fallen short of your employer's expectations of you, do you ever make excuses?
11. Do you find bawdy, sexual humor humorous?
12. Would people who know you well classify you as a single-issue Christian?

13. Do you gesture at people when they cut you off in traffic?

14. Have you ever told off a clerk or a store manager?

15. Do you look down on believers from other churches as though you understand the heart of Christ more than they do?

16. Do you tend to assume that leaders who agree with political positions are most likely believers?

17. Do you occasionally use the Lord's name in vain, such as saying, "I'll pray for you," and then not backing up that promise with actual prayer?

18. Do you have a tough time celebrating when the occasion calls for celebration?

19. Have you ever called the principal at your kids' public school and given him or her a hard time because they don't recite the Lord's Prayer?

20. Would people who know you well describe you as a "fearful" person?

As you can see, it's easy to get caught out of uniform. Guess what? It's even easier to flunk bunk inspection.

YOUR BUNK

This won't take long. Do you stay up late and either get up early or constantly catch yourself oversleeping? An amazing problem plaguing a lot of Christian men today is that they simply don't get enough rest. They take on more responsibilities than they are capable of effectively doing. They don't know how to say either "no" or "yes" at the right time. They fall behind in their responsibilities, so they deprive themselves of sleep in order to catch up. Here's the point: it's easy to find yourself unfit for duty because you are too busy. If busyness is anything, it is slothfulness. It's putting your confidence in your own abilities rather than God's. It's pushing your agenda over his. It's taking charge.

YOUR LOCKERBOX

In most barracks, it's either beside the bunk or at the foot of it. It's usually painted dull green or gray. And when it has everything in it that the army says belongs in it, there is usually not much space left. When the drill sergeant orders you to open your lockerbox, he looks for several things. He first wants to see if you have all the gear in it that you are supposed to have in it. He also wants to see if you have it stored the proper way so that when you have to use it, it's ready to go. The last thing he looks for is contraband—things in your lockerbox that would distract you from being a good soldier or outright destroy your ability to serve.

The lockerbox is the most likely place that someone would store something he shouldn't have. In the spartan surroundings of a barracks, it's about the only place a soldier could hide something he shouldn't have. During these surprise inspections, drill sergeants discover things that are perfectly legitimate for a civilian, but have no place in the lockerbox of a soldier. Also during these probes into lockerboxes, stolen articles have been found, alcohol or drugs have been confiscated, and candy has been found among the heavily starched uniforms. Candy. You say, "What's the big deal? So the guy had a Snickers bar rolled up in his socks." It's not okay if a soldier reported for duty overweight and was supposed to be on a strict eating regimen. Many platoons have had to do some extra running because one guy wanted to be able to pop a few M&M's during the night.

In Christ's army, the lockerbox represents the things that make up the personal and private life. The lockerbox is designed to hold the essentials of an unencumbered soldier of the Cross. But that doesn't stop us from trying to wedge some things into it that don't fit. Let me mention a few.

1. HOBBIES

Nothing is wrong with hobbies. My observation is that people who lack hobbies are generally not much fun to be around. The issue here is not hobbies, but the right kind of hobbies done in balance. Camping is a wonderful hobby. But what if you camp almost every weekend of the summer and withhold your spiritual gifts as well as your children from the ongoing training of the church? Any hobby that requires you to give up time that you would otherwise be using to either grow in Christ or serve his body should be modified. Or maybe you love to hunt and fish. I do too. But what if you have young children who can't safely participate with you, or you have children (whether boys or girls) who don't enjoy your hobby? It doesn't mean you can't participate in your hobby. It might, however, say how much you should participate in it. Being a good dad, as we shall see later, takes a deliberate commitment of time and energy. There is only so much room in the lockerbox.

2. CONTRABAND OR STOLEN ARTICLES

Do you ever steal peeks up your secretary's dress or down her blouse? Have you ever borrowed a good idea from a fellow employee but forgot to mention where it came from when you brought it up at the VP meeting? If you happen to teach a Bible lesson, have you ever heard another Bible teacher tell of an incident in his life and then you retold it in your next lesson as though it happened to you? Do you rob time from your wife, kids, and the Lord to give to your cronies? Have you ever held a lie about someone else in your heart long enough to believe it to be the truth? It doesn't take much to find yourself looking up at the drill sergeant with a sheepish look on your face.

3. INDULGENCES

When they look in your lockerbox, there are supposed to be a certain number of work socks (cushioned sole, OD green), dress socks, fatigue tops, jars of boot and brass polish, and so on. A problem with affluent Christianity is that we try to crowd more of the right stuff into the lockerbox than an unencumbered soldier would want to have or could possibly use. We get so used to having so much of the good stuff that we refuse to accept anything less.

I've seen this when it comes to activities specifically designed to help men grow in Christ or serve others. They don't want to go on the men's retreat because they'll have to sleep on a GI bunk. It's just for one night, but they still don't want to give up the bed at home. Or they go, but they check in to the local hotel and only come over for the meetings. Or consider this one: they have agreed to spend a Saturday on a work crew at an inner-city church. But when it is time to sit down to the lunch the people from the church prepared for them, they use some excuse about an errand they have to run so they can drive to a nice restaurant and order à la carte.

When we put more of what we want in the lockerbox, we have to take out something else that we need. Too often our affluence blinds us to the basics of the Christian walk and distracts us from our ability to meet the needs of the people around us. It tends to make us self-centered rather than Christ-centered—to put our needs over the needs of others.

4. CANDY

It's easy to stuff candy in between the socks, for example:

- Standing out in the parking lot at church talking to a friend while the choir is doing its special
- Using the *Sports Illustrated* swimsuit edition screen saver on your computer
- Keeping that old *Penthouse* in the back of your closet that you find on a regular basis
- Having talks over the backyard fence with your beautiful neighbor just as she comes out to sit by her pool

A soldier's life is hard, and the demands on his body are great. His body is to be carefully fed the right things so that it will respond as it should when the bullets start flying. In the same way, emotional and sexual junk food can find you unprepared for the sneak attacks of the enemy. And the person next to you (your wife or child) might be the one who gets hurt.

Your lockerbox is your private life. What's in it determines how well you'll function in your public life. But even though it is private, it is not off-limits to the Savior's inspection. Since he is going to be spot-checking to see how you're doing, it behooves you to keep it stowed properly with the right stuff in the right proportions.

YOUR WEAPON

A soldier without his weapon is nothing more than a fool in a camouflaged outfit. From the first day he arrives at basic training, a soldier has the sovereign importance of his weapon pounded into him. He and his weapon are to be inseparable. He recites poems and creeds about it. He is to give it a name (usually a woman's name). Some nights he is required to sleep with it by his side. He has to know its serial number and be able to take it apart and put it back together blindfolded and in a specified amount of time. He is to keep it absolutely clean and functional. But most important, he is supposed to be able to shoot it accurately under all kinds of conditions. Instructors are notorious for taking soldiers out to the rifle range when it snows, rains, or freezes, or the temperature exceeds 100°F.

Your weapon is the Word of God. It is your sword (Eph. 6:17). The writer of Hebrews said that it is "living and powerful, and sharper than any two-edged sword, piercing even to the division of soul and spirit, and of joints and marrow, and is a discerner of the thoughts and intents of the heart" (Heb. 4:12 NKJV). The number one weapon of the enemy is lies. The best way to counter his lies is with the truth. So, how well do you know your weapon? And are you a good shot?

Let me try some scenarios with you, and you be the judge:

You're bypassing the elevator and taking the stairs from the lobby of the hotel to your room. As you hit the third-floor landing, a *Playboy* magazine is lying open on the floor. You need to claim a verse to help you resist the temptation to pick it up and take it with you. You have exactly two seconds.

The Annual Mayor's Prayer Breakfast has a slight problem. The guy who was supposed to read Scripture and pray just called from his car to inform the emcee that his radiator hose broke and he will be stranded for at least two hours. The emcee turns to you, hands you the Bible, and says, "I need you to pinch-hit. Read some passage that talks about hope or faith and then lead us in prayer. I'll be calling on you in about three minutes."

You're sitting next to a very talkative New Age guru on the airplane who informs you that she feels the flight will be safe because, "I covered the plane in 'white light' as I was walking down the jetway to come on board." You have two hours and eighteen minutes.

You're visiting your best friend in the hospital. He is sharing a room with a guy who has been taking treatments for cancer.

Although the curtain is drawn, and neither of you is deliberately trying to eavesdrop, you can't help hearing the doctor tell him that the chemotherapy has proven useless. He feels that they have exhausted their options. He has set up an appointment with the hospice in the morning so the fellow can spend his last days at home with his family. He does his best to slip some hope into the scenario but the harsh reality of his crisis is impossible to veil. After the doctor leaves and a nurse changes his IV, you sit silently with your friend wondering what to do. After a while the silence is broken by the sound of crying. You peek your head around the curtain and ask him if there is anything you can do. He asks you if you know Jesus Christ as your Savior. When you tell him that you do, he asks you if you could take his Bible and read him some verses of hope. You have forty-five seconds to find some good ones.

How would you do in these situations? Did you hit the target? Are you near the center? The ability to use the Word of God as an offensive and defensive weapon is crucial to your ability to stand your post in the cause of Christ.

The situations I listed above *happen*. Life doesn't conveniently let all of these things happen to seminary-trained Bible scholars. They happen to ground pounders like you. Let me close out this last part of the four-part inspection with twenty questions about your Bible knowledge. Inspect yourself.

TWENTY QUESTIONS
ABOUT THE WORD

1. How many books are there in the Bible?
2. How many are in the Old Testament, and how many are in the New Testament?
3. Can you recite them in order?
4. Where would you find the story of the Creation (book and chapters)?
5. Where would you find the Shepherd Psalm?
6. If you wanted to read your kids the Ten Commandments, where would you turn?
7. How many books of the Bible did John write?
8. How many did Luke write?

9. If you wanted to read about David killing Goliath, what book(s) would you turn to?
10. Where would you find the new covenant mentioned in the Old Testament?
11. If you wanted to read the Christmas story, where would you turn?
12. What is the theme of the book of Matthew?
13. If your son said, "Dad, I'm having a hard time understanding why I'm supposed to love my enemies. Why should I?" where are you going to take him?
14. Where was Paul imprisoned when he wrote his famous prison epistles?
15. Who was the first king of Israel?
16. Where would you read about the famous day of pentecost?
17. If you wanted to read about the Crucifixion and Resurrection, where would you turn?
18. If someone said to you, "Why do you feel you have to believe in Jesus?" and you could share only one verse, which one would you share?
19. Where would you find the Love Chapter?
20. If someone said to you, "What must I do to be saved?" which verse would you take him to first?

How did you do? If you didn't do very well, don't feel guilty. Instead, get excited about the process of turning your Bible from a book you carry to church to power you carry in your heart. You don't have to quit your day job and go to seminary. You just have to start heading to the rifle range on a regular basis and then keep moving among hurting people. You'll get plenty of opportunity to put your skill to work.

AT EASE

Inspection is over. You see where you're strong and where you need to put forth a little more effort. A soldier's skill is acquired through repetitious training. You have the rest of your life to wear your uniform properly, maintain alertness, keep your personal gear in order, and learn how to fire your weapon with pinpoint accuracy.

This will help when you're bivouacked with the platoon. But what about times when you look around and find that you're all alone, behind enemy lines, they know you're there, and they're searching for you? Next up: survival training behind the lines!

STUDY AND DISCUSSION QUESTIONS

UP FRONT AND PERSONAL

1. Would you agree or disagree that how your behavior appears to others is your Christian "uniform"?

2. Do people identify you with a Christian lifestyle even though you don't bring it up first? Whether your answer is yes or no, why?

3. Write down the names of five people in your life from family, work, or the neighborhood. Identify their "lifestyle uniform" according to Paul's writing in Galatians 5:22–23.

FOR THE GROUP TO DISCUSS

1. What lifestyle characteristics should be obvious for a man clothed in God's uniform?

2. In Romans 13:13–14, Paul referred to behaving "as in the daytime." Why? What is the significance of daytime behavior?

3. Can a Christian become so engrossed in a special purpose ministry that he becomes insensitive to people with different needs? Can you think of prominent religious leaders who have become insensitive in this way?

4. Some people feel it is okay to convey their own political agenda (on issues such as the merits or demerits of a political candidate or a military conflict) from a Christian viewpoint. What do you think?

5. Have we made God a Republican or a Democrat? Explain.

6. Do we wear the "parade uniform" of Christ, as when we are at church; or the work fatigues of the Spirit to do God's work every day?

7. Describe our spiritual lockerboxes.

8. What are some contraband items that may find their way into our lockerboxes?

9. Do you think that God is spot-checking the contents of our spiritual lockerboxes? Would he be pleased with the results of a surprise inspection?

10. What is the weapon of the Christian?

11. What is the weapon of the devil?

12. Turn in this chapter to the section called "Twenty Questions About the Word." Call out each question for anyone to answer. You have five minutes to finish.

APPLYING GOD'S WORD

1. Read now 2 Timothy 4:1–2. Does there remain any doubt that you should armor yourself with the Word of God?

2. If you are not already doing so, set aside a time each day to gird yourself with God's Word.

CHAPTER 5

SURVIVAL TRAINING

J UNE 2, 1995. THE NO-FLY
ZONE SOMEWHERE IN THE AERIAL CORRIDOR OVER THE FORMER
YUGOSLAVIA. Earlier that day, U.S. Air Force Captain Scott
O'Grady had kicked in the afterburner and shot his F-16 off the
runway in Aviano, Italy, to do a milk run over the territory that
news reporters all over the world were calling Bosnia. A
decade earlier, the country (known then as Yugoslavia) had
hosted the Winter Olympics in its capital of Sarajevo. If you
could stand at street level in that town now, you wouldn't
believe that the event ever happened—or could have happened—there. The picture-postcard mountain town that had
provided such a spectacular backdrop to that world event was
now devoid of its color and its spirit. Its buildings were pock-
marked and cratered from the years of civil strife. Its people
were hardened by hopelessness, and too many of its children
lay in shallow unmarked graves in the hills around it.

Captain O'Grady was part of a multination peacekeeping
force that was sent in to police the skies over the war-riven
country. The two opposing forces still hunted each other at
ground level. But at least with O'Grady and Company screaming back and forth overhead one side couldn't obtain aerial
superiority over the other. The hope had been that by shutting
down the skies, supplies would dwindle, new weapons
couldn't be brought in from bordering nations, and maybe—

just maybe—both sides might calm down long enough to try to come up with a truce.

Somewhere in the forest below, someone aimed a surface-to-air missile at Captain O'Grady's F-16. An alarm started beeping in his helmet, informing him that a radar had locked onto his plane. He took the prescribed evasive measures, but they proved useless. The missile was locked on and screaming its way toward him and his aircraft. In an instant his jet started to disintegrate around him. A hard tug on the ring at the base of his seat fired Captain O'Grady high above his destroyed plane. When he finally had time to realize what was happening, he was sitting in his cockpit seat tumbling in open sky five miles above hostile land. It would be six days before his muscles relaxed.

Most of the readers of this chapter will remember the exciting story of the survival and heroic rescue of Scott O'Grady. It's a great one to tell your kids and grandkids. Captain O'Grady managed to evade capture while subsisting on a diet of leaves and insects. He maintained his composure in spite of the hostile climate, dangerous terrain, and the enemy guerrillas who were searching for him the entire time.

Finally, after receiving faint signals from his locator, the Tactical Recovery Aircraft Personnel (TRAP), made up of marines who volunteered for the mission, launched from the USS *Kearsarge* to make their rescue. It's the kind of stuff movies are made of. But for six days, there was nothing glamorous about the nightmare Captain O'Grady found himself in.

Although he experienced frightening conditions, Scott O'Grady found his time at ground level in Bosnia to be the most profound week of his life:

> Those six days in Bosnia became a religious retreat for me, a total spiritual renewal. I'm not recommending near-death experience for its own sake. It's a ride I wouldn't care to take again. But I will say that my time in Bosnia was completely positive—nothing bad has come out of it. From the instant that my plane blew up around me, *I opened my heart to God's love.*[1]

COVERT MISSIONS

A lot of good men find themselves in spiritually hostile territory. Maybe you find yourself there every Monday through Friday at 8:30 when you sit down at your desk in your office and try to make a living. You may be the only person in the entire office who believes in Jesus Christ, and you may have a few people in that office who can't stand the fact that you do.

You may wear a flannel blue-collared shirt to work each day and carry your lunch in an Igloo cooler. Life on a construction crew can be tough on a man's faith, especially if he wants to live it out conscientiously. During my summer breaks in college, I worked construction. I was low man on the totem pole— a grunt laborer. If you count the lunchtimes and travel to and from the site with the other workers, I spent fifty-five hours a week having to listen to some of the filthiest concepts a human mind could conjure up. I worked against a backdrop of sexually explicit stories, racial bigotry, and dehumanizing imagery. There was absolutely nothing or no one sacred enough to be off-limits to those guys' ridicule—especially the Lord Jesus Christ.

One summer I carried a mud hod up and down scaffolding on a construction site in a suburb of Washington, D.C. One bricklayer literally could not make a complete sentence. I never heard him put together a subject and a predicate in a logical sequence. The only way I could figure out what he wanted was to listen closely for the word *shoot* (i.e., he needed more cement) or *shake* (i.e., his cement was drying out and he needed me to bring some water and a shovel and "shake" it up for him) to emerge from the row of expletives. One afternoon I happened to mention that it would be great if he just said "shoot" and left out all of the twenty-eight other nonessential filthy words from his statement. He instantly jumped down from the scaffolding above me (I was one below him), knocked me over against the bars, put his cement trowel to my throat (those things are sharp), and proceeded to spit a series of vulgarities at me that would have made Redd Foxx blush. When he finally satisfied his profane mind, he stepped back, laughed at the look on my face, and then climbed back up to his spot on the line to the applause of every guy on the site.

That's an example of what can happen when a nineteen-year-old kid tries to help a fellow employee with his grammar. It's a wonder I didn't wet my pants!

But I want to tell you something about that summer and the many other summers I spent like it: they were experiences that galvanized my faith and defined my convictions. God used them as laboratory experiments for my belief system. There, in the middle of some of the most godless men I had ever met, God taught me how to look beyond the external to the void at the core of the human heart. He taught me not only to work effectively side by side with those men, but also to grow to love them. I got to be good friends with many of them, and from the platform of those friendships I was able to give them a peek at the Savior who owned my heart. Even the bricklayer who feigned that he was going to slit my throat became a friend. On my last day before I was to head back to college, he bought me a soda and a Snickers from the chuck wagon that stopped by every morning around 8:30.

What we learn at the survival level of our faith are the things that are most essential to a healthy relationship with God. And we start to see people the way Jesus sees them, as scattered sheep in dire need of a shepherd (Matt. 9:36). We also learn how to process the hate of our enemies through the love and grace of God.

IT'S ALL IN THE FAMILY

Some men cross the line into enemy territory as soon as they pull the car into the garage. Maybe you became a Christian after you were married and now find yourself living with a wife who not only doesn't know Christ but also works overtime to put you in situations that challenge your core values. Maybe you have a teenage son or daughter who is being manipulated by the powers of darkness, and living under the same roof with your teen is like hell on earth.

And all of us have occasions when we have to gather around the table with relatives who embrace some of the goofiest beliefs and sorriest habits imaginable. They take inappropriateness to new heights—exactly the kind of people Jesus wants to teach us to love.

WHEN WE FORGET TO FOLLOW INSTRUCTIONS

The list of survival skills needed to consistently walk by faith isn't crowded with clever insights we have never heard before. They are as basic to our existence as breathing, eating, and sleeping. They are so basic that we take them for granted. We turn them into clichés of the Christian walk that every Christian knows about but seldom consistently does. It seems that it takes a crisis before the average Christian realizes why the pastor keeps preaching about the same essentials to a healthy walk with God.

It's the same in military training. The instructor tells a soldier that should he find himself in certain dilemmas, he should do such and such. The soldier gives him a look as if he is paying attention, but the instructor knows he isn't. The soldier figures that it's a long shot that he would ever find himself in that kind of a desperate situation. That's why the instructor tries to simulate as many of the hazardous conditions as possible, so that the soldier will already have worked himself out of the crisis before he ever faces a real one. But some dilemmas are impossible to simulate. The instructor just hopes the soldier paid enough attention during training.

Joe Foss always followed orders. He led a squadron of fighter pilots in some of the fiercest aerial combat of World War II. The skies over Henderson Field, on the island of Guadalcanal, made heroes out of many good men. They also made a lot of widows out of their wives. Joe's wife almost became one of those widows—not because he didn't follow orders, but because he didn't follow instructions.

One afternoon, Joe was leading his squadron on a bombing-and-strafing mission of a Japanese convoy when they encountered a couple of Japanese scout planes. Joe splashed one of the planes into the ocean. While he was concentrating on the one, however, the other shot a hole in his cockpit windshield and damaged his engine. He had to pull out of the fight to nurse his crippled plane back to Henderson Field. Still over the ocean but in sight of the island of Malaita, Joe realized that his plane was not going to make it home. He would have to ditch into the ocean.

There were two instructions he had been given in flight school for such situations. The first was, "If you have to ditch into the ocean, jettison your canopy." Joe was flying with his canopy in the open position (i.e., slid back behind him). The second thing his instructor said was, "Also, on a water landing, make sure you unstrap the leg straps on your parachute."

Joe found out why his flight instructor had suggested those two items be on his checklist in an emergency water landing. His wounded F4F Grumman Wildcat drilled its barely spinning propeller into a rising swell in the ocean. It was like crashing into a brick wall. The impact sent his canopy sliding forward and snapped it down into the locked position. His airplane immediately began to sink. The buoyancy of his parachute, which was under his rump, forced his head forward into his instruments. It was wanting to turn him upside down.

Had he unstrapped his leg straps, Joe could have easily slipped out of his parachute. Instead, it was forcing his upper body into his instrument panel and making it difficult to dislodge his feet from beneath his seat. Adding to his nightmare was the difficulty of trying to unlock and slide back the canopy while sucking in ocean water and sinking like a rock into the depths of a pitch-black sea. It can make for a really discouraging situation. Had he followed his instructions, Joe could have exited his plane the second it began to sink. Joe believes that only the grace of God got him out of that mess.

SIX SPIRITUAL SURVIVAL SKILLS

We can find ourselves cut off from the crowd and feeling desperately on our own because we either are forced to function behind the lines or fail to follow instructions we've been taught for survival in those situations. Regardless of where it happens or how it happens, there isn't a man of God who gets through the Christian experience without somewhere finding himself all alone in no-man's-land. You can't let those situations get the best of you. Let's learn six survival skills that can keep the spirit alive in the midst of all of this.

1. MAINTAIN YOUR NUTRITION

It's a strategy as old as warfare itself. A starving soldier will soon be vanquished. It takes energy to hold your post or stand your ground. A soldier whose stomach is empty for a prolonged period of time can't concentrate on his duty because he is so preoccupied with his hunger. He is more susceptible to diseases. Discouragement overwhelms him. A hungry soldier can easily find himself a prisoner of war—taken captive not because he lacked the skill or the courage to hold his ground, but because he lacked the energy.

In the late spring of 1942, the American forces at Fortress Corregidor and the Bataan Peninsula in the Republic of the Philippines found starvation to be a greater challenge than the constant pounding they were receiving from Japan's artillery. They were outnumbered and outgunned, but the thing that finally signaled the end was the fact that they were simply too weak to fight. They had become so weak from lack of food that only 15 percent of their force were capable of carrying a rifle one hundred yards and then firing it.[2] Shortly after General MacArthur moved his headquarters to Brisbane, Australia, the officers left in the Philippines were forced to surrender their men to the enemy. A man can only hold out so long on an empty stomach.

The obvious nourishment for a soldier of the Cross is the Word of God. And when you find yourself consistently having to function in hostile spiritual territory, you will not stand a chance of enduring without a regular diet of the Scriptures. Let me show you twenty ways that God's Word keeps you spiritually healthy and strong. All of them are from Psalm 119:

- *It keeps you from sin:* "I have hidden your word in my heart that I might not sin against you" (v. 11).
- *It gives you something to be joyful about:* "I rejoice in following your statutes as one rejoices in great riches" (v. 14).
- *It keeps you humble:* "You rebuke the arrogant, who are cursed and who stray from your commands" (v. 21).
- *It helps you when you're discouraged:* "My soul is weary with sorrow; strengthen me according to your word" (v. 28).
- *It keeps you from being deceived or deceiving yourself:*

"Keep me from deceitful ways; be gracious to me through your law" (v. 29).

- *It helps you finish well:* "Teach me, O LORD, to follow your decrees; then I will keep them to the end" (v. 33).
- *It keeps you from getting preoccupied with things that don't matter:* "Turn my heart toward your statutes and not toward selfish gain. / Turn my eyes away from worthless things; preserve my life according to your word" (vv. 36–37).
- *It takes a load off your emotions:* "I will walk about in freedom, for I have sought out your precepts" (v. 45).
- *It gives you boldness:* "I will speak of your statutes before kings and will not be put to shame" (v. 46).
- *It helps you endure suffering:* "My comfort in my suffering is this: Your promise preserves my life" (v. 50).
- *It helps you endure abuse for your faith:* "The arrogant mock me without restraint, but I do not turn from your law" (v. 51).
- *It helps you behave when you're traveling:* "Your decrees are the theme of my song wherever I lodge" (v. 54).
- *It helps you love other Christians:* "I am a friend to all who fear you, to all who follow your precepts" (v. 63).
- *It helps you show more compassion:* "Let your compassion come to me that I may live, for your law is my delight" (v. 77).
- *It helps you keep life in perspective:* "Your word, O LORD, is eternal; it stands firm in the heavens" (v. 89).
- *It gives you wisdom:* "Your commands make me wiser than my enemies, for they are ever with me" (v. 98).
- *It keeps you from tripping over obstacles to your faith:* "Your word is a lamp to my feet and a light for my path" (v. 105).
- *It makes you more valuable to your family:* "Your statutes are my heritage forever; they are the joy of my heart" (v. 111).
- *It saves you from a lot of trial and error:* "Your promises have been thoroughly tested, and your servant loves them" (v. 140).

- *It helps you pray more intelligently:* "May my supplication come before you; deliver me according to your promise" (v. 170).

Power, energy, spiritual vitality—all are waiting for the man who keeps God's Word in his heart. But that's where the problem lies. Too many Christian men don't prioritize the Bible. They love the Word, but don't read the Word. They carry their Bibles to church, but they don't take its truth to work. When they find themselves behind enemy lines, the Word of God isn't deeply embedded enough into their hearts to be able to sustain them.

There are ways to solve this problem without having to quit what you're doing and sign up for seminary. A good soldier wouldn't head out on patrol without first filling his stomach. Have a little of God's Word for breakfast every day. Read a chapter each morning, or get a devotional guide that draws a small sound bite from the Bible and distills it into a two-minute thought. Take some biblical C rations with you to work. If you drive to work alone, instead of listening to the radio, play the Bible on tape. It's a great way to go through the Bible each year. Go to your Christian bookstore, and ask to see some of the tools available to you to get reminders of God's Word throughout the day. There are flip calendars with verses and thoughts, time organizers with scriptural priorities built into them. You can get cards with verses printed on them that you can set on your desk or on the dashboard of your truck. There is no end to the ways that a man can ingest God's Word throughout his demanding day. The key is to do *something*. If you stay spiritually malnourished, it's just a matter of time before you will surrender to the enemy.

2. GUARD YOUR REST

When I worked construction during my college days, I noticed that I was more sensitive and vulnerable to the degrading banter of my workplace before lunch than I was after lunch. My guard was stronger at the beginning of my day compared to the end of my day. The reason is obvious. The more fatigued I was, the harder it was to maintain my focus.

Marshall and Brenda were new Christians. They came from pitiful families. If you looked up *dysfunction* in the dictionary, their families would be the centerfolds. Although they didn't live close enough to see their families on a daily basis, they did try to take the kids home for key holidays and a vacation each year. But they dreaded the visits. It seemed that everything started off well, but before long people were at each other's throat. They were concerned that they couldn't manage to be more long-suffering and caring toward their non-Christian family members. They wanted to be good witnesses, but they ended up shooting their testimony in the foot with their impatience.

After talking with them about some of the incidents that triggered their frustration with their families, I asked them about the schedule they kept when they were home. It was just as I thought: keeping too many appointments, having too many get-togethers, staying up late every night, getting up early every morning, playing hard, and working hard. No time for rest. As a result of this observation, they decided to do two things. First, they called different family members before their next trip back and admitted to them that they needed to change the pace of the visit. They wanted to spend good time with them but felt that the usual crowded schedule caused them to wake up tired each day. They were surprised when their parents and siblings admitted they were always tired from the pace of the visit too. After talking with their families, the second thing they did came easily. They brought family gatherings to a close earlier and slept in at least one of the days they were home. Their kids felt better, everyone enjoyed one another, and they were able to give their nonbelieving family members a gift they always wanted to give them—the patience and understanding of God's love.

When a soldier finds himself in hostile territory, he knows he is in trouble if he doesn't pace himself. Resting your body gives your emotions and spirit a badly needed break. If you find yourself more and more vulnerable to a hostile environment at work or even at home, take some deliberate steps. Get to bed at a reasonable hour. Don't crowd your schedule. Take solo breaks every once in a while at work. Eat a few lunches by yourself. Take a Walkman to work and listen to a praise tape during your free time. Go for a walk. Collect your thoughts. Read a few verses from the Word and then muse on them. Everyone wins when you guard your reserves.

3. KEEP YOUR WITS

On July 30, 1945, the USS *Indianapolis* left the island of Tinian to sail to Leyte. It had left behind the components of a weapon of destruction more fierce and deadly than anything the world had ever seen. Within a few hours, crews would begin fitting the piece of cargo into the bomb bay of the *Enola Gay*. Hiroshima would be its ultimate destination.

The officers and crew of the *Indianapolis* would meet an equally horrifying fate as the citizens of Hiroshima. In war conditions, the captain of a surface ship would order his helmsman to zigzag as they made their way through the water. The reason is obvious. If an enemy submarine happened to spot them, it would be harder to set up a torpedo shot. It was also protocol to move the ship through the night in blackout conditions. The captain of the *Indianapolis* failed to take those two fundamental defensive measures. As a result, many men were killed when Japanese torpedoes ripped into the side of their ship, and many more died in the days to come as they floated in the sea. Usually, the ship would have been reported late from its cruise, and search planes would have been sent out to find survivors. But because of the top-secret cargo the *Indianapolis* had carried to Tinian, its mission was never logged out in the first place. Their distress signal was garbled and, therefore, never received.

The officers and crew fought rough seas and repeated shark attacks for several days before a search plane happened to spot them. One thing kept the men going when everything else told them to give up: *hope*. Key officers and enlisted men kept assuring them that they would be rescued.

The U.S. prisoners of war who spent years in the Hanoi Hilton kept their wits by staying focused on the future. James Stockdale, John McCain, and hundreds of other brave men endured horrific torture by keeping their minds focused beyond the barbed wire fences that surrounded them. They reminded each other of the love of their families, the power of their nation to appeal for their release, and the faithfulness of the Lord.

The best way to summarize how those men in those horrible situations made it through is that they refused to *micro*manage their situation. They *macro*managed it. If they focused only on how bad, how unfair, how hostile, or how miserable everything was, they would have given up and died. But they looked beyond their conditions. They macromanaged their dilemma. They used the perspective of the big picture to keep from succumbing to disillusionment.

Some men have children who have strayed far from the Lord. Their kids are making horrible choices and reaping the sad consequences of their choices. It's tempting to give in to the thought that the kids are beyond hope. Maybe you work in an environment where you feel there is no way your spiritual life is going to have an impact and the price you pay for living for Christ isn't worth it. Maybe you go to sleep every night next to a wife who is intolerant of your faith. If you focus on your dilemma, you will ultimately surrender to defeat.

Choose hope! Guard your wits. Good Christian soldiers keep at least one eye on the eternal at all times. The Scriptures remind us:

For our light and momentary troubles are achieving for us an eternal glory that far outweighs them all. So we fix our eyes not on what is seen, but on what is unseen. For what is seen is temporary, but what is unseen is eternal. (2 Cor. 4:17–18)

Therefore, since we are surrounded by such a great cloud of witnesses, let us throw off everything that hinders and the sin that so easily entangles, and let us run with perseverance the race marked out for us. Let us fix our eyes on Jesus, the author and perfecter of our faith, who for the joy set before him endured the cross, scorning its shame, and sat down at the right hand of the throne of God. Consider him who endured such opposition from sinful men, so that you will not grow weary and lose heart. (Heb. 12:1–3)

An eternal perspective and a focus on Jesus help you process all of the threats around you with far more calm and confidence.

4. TREAT YOUR WOUNDS

Life in a spiritual battle zone can leave a lot of scar tissue on your emotions. Denying or trivializing this reality is the fastest way for a man of God to end up bitter, cynical, or indifferent. It hurts to take attacks on your Christian witness. It hurts when other Christians let you down. It hurts when you are forced to exist in a spiritual no-man's-land far longer than you feel is fair. That's why you shouldn't go anywhere without your spiritual survival kit.

The wounds you most often suffer when you have to function in an environment hostile to Christians include anger from being misunderstood or attacked, doubts and self-efface- ment as a result of believing what people are saying about you, and loneliness from isolation. Some basic parts of your first-aid kit—forgiveness, praise, and worship—are specifically designed to treat these wounds.

Forgiveness is one of the most powerful antibiotics in your kit. When it is applied first, it enhances the effect of praise and worship in your heart. Jesus was in his most hostile environ- ment when he hung on the cross. Evil men and women scoffed at him as he hung there bleeding and dying for their redemp- tion. He said, "Father, forgive them, for they do not know what they do" (Luke 23:34 NKJV). He wasn't implying that by forgiv- ing them they were no longer held responsible for their actions. He was saying that they were people wrapped up in their sin and rage who behaved according to their lost condi- tion. He wanted to extend mercy to them before his Father. After all, their lost condition was the reason for his coming to Calvary in the first place.

You see Stephen, the first martyr for the gospel, forgiving the people who were throwing the rocks at him that would ulti- mately take his life (Acts 7:60). Stephen's extension of forgive- ness did not absolve the mob of their personal responsibility for their actions, but forgiveness released Stephen from having to harbor the rage and bitterness of being murdered. Forgive- ness is a gift you give to the people who hurt you as well as a gift you give to yourself. It's potent medicine for a hurting heart.

One more point about forgiveness before we look at the

antiseptic nature of praise: a lot of people don't want to offer forgiveness to someone who has hurt them because they don't want to let the person off the hook for what he has done. When you forgive someone who has hurt you, it doesn't mean that he is off the hook for what he has done; it just means that he is off *your* hook. He is still on God's. By forgiving him, you're relinquishing your right to stay mad or get even with him for what he has done to you. You are leaving justice and revenge where they belong—in God's hands. As you learn in Romans 12:17–21:

> Do not repay anyone evil for evil. Be careful to do what is right in the eyes of everybody. If it is possible, as far as it depends on you, live at peace with everyone. Do not take revenge, my friends, but leave room for God's wrath, for it is written: "It is mine to avenge; I will repay," says the Lord. On the contrary:
>
> "If your enemy is hungry, feed him;
>   if he is thirsty, give him something to drink.
> In doing this, you will heap burning coals on his
>   head."
>
> Do not be overcome by evil, but overcome evil with good.

Another great antiseptic for a wounded heart is *praise*. It's a remarkable cure for doubts and self-effacement. When you are in a constant environment of antagonism toward your beliefs, you may doubt whether your beliefs are legitimate. Praise is effective medicine because it gives you a chance to remind your spirit just how much you are loved. Praise leaps from a heart that has been redeemed and rescued. When you praise God, you're brought back to the point of your salvation. You don't have to make a scene or embarrass people in order to praise God. You can praise him in your heart and in your attitudes. When people see you working hard, cheering their legitimate efforts, and working overtime to help them succeed, you point them to the Savior. They see you responding contrary to what your treatment would dictate. Only a loving God could enable you to do that.

A third item in the first-aid kit is a wonderful ointment called *worship*. It's a salve for a lonely heart. Worship can do many things for you, but one thing it does is to help you focus on the intimate relationship you have with the God of history. It views God not in a moment in time but in the larger story of his relationship with humankind from the beginning of time. It's acknowledging the God who has sustained his people through all the whims of change. Often, in the Old Testament, you read of a prophet or king referring to God as the God of Abraham, Isaac, and Jacob. He was seeing the God of the big picture. It helped him transcend the particular nightmare he was experiencing.

To worship God when you're having to operate in a non-Christian environment, you can present your body as a living sacrifice. You learn this in Romans 12:1–2:

> **Therefore, I urge you, brothers, in view of God's mercy, to offer your bodies as living sacrifices, holy and pleasing to God—this is your spiritual act of worship. Do not conform any longer to the pattern of this world, but be transformed by the renewing of your mind. Then you will be able to test and approve what God's will is—his good, pleasing and perfect will.**

Being willing to function and serve God in a hostile setting is an act of worship. You are saying, "I love you, Lord, and I'll serve you anywhere, any way, any time."

Forgiveness, praise, and worship applied together make a powerful prescription for a broken heart. But even if you aren't hurting, they're also three antibiotics you can take every day to keep yourself spiritually healthy.

5. EVADE THE ENEMY

The fifth item on your survival checklist is making sure you don't fall into the hands of the enemy. Enemy soldiers stepped within inches of Scott O'Grady when he was evading them. Even a twitch from him would have given away his hiding place. Sometimes you feel that close to spiritual danger. You need to take efforts to minimize your risk of being taken captive.

You know your situation. Every man has certain temptations and traps that he must avoid. If you work in a large office, it is easy to get pulled into cynical humor, gossip, and senseless debates. Certain places and times in your situation are tailor-made for them, such as coffee breaks, the copy room, lunchtime. Certain people are more likely to draw you into these negative conversations than others. Take drastic measures! Avoid certain people if necessary, change subjects if the talk is getting out of line, excuse yourself from the conversation, but most of all—*do something.*

Maybe you travel a lot. You're out of the accountable view of your wife, children, and friends. Take them with you! Not physically, but with you nonetheless. Call your wife and kids regularly. Always carry pictures of them that you can set up in your hotel room. Have a buddy you can call to confide in if you're struggling.

One of the problems that growing Christians face in a non-Christian environment is that they often become the company counselor. People may mock and ridicule you, but when the wheels fall off their lives, they are quick to turn to you for advice. Here's the problem: sometimes they are beautiful women. They may be having problems with a husband or boyfriend. You represent someone who is the antithesis of the person they're with. You treat women with worth, honor, and high respect. So they turn to you for help. Watch out! This is the ideal scenario for the development of an emotional affair. And the prettier they are, the easier it is.

How do you avoid this trap? It's simple. Step One: maintain a healthy relationship with your wife. If you aren't married, skip to Step Two. Step Two: don't become the adviser or confidant. If they want to talk with you about these problems, recommend a competent woman that they could call for help (perhaps your wife or sister). If there isn't a suitable female available, you should still refuse to get involved at an emotional level with them. Our God is a big God. He can find an adequate person to help them without having to put you in jeopardy. You might think that you're capable of handling these situations without falling into an emotional or sexual trap. If you think that, then you're dead meat! Look at what God's Word says:

> [Jesus gave this advice:] **"Watch and pray so that you will not fall into temptation. The spirit is willing, but the body is weak."** (Matt. 26:41)

So, if you think you are standing firm, be careful that you don't fall! (1 Cor. 10:12)

Keep in mind that when it comes to drawing you into temptations and sinful traps, Satan is not primarily trying to destroy you. That's his secondary purpose. What he wants most of all is to steal glory from God. Your sin makes God's power look ineffective to non-Christians. That's why you must take every evasive measure possible to keep from succumbing to captivity by the powers of darkness.

6. PREPARE FOR RESCUE

When a soldier is caught behind enemy lines, he must take one other step in order to survive his hostile situation—get rescued. Modern-day soldiers who are on a mission where they could possibly find themselves behind enemy lines are issued a homing beacon. Scott O'Grady had one. Even though its battery was starting to run down and its signal was getting weak, it was the very thing the recovery personnel used to locate him. Before the issuing of homing beacons, soldiers were taught to have signal fires ready or to spread the parachute out in such a way as to alert a search-and-rescue plane.

Men of God have been issued a homing signal to alert rescue forces that we are in trouble and need help—we have prayer. Daniel consistently prayed as he lived behind enemy lines (Dan. 6:10). Elijah prayed when he was being hunted by wicked Queen Jezebel (1 Kings 19:3–9). David prayed when he was running from Absalom (2 Sam. 15:31). When the pressure is on, pray.

Jesus said we "always ought to pray and not lose heart" (Luke 18:1 NKJV). When he knew the time had come for him to have to endure the agony of the cross, he isolated himself to pray and ask the heavenly Father for strength (Luke 22:39–46). Paul summarized it this way: "Don't worry about anything; pray about everything." He declared in Philippians 4:6–7: "Do not be anxious about anything, but in everything, by prayer and petition, with thanksgiving, present your requests to God. And the peace of God, which transcends all understanding, will guard your hearts and your minds in Christ Jesus."

When you're alone and afraid, two things can cause you to

get yourself into deeper problems: letting your fears get the best of you so much that you become paralyzed and give up hope, or allowing your mind to slip into irrational thinking or vain imaginations. Prayer guards you against that because Paul said that God's peace will guard your heart and your mind. Prayer takes the attention off your desperate situation and focuses on an awesome God. God's power can overcome any situation. Paul told you what the attitude of the heart is supposed to be when you pray: it is to be an attitude of thankfulness. That assumes confidence in the power of the God you are praying to.

That requires faith. God's Word says that "without faith it is impossible to please God, because anyone who comes to him must believe that he exists and that he rewards those who earnestly seek him" (Heb. 11:6). Proverbs 4:23 urges, "Above all else, guard your heart, for it is the wellspring of life." So the process works like this:

You find yourself in a hostile spiritual environment.
God wants you to guard your heart because . . .
it is from the depths of the heart that the joy of life comes,
so you exercise faith in an all-powerful God,
for whom you are thankful, and
he turns around and guards your heart and mind from the
    discouragement and fear that could finish you off.

Let me mention two other powerful passages for you when you feel frightened and alone:

For the eyes of the LORD range throughout the earth to strengthen those whose hearts are fully committed to him. (2 Chron. 16:9)

> **Do you not know?**
>   **Have you not heard?**
> **The LORD is the everlasting God,**
>   **the Creator of the ends of the earth.**
> **He will not grow tired or weary,**
>   **and his understanding no one can fathom.**
> **He gives strength to the weary**
>   **and increases the power of the weak.**

> Even youths grow tired and weary,
>   and young men stumble and fall;
> but those who hope in the LORD will renew their strength.
> They will soar on wings like eagles;
>   they will run and not grow weary,
>   they will walk and not be faint. (Isa. 40:28–31)

No matter what the odds, no matter how isolated you feel, don't worry about anything. Instead, pray about everything.

Maintaining spiritual nutrition, guarding your rest, keeping your wits, treating your wounds, evading the enemy, and always being prepared for God to rescue you from the traps set for you are nonnegotiables to spiritual survival. If you are going to live on the front lines of the cause of Christ, you're going to find yourself behind enemy lines more often than not. Don't panic. Like Scott O'Grady, you will find that relying on your spiritual training and trusting in a God who has everything under control could turn out to be the biggest spiritual victory you could ever experience.

STUDY AND DISCUSSION QUESTIONS

UP FRONT AND PERSONAL

1. Are you forced to function in a spiritually hostile environment? Is it at work or home?

2. Has God taught you to look beyond the outer shell of a spiritually hostile person and into an empty heart? If so, how?

3. Do you have a spouse or a child living under the powers of darkness? Have you talked with your pastor and other men of God about what the Scriptures say your actions should be? If not, have that talk right away.

FOR THE GROUP TO DISCUSS

1. We may succumb to temptation because we suffer from spiritual malnutrition. What is the food of the spirit that enables us to overcome?

2. Have you "prioritized" the Bible? What does that mean?

3. List five ways to easily absorb a little of God's Word every day.

4. There are six spiritual survival skills. The first is to *maintain your nutrition*. Discuss how you would develop a personal plan to study the Word. If you already have a plan, share it with the group.

5. The second is to *guard your rest*. How many hours of sleep should you have each night to be at your best the next day?

6. The third survival skill is to *keep your wits*. State how you can use a Christian perspective of the "big picture" to stay focused on what is ahead.

7. The fourth is to *treat your wounds*. The three spiritual ingredients for treating your emotional and spiritual wounds are forgiveness, praise, and worship. Is one of these more important? If so, which one, and why?

8. The fifth skill is to *evade the enemy*. What enemy are we talking about? Discuss how the company of our Christian brethren helps us.

9. The sixth survival skill is to *prepare for rescue*. What is our "homing signal" for a spiritual rescue?

APPLYING GOD'S WORD

1. Do you carry your Bible to church but leave its truth behind? Carry the Word in your heart where it will never be lost.

2. Study Psalm 139.

3. Focus not on your problems but on their solutions. Ponder Psalm 37:5, which says, "Commit your way to the LORD, / Trust also in Him, / And He shall bring it to pass" (NKJV).

4. Pray about everything.

CHAPTER 6

BATTLE-GROUND

It's hard to say what in Wendell Fertig's childhood and engineering studies prepared him for the role he would play fighting his part of the war in the South Pacific. He was a recently promoted light colonel when he reported to Brigadier General William Sharp on the island of Mindanao, Republic of the Philippines. His last assignment had been to rig for demolition all of the ordnance on the Bataan Peninsula in order to keep it from being seized by the enemy.

General Sharp decided to surrender his forces on Mindanao to the Japanese shortly after Fertig's arrival. Fertig had other plans. Rather than sit out the war in a Japanese prison camp, Lieutenant Colonel Fertig slipped into the jungle (in obedience to the wishes of General Sharp), along with a handful of other men, to set up an insurgent army against the Japanese.

Before long he assembled a small army of men who had escaped from the other Philippine islands. As their commander, Fertig organized an effective campaign of harassing and distracting the Japanese army until General MacArthur could finally fulfill his promise to the Philippine people to return.

Wendell Fertig and the U.S. Forces in the Philippines (USFIP) had to constantly contend with three threats. They illustrate the same three enemies we have in our day-to-day battle to live for Christ.

KNOW YOUR ENEMY

This chapter is about the ways in which you as a Christian could find yourself compromised, neutralized, and demoralized in your walk with God. There are three basic threats to your ability to stay faithful to your convictions and four basic ways these threats can attack you. We'll deal with them in a way that should leave you adequately forewarned and, I hope, forearmed. But before we talk about the battleground of the Christian faith, I need to make sure one essential point is clear at the outset of this study. *Our conflict is not with people.* People may be used by the various forces to bring us down, but they are not the enemy.

I'm bringing up this point because too many within the ranks of the Christian movement make the mistake of viewing people as their primary threat. How am I defining *people* at this point? Anybody, whether Christian or non-Christian, who fails to fall within a particular Christian's definition of spiritual acceptability. I've known Christians who viewed as their enemies their neighbors, their child's teacher or principal, their son's science professor, a Hollywood celebrity, a politician, a rock star, or their bosses, you name it. And they treat them as enemies. They speak caustically about them, show them dishonor and disrespect, and sometimes even threaten them in Jesus' name. They justify this behavior by quoting 2 Corinthians 6:17:

> **Therefore come out from them**
> **and be separate,**
>> **says the Lord.**
> **Touch no unclean thing,**
> **and I will receive you.**

There is no way this verse justifies any Christian treating another person, whether Christian or non-Christian, as an enemy. They may treat us as their enemies, but we are not to treat them as ours. We are told to "love your enemies and pray for those who persecute you, that you may be sons of your Father in heaven" (Matt. 5:44–45).

The Bible definitely teaches that certain kinds of people who embrace certain kinds of thinking can have a negative effect on us. For example, we read in 1 Corinthians 15:33: "Do not be misled: 'Bad company corrupts good character.'" It even teaches that there are times when we should not associate with them. But at no time are we to treat them as our enemies. Our ultimate goal is to reach them for Christ. That's hard to do if they feel we view them as "beneath us." We are told to be the "salt of the earth" and the "light of the world" (Matt. 5:13–14 NKJV). We can't be salt unless we first get out of the salt shaker. We can't be light if we are holed up in our church fortresses and fire salvos at all the people surrounding us.

When it comes to a fellow Christian with whom we disagree or we view as a threat to our belief system, God's Word says,

> **If anyone does not obey our instruction in this letter, take special note of him. Do not associate with him, in order that he may feel ashamed. Yet do not regard him as an enemy, but warn him as a brother. (2 Thess. 3:14–15)**

> **I have written you in my letter not to associate with sexually immoral people—not at all meaning the people of this world who are immoral, or the greedy and swindlers, or idolaters. In that case you would have to leave this world. But now I am writing you that you must not associate with anyone who calls himself a brother but is sexually immoral or greedy, an idolater or a slanderer, a drunkard or a swindler. With such a man do not even eat. (1 Cor. 5:9–11)**

People, whether they are errant believers or nonbelievers, need to be reached with the hope of Christ's forgiveness, mercy, and love. Therefore, as we develop our skill to combat the enemies to our righteousness, we want to make sure that we at no time view people as our enemies. Rather the forces that are at work behind them, in them, or through them are our enemies.

THE TRIUNE ENEMY

The men who made up the U.S. Forces in the Philippines had to contend with three enemies. Their first enemy was a hostile environment. The jungle was hot, humid, and crawling with every kind of animal and insect capable of ruining a man's day. Mosquitoes were a constant nuisance, venomous reptiles could surprise them while they were bivouacked at night, and they had a few spiders that made life miserable. If the soldiers tried to move around by water, they had to contend with sharks. The natives were a mixed bag. Some were allied with the American interests and were willing to do everything they could to aid Fertig's troops. Others were more mercenary in their loyalties and sold their aid to the highest bidder. They had many supplies the Americans needed but didn't produce them until a shipment of gold arrived by submarine. Then there were those who were antagonistic to the American interests. They could be counted on to betray Fertig's plans to the Japanese.

The second enemy of the men of USFIP was disease. Malaria was rampant among the troops. And without adequate medicine to treat it, the ranks of Fertig's army were decimated. Add to the disease problem the fact that they didn't have enough food. Malnutrition was a constant threat. That caused discouragement and morale problems.

The third enemy was, of course, the presence of a couple of divisions of Japanese soldiers on the island. The Japanese had superior numbers and superior resources. Until the liberation of the island by MacArthur, Fertig and his men engaged in a constant battle of wits and might with the Japanese forces. USFIP had to live in a constant state of alertness. They were always packed and ready to flee to the jungle should their location be detected.

As a soldier of the Lord Jesus Christ, you have three similar enemies.

1. THE WORLD SYSTEM

You must operate in an environment filled with hazards to your faith. Just walk around in any town and you'll see evidence of the corruption of the world. So far, I've logged miles on four continents. I've searched high and low and I have yet to locate the Mayberry of TV's sitcom *The Andy Griffith Show*. It doesn't exist. The world is corrupted. I've chosen my words carefully here. It is corrupted, not corrupt. Originally, God made the heavens and the earth and pronounced them good

(Gen. 1:31). They were perfect until a point in time when they were corrupted by the introduction of sin into the world.

God's Word has a lot to say about the nature of the world system: "For everything in the world—the cravings of sinful man, the lust of his eyes and the boasting of what he has and does—comes not from the Father but from the world. The world and its desires pass away, but the man who does the will of God lives forever" (1 John 2:16–17).

Someday God is going to uncorrupt the world. There will be a new heaven and new earth (Rev. 21:1). In the meantime, you have to contend with antagonism of your convictions.

2. THE FLESH

Track with me here because there has been so much faulty teaching about the nature of human beings. Like the men on the island of Mindanao who had to contend with disease, we, too, have to contend with a disease—it's called sin. In fact, it's a terminal illness. Romans 5:12 plainly states, "Therefore, just as sin entered the world through one man, and death through sin, and in this way death came to all men, because all sinned." As a result, we have a corrupted nature or what the Bible calls a "sin nature." There is nothing we can do on our own to remedy this problem. We have no built-in cure for our corrupted nature.

A lot of people make a mistake in how they view the starting point of their sin problem and its ultimate effect on them. I've often heard preachers and Bible teachers say that we are sinful *by* nature. That is false. We are sinful *in* our nature. You ask, "What's the difference?" Tons!

We were not created sinful. We were created perfect. We were made in God's image—the antithesis of corruption. There was a point in time when the beautiful and perfect nature of human beings was corrupted by sin. Why is this clarification important? When we teach that we are sinful by nature, we lose the sense of our dignity. We say that we are absolutely, fundamentally flawed by nature. If we are sinners by nature, we create a host of problems within our theology.

Sit up for a minute, please, and rearrange your boxers because I'm about to give you a crash course in Theology 101 that you desperately need if you want to gain victory over your corrupted sin nature. The reason we don't want to teach that we are sinful *by* nature is that we create four huge nightmares within our understanding of the Bible.

First, it messes up our doctrine of God because it teaches that God made something imperfect. We've already seen that that isn't so.

Second, it messes up our doctrine of Christ. The Bible teaches that Christ was fully man and yet fully God (don't try to make it all add up in your mind because it's a mystery). If man is sinful by nature, then Christ, being fully man, would have been sinful too. That, we know, isn't true. Christ was fully man, yet without sin.

Third, it messes up our doctrine of human beings. If we see a pig wallowing in the mud, we don't poke it with a stick and tell it to stop, because it's not doing anything wrong. A pig has no sweat glands. The only way it can cool itself down is to wallow in mud. It's the pig's nature. However, if we see a man wallowing in sin, we can expect him to stop it because he is not behaving according to his nature. He is behaving contrary to his nature of being made in the image of God. If a man was sinful *by* nature, he wouldn't be capable of doing anything about his behavior. Which brings up the fourth problem.

Fourth, it messes up our doctrine of salvation. If we are sinful by nature, why should we be held accountable for our sin? If we can't do anything about our behavior, then it would seem quite unfair of God to punish us for it.

As you can see, we're dealing with more than semantics here. That's why we need to see that we are sinful *in* our nature. There was a point in time when sin entered into human beings. By succumbing to the temptation by Satan, human beings introduced sin into the picture. Evil is not the opposite of good; it is the corruption of good. It's like mold on bread. It has corrupted it. But what do we make out of bread mold? Penicillin!

Think of the most evil corruption of good in the history of humankind. It has to be when the Son of man, the Lord Jesus Christ, became sin for us and bared his body to the torture of Satan. But out of that evil God made the penicillin for our sin sickness. Through the very act of Christ's being destroyed on a cross, we were released from the terminal effect of our corrupted sin nature.

Once you give your life to Christ, you are declared righteous in God's eyes. That's what the pastor is talking about when using the word *justification*. As far as God is concerned, the penalty for your sin has been paid in full through the blood shed by his Son, Jesus. If this is true, then why do we continue sinning after we give our lives to Christ? That's where the word *sanctification* comes into play. Sanctification is the process of becoming more like Christ as we live for him. We don't become "like" Christ when we give our lives to him. That doesn't ultimately happen until we die and go to be with him (1 John 3:1–3). But when we give our lives to Jesus, we receive the Holy Spirit. The Holy Spirit is all the power of God made available in us to combat our propensity toward sin. Read these verses on the subject:

> So I say, live by the Spirit, and you will not gratify the desires of the sinful nature. For the sinful nature desires what is contrary to the Spirit, and the Spirit what is contrary to the sinful nature. They are in conflict with each other, so that you do not do what you want. But if you are led by the Spirit, you are not under law. The acts of the sinful nature are obvious: sexual immorality, impurity and debauchery; idolatry and witchcraft; hatred, discord, jealousy, fits of rage, selfish ambition, dissensions, factions and envy; drunkenness, orgies, and the like. I warn you, as I did before, that those who live like this will not inherit the kingdom of God. But the fruit of the Spirit is love, joy, peace, patience, kindness, goodness, faithfulness, gentleness and self-control. Against such things there is no law. Those who belong to Christ Jesus have crucified the sinful nature with its passions and desires. Since we live by the Spirit, let us keep in step with the Spirit. Let us not become conceited, provoking and envying each other. (Gal. 5:16–26)

I hope you read every word of this passage from Paul's letter to the Galatians. It's packed with a powerful message of hope. Christ has provided penicillin for our sin. But we must take it.

If you'll allow me to change the metaphor slightly, I think I might be able to show you how to gain victory over your corrupted nature through Christ. Suppose I had diabetes. Without a treatment for it, I would die. Fortunately, God enabled someone to discover the power of insulin. In most cases, people with diabetes don't die of diabetes. They have the treatment. But if I were a diabetic, I wouldn't go anywhere without taking my blood-testing kit, a couple of cans of juice, and a few vials of insulin. I know that insulin can save me from death as a diabetic, but without monitoring my insulin level and carrying some with me, I could go into insulin shock.

How does this work in my spiritual life? I find that I have far more victory over sin in my life when I approach each day realizing how capable I am of falling into sin. I assume I'm capable of lust, gossip, irrational rage, vain imaginations, lying, stealing, cheating, or laziness. By approaching the day acknowledging my propensity toward sin, I'm in a better position to guard my heart (Prov. 4:23) and appropriate the power that God has made available in me through the presence of his Holy Spirit (Gal. 5:25).

Now, take a deep breath. We've just covered some heavy, but vital stuff for an effective soldier of the Cross to understand. It's essential that you maintain a balanced view of who you are and how you were made. You have dignity. You have worth. You were fearfully and wonderfully made (Ps. 139:14). You are also totally depraved. You can't do anything in yourself or by yourself to merit God's favor. You can't solve your sin problem. You can't save yourself as a result of your good works. These two sides of you are brought into harmony through the overwhelming love of Jesus Christ on the cross. Let me present one more powerful passage for you to meditate on before we look at the third enemy we have to contend with:

> I know that nothing good lives in me, that is, in my sinful nature. For I have the desire to do what is good, but I cannot carry it out. For what I do is not the good I want to do; no, the evil I do not want to do—this I keep on doing. Now if I do what I do not want to do, it is no longer I who do it, but it is sin living in me that does it. So I find this law at work: When I want to do good, evil is right there with me. For in my inner being I

delight in God's law; but I see another law at work in the members of my body, waging war against the law of my mind and
making me a prisoner of the law of sin at work within my
members. What a wretched man I am! Who will rescue me
from this body of death? Thanks be to God—through Jesus
Christ our Lord! (Rom. 7:18–25)

3. THE DEVIL

The men in Lieutenant Colonel Fertig's corps had to deal
with hostile surroundings and contend with malaria, but their
biggest challenge was the presence of the Japanese army on the
island. Once the Japanese realized they had company (Fertig
and his men were a constant source of trouble to the Japanese),
they devoted a great deal of time and effort to trying to drive
Fertig's men out of hiding in order to destroy them.

You need to know a few things about Satan if you want to
keep from becoming his next victim. First, you need to realize
that he is bigger than you. You don't stand a chance against
him. However, when you are in Christ, you have the Holy
Spirit in you. The Scripture assures you, "He who is in you is
greater than he who is in the world" (1 John 4:4 NKJV). So even
though Satan is bigger than you, he is no match for the Holy
Spirit who is in you. Therefore, don't let him intimidate you.

It you asked most people, "What is the opposite of God?" the
likely reply would be, "Satan."

Wrong! Wrong! Wrong! God has no opposite. Satan would
love you to think that he is the opposite of God. But he isn't
even close. He is not omniscient or omnipresent; he has none
of the other attributes of God. He is just a perversion who
wants to steal glory from God. He can't read your mind. He
can't *make* you do anything!

The main thing you have to know about Satan is his *modus
operandi:* he is a liar! He started in the garden with Eve, and he
hasn't given up since then. One afternoon the Pharisees were
nitpicking Jesus. The Pharisees were Jewish legalists. All rules,
no grace. They're still around. Just about every church has a
delegation of them. They'll drive you nuts if you let them.
Jesus did one of three things when it came to the Pharisees: he
put them in their place, he exposed their hypocrisy to others
(Luke 12:1–2), or he ignored them. On the occasion I'm about

to discuss, they needed to be rebuked. But in the process of rebuking them, Jesus gave us insight into the way Satan operates. Addressing the Pharisees, he said, "You belong to your father, the devil, and you want to carry out your father's desire. He was a murderer from the beginning, not holding to the truth, for there is no truth in him. When he lies, he speaks his native language, for he is a liar and the father of lies" (John 8:44).

There is a simple way, outlined in Scripture, to deal with Satan. Look at this: "Submit yourselves, then, to God. Resist the devil, and he will flee from you" (James 4:7).

If you could talk to me at this point, you might want to have an emotional word with me. "A simple way to deal with Satan?" you might ask. Yes, it's simple. You simply submit to God, then resist the devil. He'll not only back off; he'll flee.

The key here is not resisting the devil—it's submitting to God. Submitting to God means you'll obey him. Obeying him assumes something. It assumes that you know how he expects you to act and think. That's where you have your work cut out for you. The only way you can know how God expects you to act or think is to study his Word. His Word is truth. Lies are a corruption of the truth. If Satan gets the best of you through lies, then you can keep him from getting the best of you by knowing the truth.

The best way to spot a counterfeit twenty-dollar bill is to study an authentic one. That's why you are always encouraged to study God's Word. Jesus said, "If you hold to my teaching, you are really my disciples. Then you will know the truth, and the truth will set you free" (John 8:31–32).

Satan trips up men all the time simply by lying to them. He says things such as the following:

- "The situation between you and your wife is hopeless."
- "It won't matter one bit if you inflate a few of those numbers on your expense account."
- "You can play catch with your son tomorrow evening."
- "Forget how much the payments are. You deserve a new truck."

- "Your dad was a horrible role model; therefore, there is no way you could ever be an effective father."
- "If you don't have $1 million in liquid assets in the bank by the time you're fifty, your future is doomed."
- "Good boy, you're not even noticing that woman's gorgeous figure."

If you know what God's Word teaches, you can see through every one of these lies. As you study God's Word year after year, you become better at discerning Satan's cunning deceptions. When you sense one of his lies crossing your brain, God's Word tells you something specific to do at that point: "We demolish arguments and every pretension that sets itself up against the knowledge of God, and we take captive every thought to make it obedient to Christ" (2 Cor. 10:5). The more you know God's truth, the more you can take thoughts captive and make them obedient to Christ.

As you can see, keeping Satan in check and out of your face is well within the grasp of a man who walks with God. The apostle John put it better than I ever could when he wrote,

> **This is the message we have heard from him and declare to you: God is light; in him there is no darkness at all. If we claim to have fellowship with him yet walk in the darkness, we lie and do not live by the truth. But if we walk in the light, as he is in the light, we have fellowship with one another, and the blood of Jesus, his Son, purifies us from all sin.** (1 John 1:5–7)

The world, the flesh, and the devil make up a triune enemy that is vanquished by a triune God: the Father, the Son, and the Holy Spirit.

WAR GAMES

Our three enemies have four basic ways that they can attack us. They're as old as warfare itself.

1. THE FRONTAL ATTACK

On July 3, 1863, Winfield Scott Hancock sat on his horse at the brim of Cemetery Ridge in Gettysburg, Pennsylvania, and watched through his field glasses as the Army of Northern

Virginia mustered by regiments more than a mile away. One of
the flags he saw waving in the afternoon breeze was under the
command of his dear friend, General Lothario "Lo" Armistead.

The Confederates' grand charge was straight out of
Napoleon's strategy manual. The plan called for a division of
Confederate soldiers to charge across the mile that divided
them from Hancock and the Army of the Potomac, seize the
high ground, and settle the issue of states' rights once and for
all. Instead, it became Pickett's charge, a logistical debacle
that would haunt Robert E. Lee all the way to the end of his
life.

Hancock was wounded while leading his men in defense of
the hill. His good friend General Lo Armistead was wounded
as he reached the Union line. He was removed from the battlefield and taken to a home in downtown Gettysburg where he
died on the kitchen floor.[1]

Frontal attacks are extremely dangerous, but when it comes
to frontal attacks on the spiritual life, we have the high
ground.

Sometimes we get a frontal attack from the world system.
One summer, I went to Amsterdam to participate in a conference sponsored by the Billy Graham Evangelistic Association. It was hard to go from point A to point B without being
exposed to sights that I've never seen in the United States.
Women wearing nothing but a seductive smile would stand
in bay windows jutting out into the sidewalk. I was assigned
to a street-level outreach on a couple of afternoons. Our turf
was right in the heart of the red-light district. But I had the
high ground while I worked among those sights. I prayed
myself up before I went down there, I worked with a team of
fellow soldiers of the Cross, and everywhere I went I was holding hands with my wife, Darcy.

Sometimes the world makes a full-scale frontal assault on
you, and you aren't given the option to run. In times like these,
follow Paul's advice in Ephesians 6:10–12:

> **Finally, be strong in the Lord and in his mighty power. Put on
> the full armor of God so that you can take your stand against
> the devil's schemes. For our struggle is not against flesh and**

blood, but against the rulers, against the authorities, against the powers of this dark world and against the spiritual forces of evil in the heavenly realms.

Notice Paul's reminder in verse 12 that I emphasized at the outset of this chapter: it's not people you're fighting but the forces behind them. In many cases, the people are merely pawns. They're wrapped up in their sin, they're lost, and they need a Savior.

You can stand up against frontal assaults by putting on the full armor of God. Paul listed the pieces of this armor in Ephesians 6:13–17:

- Belt of Truth
- Flak Jacket of Righteousness
- Combat Boots of the Gospel of Peace
- Shield of Faith
- Kevlar Helmet of Salvation
- M16 of the Word of God

After you have all of your armor on, Paul said, "Pray in the Spirit on all occasions with all kinds of prayers and requests. With this in mind, be alert and always keep on praying" (Eph. 6:18).

Keep in mind that you can get a frontal attack from the world, the flesh, or the devil. Don't panic. If you are in Christ, you've got bigger guns and you've got the high ground.

2. THE SNEAK ATTACK

I stood on the edge of the floating memorial spanning the deck of the USS *Arizona* and tried to imagine how horrifying it must have been that Sunday morning back in 1941 when the Japanese fighter planes and bombers screamed down the valley, over Schefield Barracks, and then across the waters of Pearl Harbor and caught the U.S. Navy and U.S. Air Corps asleep. The old black-and-white films, though shocking, still can't capture how absolutely frightening it must have been. That's the nature of the sneak attack.

Anger has a bad habit of sneaking up on you. So do lustful

thoughts. Most temptations spring up on you when you aren't expecting them. Wise armies always post a guard to warn them of danger.

God has given you a radar system to forewarn you of a possible sneak attack from the world, the flesh, or the devil. In fact, you have several:

- Your conscience. God might give you a bad feeling about a movie you are driving to the mall to see. There is a good chance he is trying to spare you giving your flesh more garbage than it needs. There are all kinds of ways that God tips you off that you're walking into a trap. You have got to be prepared to respond to the warnings.

- The Word. It's fairly common to be reading the Scripture and have the Holy Spirit give you an insight into a possible nightmare that is developing in a certain area of your life. For instance, if you study David and Bathsheba in Sunday school and then a beautiful woman, whose husband is away a lot on business, moves into the house next door, beware.

- Your spouse. Your wife has two things going for her that enable her to be excellent radar warning you of possible danger. First, she has God-given intuitive skills that often make her more cautious. You may look on this as a negative—that is, she is a lousy risk taker. But God may use your wife's caution to keep you out of harm's way. A second advantage she brings to the table is that she knows your strengths as well as your weaknesses. She can analyze your weaknesses in light of the things happening around you and see a problem long before it has time to take place. A man who listens to his wife's concerns loses less money in bad investments, gets involved in fewer bad associations, and spends a lot less time asking God to forgive him for being so foolish.

- Mentors. A wise officer asks the advice of his fellow officers. When you allow a few trustworthy men access to the inner regions of your heart, they can often anticipate the way traps may be set for you and warn you away from the direction you are going.

What happens, however, if you walk into an ambush? Training rules teach you to drop to cover and then defend yourself. In spiritual terms that adds up to dropping to your knees in prayer and then firing back at the attack with the truth of the Word of God. Usually, the mere presence of the Word of God in your daily life is enough to keep your three enemies from trying much.

3. GUERRILLA WARFARE

A typical story from Vietnam would go something like this: you're riding along in your jeep. You happen upon a disabled child hobbling along a lonely road carrying a heavy load. You take pity on him, so you stop to give him a ride to the next village. You give him a candy bar and some water from your canteen to perk him up. Just shy of the village the little boy starts pointing in an animated way to the jungle and saying something you can't understand. You slow down to see what he is pointing to, and suddenly, he jumps out of the jeep and runs without any trouble into the underbrush. A few seconds after he disappears, the canvas sack he left behind on the floor of your jeep blows up.

Some of the most enraging stories of warfare come from the catalog of guerrilla tactics. The thing that makes guerrilla warfare so frustrating is that you can't figure out who your enemy is or how he is going to hit you next.

It's terrorism. Terrorists prey on innocent people who don't know they are about to get nailed and have no way of defending themselves when it happens. Your best friend stabs you in the back financially; your pastor takes off with a young woman from the college group; you have to give a woman at work an inferior review for her poor work performance and the next thing you know she accuses you of sexual harassment; your mother-in-law turns your wife completely against you; your boss fires you because you brought up some ethical concerns with the way a product is being marketed. These are all serious attacks on you that come out of the blue, from people you don't expect them from, at a time when you feel you are doing the right thing.

There are ways to endure acts of terrorism against your spirit. Let me list them for you:

- You need to assume that they can and will happen to you somewhere along the line so that you aren't so shocked when they do take place. At the 1996 Olympics in Atlanta, there was an assumption that someone might attempt a terrorist act against the backdrop of the Games. The authorities built contingency plans, beefed up their police force, installed more detection devices, and had medical centers waiting in the wings just in case. Sure enough, someone detonated a bomb in one of the public venues. But the intended effect of the bomb on the Olympics wasn't realized. They went right ahead with the Games. A lesson you can learn from this is that you minimize the shock of terrorist acts against your spirit by overcoming your naivete. People let you down; family members sometimes betray you; you can be unjustly accused or unfairly dismissed. These things happen. They hurt when they happen. But that hurt is minimized and the healing accelerated if you approach life assuming that terrorist attacks can and do happen to people like you.

- Don't negotiate. Sometimes the attacks against your spirit are designed to get you to water down your convictions or soft-pedal your concerns. Don't let it happen. If the United States negotiated with terrorists, the number of terrorist acts against us would increase.

- The safest way to endure unfair acts against you is to maintain a good reputation. When the smoke clears and people try to figure out who is right and who is wrong, a clean reputation will give you the moral high ground.

- Sometimes you have to show tough love with people. You can't accommodate their demands. Most of all, don't roll over and play dead. Hold your ground. Speak the truth in love, but by all means speak it.

Then we will no longer be infants, tossed back and forth by the waves, and blown here and there by every wind of teaching and by the cunning and craftiness of men in their deceitful scheming. Instead, speaking the truth in love, we

will in all things grow up into him who is the Head, that is,
Christ. (Eph. 4:14–15)

• Show courage through your position in Christ. Don't let
your fear get the best of you. Listen to the way the apostle
Peter discussed the issue:

Who is going to harm you if you are eager to do good? But
even if you should suffer for what is right, you are blessed.
"Do not fear what they fear; do not be frightened." But in
your hearts set apart Christ as Lord. Always be prepared to
give an answer to everyone who asks you to give the reason
for the hope that you have. But do this with gentleness and
respect, keeping a clear conscience, so that those who speak
maliciously against your good behavior in Christ may be
ashamed of their slander. (1 Peter 3:13–16)

4. CONSTANT BARRAGE

Late in the war against Adolf Hitler, the Russians wanted to
make a move across Germany from the east. The city of Dresden stood in their path. The ancient city was one of the true
jewels of Europe. Its palaces, opera house, majestic churches,
and picturesque setting on the Elbe River made it the envy of
Germany. But there was a war on. The city was in the path of
the attacking army, and intelligence reported that it harbored
up to fifteen thousand of Hitler's feared SS troops. It had to be
flattened before the Russian army got too close.

For seventy-two hours, bombs rained from the sky onto Dresden. The first two days of pounding came from the Royal Air
Force. The last day was from the U.S. Air Force. When the
smoke cleared, there wasn't a single roof left on a building or a
single pane of glass left in a window. Dresden burned for many
days afterward. The number of dead as a result of the bombing
is estimated at 120,000.

I've been to Dresden. I've seen many of the aerial photos
taken after the bombing. It was devastation as far as the eye
could see. Even though the bombing happened more than fifty
years ago, some of the cratered buildings are still standing just
as they were after the bombing. Their outer walls stand like

ghosts surrounding the heap of rubble that once was their splendor.

You can find yourself on the wrong side of a constant barrage from the world, the flesh, and the devil. When they feel like it, they can be relentless. Maybe you sit on a school board and want to take a stand for morality in education. Brace yourself, you're going to get hammered. People have found themselves hauled into court for exercising what they thought was their freedom of religion. Many politicians have had to face vitriolic attacks on their character by people in the gaming industry, the gay-lesbian lobby, the pro-choice contingents, or the other party simply because they took a moral stand on an issue. When the bombs rain down, and there doesn't seem to be any end in sight, it's human nature to want to give up. Don't. There is hope.

God has provided safe places for you to hide in while you ride out the firestorm. God has provided protective bunkers:

- The church. The love and support of a church have been the salvation of many people who have had to face a constant barrage. The ongoing teaching, advice, and perspective of your local church can keep you from surrendering to the assaults on your convictions.
- The family. The love and encouragement of your wife, your teenagers, and even the tyke who sits on your knee can galvanize your resolve not to succumb to the relentless pounding of your enemies. A constant barrage against a member of the family (or even the entire family) can be used by God to increase the level of commitment within the family too.
- Prayer teams. A wise man shouldn't face any day without adequate prayer. Spouses who pray for each other can hold each other up when the missiles from the world, the flesh, and the devil are exploding all around them. It's a good idea to recruit a team of people to pray for you every day. I have one, and I'm convinced that there have been times when I have been able to endure a constant pounding to my beliefs because of them. Prayer protects you. It covers you with a shield of love and support that includes

not only the people who are praying for you, but the entire heavenly host as well.

- The Word of God. It's almost a cliché, but when you're in God's Word, it's hard for your enemies to lay a glove on you.
- An intimate relationship with the Lord Jesus. The more you commune with Jesus on a step-by-step basis, the more you get to embrace hope. Walking with Christ reminds you that someday there will be relief from the relentless barrages of the enemy. The prophet Habakkuk painted a bleak picture of life at "ground zero" in Israel. The enemy was bent on Israel's total annihilation. The prophet poured out his lament. And then he summarized their situation with these words:

I heard and my heart pounded,
  my lips quivered at the sound;
decay crept into my bones,
  and my legs trembled.
Yet I will wait patiently for the day of calamity
  to come on the nation invading us.
Though the fig tree does not bud
  and there are no grapes on the vines,
though the olive crop fails
  and the fields produce no food,
though there are no sheep in the pen
  and no cattle in the stalls,
yet I will rejoice in the LORD,
  I will be joyful in God my Savior.
The Sovereign LORD is my strength;
  he makes my feet like the feet of a deer,
  he enables me to go on the heights. (Hab. 3:16–19)

After you have endured a constant barrage, there is usually some rebuilding to do. There is hope for this process too. In Dresden, my wife and I toured the Semper Opera House, Zwinger Palace of King Frederick Augustus I (August the Strong), and a Catholic church that were piles of rubble after the Allied bombings. They have been rebuilt to their original splendor.

Just beyond the Catholic church is the site of a famous Lutheran church that is being rebuilt. We viewed acres of shelves holding the thousands of pieces of the original building. Each block had a number on it. Through computer re-creation, workmen were able to determine exactly where each piece once belonged in the building. They were also able to determine which pieces were completely destroyed by the impact of the bombs. They are being cut out in nearby quarries. Slowly but certainly, they are rebuilding that Lutheran church. But there will be a major difference between the one rebuilt and the one destroyed. The rebuilt church will be stronger. Through all that they learned from studying the devastation of the buildings, they are able to restore them with much greater strength and resiliency than they had originally. On the day we toured the Lutheran church site, they were dedicating the foundation and basement that had been completed.

Even after you take a pounding, there is hope for you to come back stronger and with much more splendor than you had before you took the beating. An excellent biblical parallel to this is the restoration of Job after he endured the constant barrage from the devil:

> **The LORD blessed the latter part of Job's life more than the first. He had fourteen thousand sheep, six thousand camels, a thousand yoke of oxen and a thousand donkeys. And he also had seven sons and three daughters. The first daughter he named Jemimah, the second Keziah and the third Keren-Happuch. Nowhere in all the land were there found women as beautiful as Job's daughters, and their father granted them an inheritance along with their brothers. After this, Job lived a hundred and forty years; he saw his children and their children to the fourth generation. And so he died, old and full of years. (Job 42:12–17)**

SEEKING SOLID GROUND

Whether it's the world, the flesh, or the devil, whether it's through a frontal assault, a sneak attack, guerrilla tactics, or a constant barrage, you have a citadel that cannot be moved, a hope that cannot be shaken, and a God who cannot be defeated. One of the best doxologies for a Christian warrior was the one we received from a man who shared a bedroom with Jesus as a kid, Jesus' earthly half brother, Jude:

> **To him who is able to keep you from falling and to present you before his glorious presence without fault and with great joy— to the only God our Savior be glory, majesty, power and authority, through Jesus Christ our Lord, before all ages, now and forevermore! Amen. (Jude 24–25)**

STUDY AND DISCUSSION QUESTIONS

UP FRONT AND PERSONAL

1. If we are not to treat as enemies others who have a lifestyle we see as sinful, how are we to treat them? What is our ultimate goal for them?

2. As a soldier of Christ, you have three enemies: the world system, the flesh, and the devil. Describe the form and substance they take in your life.

3. Do you have an intimate relationship with the Lord? Describe what that means to you.

FOR THE GROUP TO DISCUSS

1. Explain the difference between being sinful *in* nature and sinful *by* nature.

2. What does the author mean when he says, "Our conflict is not with people"?

3. Cite an example of how you have considered someone as "the enemy" because he or she disagreed with your view of a Christian lifestyle.

4. Is saying that the world is corrupted taking too pessimistic an attitude toward things? Why, or why not?

5. If God created us in his likeness and created us perfectly, why do we continue to sin? Even after salvation?

6. Complete the sentence: "Evil is not the opposite of good; it is _____ _____ _____ _____."

7. On a scale of 1 to 5 (with 1 being strong and 5 being not-so-strong), rank yourself on your propensity to continue sinful patterns in your life. Now read Galatians 5:16–17 and relate it to where you have placed yourself on the scale.

8. What is your opinion about Satan being God's opposite, on the side of evil?

9. Complete this sentence: "The best way to spot a lie is to compare it with _____ _____." Relate this to discerning evil.

10. Explain what the author means when he says we have a "triune enemy."

11. Name at least three things that can serve as your early warning system that you are, or are about to be, under attack by the enemy.

12. When the enemy attacks, God has provided spiritual fortresses for us to find refuge. What are they, and just how can they help us?

APPLYING GOD'S WORD

1. Memorize 2 Timothy 1:7.

2. Think of ways that your spiritual strength can be a fortress and a refuge for others who are under attack by the enemy. Can you think of someone you could help right now?

CHAPTER 7

AWOL

$\boxed{\text{O}}$ur Humvee stopped in front of a collection of small buildings on the edge of the complex. The corporal who had driven me from the other side of the fort pointed to a guard shack and told me the sergeant I was to meet would be waiting for me on the other side. I studied the razor wire coiled at the top of the twelve-foot chain-link fence and wondered if any of the occupants of these buildings had ever tried to take their chances with it.

I was at an army base in Washington State, and among my duties that week, I was to address the MPs who guarded the prisoners at the stockade. We would be meeting in one of the rooms within the lockup. The sergeant who met me after I cleared the checkpoint was not what I expected. First of all, *he* was a *she*. And she was extremely small for a sergeant. If you had to outfit her you would probably start in the section of clothing labeled size 5. But as the saying goes, "looks are deceiving." Two seconds after we met, I knew she was not a woman that anyone would think to mess with. Her voice was strong, deep, and confident. Her brown eyes locked on my blue eyes as she extended her tiny hand to me and proceeded to put a viselike grip on my hand as we shook. The patch on her sleeve told me she was part of a mechanized division. She looked as if she could hold her own just fine in one of the army's heavily armed recreational vehicles (i.e., a tank).

As we came into the room, the MPs sitting at the individual desks were ordered to attention. Instantly, they jumped to their feet and assumed the braced position. I didn't understand why they did that for a noncom. Later someone explained that the sergeant had ordered it as a way of showing respect to me. She put them at ease and then proceeded to introduce me. My job was to help the men understand better why so many more of the newer recruits were having a tough time finishing basic training or carrying out their assignments. We talked for an hour and a half. As the dialogue proceeded I realized that the U.S. Army deals with some of the same problems as the army of the Lord Jesus Christ. Most of the soldiers in the stockade were there because they had gone AWOL. If it's been a while since you were around military acronyms, that stands for absent without leave. I was surrounded by cells filled with men who had donned a uniform, taken an oath, and then turned tail and ran when duty called.

DISOBEYING ORDERS

Whether it's leaving a post, ignoring orders, being insubordinate, or deserting in the face of the enemy, too many Christian men have failed to meet the minimal demands of a good soldier of the Cross. I know. I've fallen short. And so have you. There isn't a man who hasn't at some point deliberately disobeyed his marching orders. But every time we do, we weaken the ranks and give ground to the enemy.

Every time a man turns his back on his wife, his kids, his reputation, or his dignity, we all lose. The building blocks of any culture are the families at its core. When a family's stability is jeopardized, that building block is unreliable. Therefore, the blocks around it can't depend on it to hold up its share of the load. We all end up compensating for or paying the negative price for a man's failure to live up to his obligations in the home. For proof, just check out the statistics on how many kids in gangs come from homes where a dad has shirked his responsibilities.

When a man is directed by his urges, he'll find that his glands and his lusts have no conscience. When he is directed by his fears, the enemy seems more imposing than he really is. When he is ruled by his regrets, he can't see what he is capable of being in Christ. When a man is ruled by self-pity, he is too busy being angry to be effective. Men, I could go into a long list of the things that are expected of us. I don't think it's necessary. You already know what God expects of you. I could go into a long list of ways we fall short. I think men feel guilty enough. The purpose of this chapter isn't to point out our inadequacies; it's to show us how to overcome them.

THE "PASS THE BUCK" GENERATION

One of the things we've seen rise out of the ashes of the generation that threw right and wrong out the window is a complete abandonment of the sense of personal responsibility. As mentioned earlier, we have become a generation that doesn't believe there are any accidents. No matter what happens, someone, other than ourselves or circumstances, must take the blame. It only figures that trying to place blame on the innocent will lead to absolving the guilty of responsibility.

I'll give you an example: a mom and a dad work outside the home, the kids grow up in day care and all-day school, and when family members show up at the end of the day, they're on "empty." They eat in shifts, hole up in their different corners of the house, and tensions run high. The next thing you know, the parents get a notice that their child is struggling in school. He can't seem to pay attention. He isn't cooperating with other students. He is a discipline problem.

After a careful and expensive analysis of the situation by experts, it's determined that the cause of the kid's problem is lead in the paint, holes in the ozone, acid rain, or the fact that we're losing thousands of square miles of rain forest every day. Or maybe it's the result of incompetent teachers and lousy peer influence. If a counselor happens to suggest to the parents that maybe the child is struggling in school because the child's parents have a thoroughly messed-up set of priorities and they need to rearrange their lives around the things that are eternally important instead of things that are temporarily gratifying, the parents pick up the nearest phone and call their attorney.

The grand-scale refusal to bear the responsibility of our actions as individuals is slowly but certainly wiping us out as a people.

This behavior has waltzed its way into Christian circles too. Pastors who are committed to obeying God by confronting people regarding their sin learn to keep their résumés up to date. There is nothing new about this. Paul warned his young understudy, Timothy, about the same thing:

> **For the time will come when men will not put up with sound doctrine. Instead, to suit their own desires, they will gather around them a great number of teachers to say what their itching ears want to hear. They will turn their ears away from the truth and turn aside to myths. But you, keep your head in all situations, endure hardship, do the work of an evangelist, discharge all the duties of your ministry. (2 Tim. 4:3–5)**

"NO EXCUSE, SIR"

If you are serious about being a soldier for Jesus Christ, then you have to be absolutely committed to personal character. Character trickles down. Men of character create marriages with character. Men of character have a lot easier time expecting and receiving high standards of character from their kids.

All of us occasionally fall short. The way we handle our shortcomings, mistakes, and sins has everything to do with the level of respect and responsibility we will enjoy as servants and leaders in Christ's army. There is a powerful principle you need to learn and exercise when you fall short of God's mark. It's uncomplicated, it's redeeming, and it has enormous power to free you from the tyranny that disobedience to God's orders can hold on your life. And when you exercise it, everybody wins. God can actually use this powerful action in your life to move you beyond your sin to higher levels of fellowship and service with him.

At West Point, the cadets are taught that only four appropriate answers can be given to an officer who inquires about the status of a given order. Here are the answers available to them:

1. "Yes, sir."
2. "No, sir."
3. "No excuse, sir."
4. "Sir, I do not understand."

It doesn't matter what the extenuating circumstances are. When they are faced with an infraction, shortcoming, or inadequacy, cadets are to be absolutely and personally ready to confess responsibility. Maybe an upperclassman notices that a cadet's belt buckle has a smudge on it, and he asks him if he thinks his buckle is polished to standard. The cadet might have worked overtime making sure it was polished to standard. His belt buckle might have a smudge on it because another cadet brushed up against him on the way to formation. It doesn't matter. If it isn't up to standard, he is to reply, "No, sir." If the upperclassman asks him why, he is to reply, "No excuse, sir."

If he doesn't understand what was expected of him, he has an option to let the upperclassman or superior officer know that he doesn't understand. Once the orders are clarified, he is limited to the first three responses to the question: yes, no, or no excuse.

One source states, "The cadet learns to live with the injustice; life isn't always fair. He is learning that no matter what the circumstances, he is expected to live up to his obligations. At this early stage in his career, that may only mean presenting himself with proper military dress and bearing. Later, he will hold other lives in his hands."[1]

When it comes to what God expects of us, we really don't have the option to say, "Sir, I do not understand." God has made his expectations for us crystal clear in his Word. As soldiers of the Lord Jesus, we should restrict ourselves to the first three options. And when we refuse to give excuses and pass blame for our choices to other people, we accelerate the level of responsibility God can place in us as leaders in his cause.

God doesn't want to hear our excuses. He wants us to own up to our responsibility for our actions.

God Doesn't Want to Hear . . .

God doesn't want to hear, "But I had a horrible childhood." He wants to hear, "No excuse, sir."

God doesn't want to hear, "It was my wife's idea." He wants to hear, "No excuse, sir."

God doesn't want to hear, "Everybody in my department turns in reports that way." He wants to hear, "No excuse, sir."

God doesn't want to hear, "But I haven't had sex with my wife in six months." He wants to hear, "No excuse, sir."

God doesn't want to hear, "I stayed up too late Saturday night and was too tired." He wants to hear, "No excuse, sir."

God doesn't want to hear, "My friends started me drinking." He wants to hear, "No excuse, sir."

MEN OF CHARACTER

Wimps make excuses. Real men don't.

What we fail to realize about our excuses is how much we have to lose when we make them and how many innocent people suffer when we use them. We also don't realize how much we have to gain and how much the people we love get to benefit when we own up to our responsibilities. We will all fare far better in our walk with Christ if we eliminate from our system any defense mechanism that tries to limit the honest handling of our actions.

THE MOST POWERFUL
SURVIVAL SKILL OF ALL

In a few years, I will have lived a half century. I have lived all of my life under the influence of Christian leaders and mentors. From my almost half century of observation, I have noticed one quality that sets the great men of God I have known apart from the not-so-great men of God I have known. Great men of God know how to repent.

They don't make excuses, and they don't wait to be confronted. They just drop to their knees and repent. And because of their transparent attitude before God, they get to enjoy several qualities that most men who play games with the truth don't get to enjoy:

- Freedom. They have an absolute sense of acceptance in the Lord because they have not tried to live a pretentious life with him.
- Peace. They sleep like babies at night and don't worry about their past catching up with them during the day.
- A noble reputation. People know they can trust them. Their track record of honesty and responsibility ultimately precedes them wherever they go.

- The respect of their loved ones. Spouse, kids, friends, you name it, they all appreciate the fact that this person is a stand-up guy.
- Joy. They have a genuine appreciation for life. It's a by-product of not having to catalog all of the excuses or project all of the blame onto others.
- Humility. Because of their honest attitude toward themselves, they know better than to put on airs toward others.

YOU, TOO, CAN BE SET FREE

Repenting isn't easy. You have to develop a taste for crow. You have to hear a few "I told you so's." You may have to get on your knees to be at eye level with your kids when you tell them you have been a jerk. You may have to process some shame. You may have to lose (either temporarily or permanently) the fellowship of a few people close to you. You probably will have to endure some punishment.

Take your lumps. Swallow your pride. Get it over with. Move on with your life. In the macromanaged life, you ultimately process less guilt, anger, shame, and regret when you simply confess and repent.

If you let your pride dominate you, you close the door on an effective future. You also resign yourself to dishonest relationships with the people you are supposed to love. God offers you a gift when he gives you the opportunity to repent. He says, "Take responsibility, and in the process, save me from having to expose you." Because eventually, everyone will be found out. Hear what his Word says:

> **There is nothing concealed that will not be disclosed, or hidden that will not be made known. What you have said in the dark will be heard in the daylight, and what you have whispered in the ear in the inner rooms will be proclaimed from the roofs.** (Luke 12:2–3)

> **But if you fail to do this, you will be sinning against the LORD; and you may be sure that your sin will find you out.** (Num. 32:23)

God loves it when you repent. David taught that in Psalm 51:

> Restore to me the joy of your salvation
>   and grant me a willing spirit, to sustain me. . . .
> You do not delight in sacrifice, or I would bring it;
>   you do not take pleasure in burnt offerings.
> The sacrifices of God are a broken spirit;
>   a broken and contrite heart,
> O God, you will not despise. (vv. 12, 16–17)

When you repent, you get to enjoy God's forgiveness: "If we say that we have no sin, we deceive ourselves, and the truth is not in us. If we confess our sins, He is faithful and just to forgive us our sins and to cleanse us from all unrighteousness" (1 John 1:8–9 NKJV).

Freedom, a heart at rest, a noble reputation, the respect of the family, joy, and the ability to practice humility—they're all wonderful rewards to the soldier who can repent.

THE LAST CHAPTER
OF A PRIDEFUL HEART

When we resist assuming responsibility for our actions, innocent people end up paying for our folly. The pride that drives us to maintain our false sense of innocence can even cause us to sell the people we love most down the river. In the end, however, we lose. After our pride and the arrogance that so often accompanies it are exposed, we find ourselves with no place to hide and no one but ourselves to blame.

A story is told to the cadets at West Point that sadly but powerfully illustrates the effect of pride and dishonesty on a man's reputation:

It is really two entwined stories of men who, during the American Revolutionary War, distinguished themselves by their brilliant leadership of soldiers—generals George Washington and Benedict Arnold—men whose stories make plain the virtue of choosing the harder right.

In the early days of the war, both men showed extraordinary skill, courage, and heroism. Of Arnold's victory at Bemis Heights, leading to the British surrender at Saratoga, the historian Herman Beukema reluctantly acknowledged, "the laurels for one of the decisive victories of all history rest on Arnold's brow."

But only one of the two men stayed the course through the dark, discouraging days of the war, having the personal character to persevere in the face of overwhelming difficulty. The other man collapsed under pressure [fueled, among other things, by jealousy for not being promoted fast enough—author's editorial comment] and sought to sell the British the plans for the strategically key fortresses he commanded at West Point—which had been built and supplied to maintain control of the Hudson River, vital to the security of New York. Fortunately, Washington discovered Arnold's treacherous plot before the damage was done (although Arnold himself escaped).

Of the two men, one is revered as the father of his country; the other is a man without a country, his name remembered only as a synonym for treason.

At West Point, Washington is honored in numerous ways. The most prominent memorial is seen by cadets three times daily. In front of the Cadet Dining Hall, in the center of the Plain, stands a larger-than-life statue of the general on horseback, elevated by a ten-foot-high pedestal. It is quite intentional that he is featured at the very center of the grand stage formed by the campus buildings and the surrounding mountains.

Arnold is remembered, too—in stark terms that remind us all how much rests on a leader's character. On the east wall of the old cadet chapel, located in the West Point cemetery, hangs a collection of plaques naming the senior officers of the Revolutionary War. At the front in the most prominent position, as one would expect, is Washington's plaque. Concluding the collection, in an inconspicuous position at the rear of the building, hangs a mysterious plaque bearing only the words "Major General," followed by a chiseled blank space where a name would have been carved, then a date of birth, "1741," and another chiseled blank space where the date of death would have been carved. Arnold's plaque represents the symbolic obliteration of his name from the honor rolls of American history.[2]

Life is too short, men. Eternity is a long time. Own up. Confess up. Repent. Set yourself free.

STUDY AND DISCUSSION QUESTIONS

UP FRONT AND PERSONAL

1. Explain what this statement means: "Lust has no conscience."

2. Make a list with two columns. In one, list the things in your life that are temporarily gratifying to you. In the other, list the things that are eternally important to your life. When you have finished, compare the lists.

3. When was the last time you were on your knees and repenting? Why is it so important for you to do this?

FOR THE GROUP TO DISCUSS

1. Discuss how ordinary men with families and jobs can do the work of an evangelist. Refer to 2 Timothy 4:3–5.

2. Match these three emotions with their consequences:
   (1) directed by fear   a) can't see your Christlike capabilities
   (2) ruled by regrets   b) the enemy seems more imposing
   (3) ruled by self-pity c) too angry to be effective

3. If asked to make a statement about this generation's refusal to bear their responsibilities, what would you say?

4. Does taking a stand on issues naturally lead to confrontations? Explain your response.

5. Name three benefits for men who are quick to repent their sins.

6. What is "blame shifting," and how do we recognize it?

7. Describe masculine defense mechanisms men use to avoid facing the honesty of handling our actions.

8. Ending dishonest relationships, apologizing to your kids for being a jerk, and feeling shame about one of your actions are all signs of . . . what?

APPLYING GOD'S WORD

1. The author states, "Life is too short; eternity is a long time." With that truth in mind, what should be the next spiritual step in your life?

CHAPTER 8

OFFICER CANDIDATE SCHOOL: A FEW GOOD MEN

It's been a while since it happened. In fact, the last time it occurred on a grand scale was on December 8, 1941—the day after the day that would live in infamy. Most of our navy was still burning, listing, or settling into the bottom of Pearl Harbor. Admiral Husband Kimmel (no relation) was trying to explain to the powers that be how he and his navy were caught so unaware by the Japanese, while the Washington war machine geared up to even the score.

UNCLE SAM WANTS YOU! posters started popping up from Main Street USA to the most obscure back roads of the hinterland. A foreign nation had pushed America up against the wall and put a knife to its throat. The only way out was to stand and fight. It was a wholesale appeal for manpower that dwarfed any appeal before or since. Hundreds of thousands of men answered the call.

In spite of the magnitude of the responsibility of equipping, training, and putting an army on the front lines, the people in charge of fighting the war had an even bigger problem. It's the problem that haunted FDR as he sat in the White House at night thinking about the mighty army that was mustering across the country. It caused the parents who were offering up their young men more than their fair share of fitful nights' sleep. Leadership. Where would they get the leaders necessary to command the armed forces and guide them to victory?

Officer Candidate School was one of the main answers. OCS was not an invention of World War II. It not only predated that war, but the concept behind it predated America. Ever since the first army was formed, there has been a need to identify and train competent leaders to stand before the warriors. They had to be men who could communicate, educate, delegate, and motivate. They had to be able to take orders as well as give them, follow as well as lead.

In peacetime, the requirements for getting into Officer Candidate School were far more strict than in times of war. Some of the standards were superficial and often eliminated great potential leaders. Often the results of the arbitrary standards turned the officers' ranks into little more than gentlemen's clubs outfitted with nice uniforms. But when a war broke out, the sheer size of the demand caused them to peel away the extraneous requirements and draw in virtually any man who showed promise.

THE HEAVENLY FATHER WANTS YOU!

In his classic film *High Noon*, Gary Cooper finds himself in a life-or-death dilemma. He represents the law in a small western town. He has boldly stood behind his badge and in the process has incurred the wrath of some desperate outlaws. One was sent to prison, but a higher court pardoned him. He is arriving on the noon train and, along with three of his lawless friends, is planning on gunning down the sheriff and then terrorizing the town.

Gary Cooper is but one man—no match for four guns—so he sets out to recruit some other men to stand alongside him to face down these desperate outlaws. He wants to form an instant Officer Candidate School, but no one will join him to help him in taking a stand. The most telling scene in the entire movie happens when he comes to the church. The townsfolk are meeting for worship on Sunday. They are all aware of the crisis. They are all indebted to the sheriff for his bravery in carrying out law and order. But to the man, no one is willing to join him. Even the minister and church leaders give emotional defenses for their cowardly positions. They leave him to face the noon train, and the revenge arriving with it, by himself.

Throughout the movie, the director pans down the lonely railroad tracks that stretch out across the prairie, reminding us that off in the distance, out of sight and earshot, is a train thundering its way toward its noon appointment. Unfortunately, one good man can't find any other good men to help him face and defeat the forces of evil.

It's "high noon" in our country. The forces of evil have been harassing, destabilizing, and destroying our nation for decades. Lately, they have been at work as though they were totally unbridled. They have cratered marriages, estranged kids from their parents, saturated minds with lies, ravaged bodies with drugs, alcohol, disease, and the bitter residue that accompanies promiscuity. Jesus carried out justice two thousand years ago against the forces of darkness. Now they are coming back to seek their revenge. Once they overwhelm his work, they want to destroy his people. And so he searches for the brave but few good men who will take rank with him, allow him to train them as leaders, and then take their stand with him against the prince of the power of the air.

If it were technically possible to slip through a time warp and go back to a little cottage along Nebuchadnezzar's Canal in ancient Babylon, an outspoken prophet of Judah would feel quite an affinity with Gary Cooper. Ezekiel grew up in Jerusalem. He was there during the siege of the city, and he was carried away, along with most of his fellow Jews, to the captivity in Babylon. God raised him up in that foreign land to be a strategic voice to the apathetic remnant. He was to remind them of the sins that got them into their dilemma and challenge them to get out of there. Their time in Babylon was to be temporary. His job was to use that time to enlist an army of volunteers who would be ready to let Jehovah God be their God once again. He knew that if the sins that had caused their nightmare were not defeated, they were certain to find themselves in the same crisis in the future.

Ezekiel 22:30 tells the whole story. It had been "high noon" in Jerusalem. God had wanted to face down the coming judgment with men who were willing to surrender to his ordinances and laws, and once again make the city a safe and righteous place to raise families. Here's what he found: "So I sought for a man among them who would make a wall, and stand in the gap before Me on behalf of the land, that I should not destroy it; but I found no one" (Ezek. 22:30 NKJV).

For our nation, the train carrying the powers of evil isn't thundering its way toward us. It's sitting in the station, and the evil has long since made its way down Main Street for the showdown. Will you heed the call to arms? And not just that, but will you heed the call to be trained to lead others to stand and fight?

In 1980, Dr. James Dobson put it this way: "The Western world stands at a great crossroads in its history. It is my opinion that our very survival as a people will depend upon the presence or absence of masculine leadership in millions of homes. . . . I believe, with everything within me, that husbands hold the keys to the preservation of the family."[1] Years have passed since Dr. Dobson made that statement, and its truth is even greater now than when he first said it.

The Scriptures give us an excellent guideline for reviewing the résumés of men who would enlist in God's Officer Candidate School. It's some sound advice given to Moses by his father-in-law, Jethro. Moses was experiencing a bit of a "high noon" dilemma himself. But instead of pulling a Gary Cooper and trying to enlist help to face the challenges before him, he was behaving more like the Lone Ranger. He was trying to do it all by himself. When Jethro saw the demands on Moses, he got right in his face with the ice-cold truth.

[Jethro said,] **"What you are doing is not good. You and these people who come to you will only wear yourselves out. The work is too heavy for you; you cannot handle it alone. . . . But select capable men from all the people—men who fear God,**

trustworthy men who hate dishonest gain—and appoint them
as officials over thousands, hundreds, fifties and tens. . . ."
Moses listened to his father-in-law and did everything he said.
(Ex. 18:17–18, 21, 24)

It was critical to the survival of the nation of Israel that
Moses enlist an army of godly men to lead the work of God
before the people. He was advised to put them over groups of
thousands, hundreds, fifties, and tens. By assigning the men to
manageable groups of people, the entire nation's spiritual,
emotional, and physical needs could be met effectively.

But leading on the battlefield is a lot easier if you feel confident about your chances of victory. Many decades later, shortly
before Moses handed the mantle of leadership over to General
Joshua, he shared some poignant and powerful words of challenge to the army that would cross the Jordan and conquer the
land:

When you go to war against your enemies and see horses and
chariots and an army greater than yours, do not be afraid of
them, because the LORD your God, who brought you up out of
Egypt, will be with you. When you are about to go into battle,
the priest shall come forward and address the army. He shall
say: "Hear, O Israel, today you are going into battle against
your enemies. Do not be fainthearted or afraid; do not be ter-
rified or give way to panic before them. For the LORD your God
is the one who goes with you to fight for you against your enemies to give you victory." (Deut. 20:1–4)

His encouragement was based on God's track record in bringing them safely past and through myriad obstacles.

Nothing has changed. The odds are still the same: God and
you make a majority. The final score is still the same: we win!
I've read the last chapter of the incredible story. The God who
had the first word will have the last (Rev. 22:13).

DIVIDE AND CONQUER

Civilization lives or dies by the strength of its families. The
family lives or dies by the strength of its leadership. The
strength of the leadership within the family has everything to

do with the character of the man at its head. That's why you're reading this book.

You're reading this book because you want to make a difference. You're reading this book because there is unrighteousness in the streets, in the hallways at your kids' school, and in the back rooms at the office. It's calling for a showdown and God has recruited you.

I want to mention a few qualities you might want to tuck inside your heart before you go out to face your enemies—four offensive weapons that will ensure that you'll still be standing after the smoke clears. When it comes down to it, these characteristics set real men of honor apart from the rest.

1. MEN OF HONOR HOLD TO THEIR *CONVICTIONS*

When you look up most words in the dictionary, you'll find more than one definition. The word *conviction* is a good example. If you'll allow me, I'd like to offer one definition that doesn't appear in any dictionary I've read lately but, nonetheless, applies perfectly to the word. I like to define *convictions* as "what you are willing to die for."

Obviously, if you define the word this way, I advise you not to have a long list of convictions. After all, life is precious. You shouldn't have a flippant attitude toward it. And you would cheapen it if you were willing to sacrifice it for any little thing that came along. But the big problem with most people is not that their list of convictions is too long; rather, there isn't anything on their list.

And that crisis equally cheapens life. An old principle has probably been used so much that it's worn out in some circles. But it's still true. It goes like this: until you have something worth dying for, you really don't have anything worth living for.

Joshua understood this principle. It was toward the end of his life, after his childhood in Egypt, his forty years' experience as understudy to Moses, and his forty-year career as commander in chief of the conquering Israelite army. He had been there when God parted the waters; he had been there when water gushed from the solid rock; he had spied out the land; he had watched the walls of Jericho crumble. He knew what was and what wasn't, who was and who wasn't. As peace was settling over the land, he had seen the cancer of compromise creeping back into the mainstream of Israel's life. And he despised the thought. He knew what the moral infection had done in the past and was certain of what it would do in the future if God's people refused to back away from it.

If you want to get a real feel for the story, read Joshua 23. I have a feeling that if you could see the original parchment on which Joshua wrote that chapter, it would have teardrops on the edges. In the closing paragraphs of his book he reminded them how much God had done, and he warned them of what would happen to them if they turned their backs on God's grace. It was as though he had already anticipated that they would surrender to the temptations and intoxications of the pagan practices surrounding them in the new, conquered land.

That was when he drew his line in the sand and stated his convictions before the people. Look at what he said:

> **And if it seems evil to you to serve the LORD, choose for yourselves this day whom you will serve, whether the gods which your fathers served that were on the other side of the River, or the gods of the Amorites, in whose land you dwell. But as for me and my house, we will serve the LORD.** (Josh. 24:15 NKJV)

Convictions cause you to take stands in life, and sometimes they require you to take them alone. Joshua was prepared to do just that. But look at the confidence he had in his role as a husband and father; he said, "As for me and *my house.*" Joshua spoke for his wife and kids. He knew that he, for one, wasn't about to surrender to compromise his convictions, and if he didn't, he knew his family would stand with him. What made him so certain? Maybe it was the fact that his uncompromising stand had been his track record for more than a hundred years! He knew that his family had been able to count on him to do what was right in the past, and that they could count on him to make the right choices for them in the future.

As I mentioned in the opening chapter, I went through my

high school years at the same time my country was going through one of the most difficult periods of this century's history. I graduated in 1968. During my senior year, I sat in our school's auditorium and listened to the recruiters from the four branches of the armed services tell me why I should cast my lot with them. At other times I sat in that same auditorium and listened to heated debates about why we were justified in trying to undermine our "corrupt government" and have nothing to do with the war in Southeast Asia. Above the stage, and etched on the frieze, was a motto that we all would have done better to take to heart. It read,

> The measure of a man is the depth of his convictions, the breadth of his interests, and the height of his ideals.[2]

In a time when too many people feel that there is absolutely nothing worth dying for, I'd like to offer these things that I think are worth dying for:

- Our faith
- Our family
- Our friends
- Our freedom

These parts of our lives are high-ticket items. They don't come cheaply. But the day we think that we can have contentment and a meaningful life without paying a high price at the conviction level is the day we cease to have significance as individuals. Gandhi might not have shared our theology, but he had figured out some important things about life. He said, "The things that will destroy us are: politics without principle; pleasure without conscience; wealth without work; knowledge without character; business without morality; science without humanity; and worship without sacrifice."

Recruiting volunteers to stand alongside you to face down the forces that are undermining you is going to be a lonely job. If you're going to join the Lord Jesus in his shoot-out at "high noon," you'd better be a man who holds to your convictions.

2. MEN OF HONOR
MAINTAIN THEIR *COMMITMENTS*

A quality needed to overcome the forces that want to undermine the family (and, therefore, the community and the country) is our tenacious resolve to maintain our commitments. We're desperately in need of men who give their word and then back it up with consistent action.

We have become a nation of men who feel justified in renegotiating our contracts when commitments we have made don't work out as well as we anticipated. Professional athletes sign on the dotted line to play ball for four years for some eleven-figure salary and then halfway through the contract say they want to renegotiate it because they have learned that some other athlete is making more than they are. They feel they can't put their hearts into the game when they know other people doing the same job are viewed as more valuable. Others do the same thing with their marriage vows. Some men want to back out of business deals that didn't turn out as well as they anticipated and leave some other guy to absorb their financial loss for them. It's happening all around us—and it's killing us as a nation.

It's time for us to grow up and be men. If you look a man in the eye, shake hands, and say it's a deal, then it's a deal. That man might be your employer, your partner, or your father-in-law. We make commitments because of the outside chance that things won't go as well as we plan. And just in case, we agree in advance to be men of our word.

Two structural crossbeams give our commitments their ultimate strength. One supports our emotions; the other supports our spirits. Let's look at the spiritual support beam first.

THE FIRST SUPPORT BEAM: INTEGRITY

Without integrity, commitments don't stand a chance. We all have a private life and a public life. Integrity is the quality in the private life that assures others that they can count on us to maintain our commitments in the public life. Which reminds me of the best definition of integrity I've ever run across: *Integrity* is "what you are when no one is looking."

The goal of the heart of integrity is aligning behavior in the private life with behavior in the public life in such a way that if you see one, you see them both. Some public figures illustrate this better than others.

Senator Gary Hart was zeroing in on the Oval Office, running way ahead of his fellow Democratic contenders. If he had maintained his momentum and avoided doing anything unusually foolish, he could have made it. But a reporter from the *Miami Herald* had reason to believe that the senator was cheating on his wife. The reporter believed that Senator Hart was holding his wife's hand on the platform by day while talking about the need for strong families in America, but sleeping with his mistress at night.

Senator Hart not only denied the accusations, but he offered a challenge to the reporter. I remember watching a clip of him on *Nightline*. He was making an impromptu statement to the reporter. He said, "Follow me. You'll be bored."

So the reporter followed him, with a camera. He wasn't bored. The pictures of Senator Hart holding the young, the blonde, the single, the "Hey-buddy-that's-not-your-wife" Donna Rice brought his house of cards toppling to the bottom of the political heap. The truth finished him. His private life didn't align with his public life. And he ended up paying a hefty price for his lack of integrity. (Donna Rice, on the other hand, has shown a contrite heart about the role she played in this chapter of her life, and as a result, God is using her to minister to others.)

As David neared the end of his life, he prepared his government for the transfer of power from himself to his son, Solomon. Although David had made some mistakes in his private life that cost him dearly in his public life, he had also demonstrated the broken and contrite heart that helps correct mistakes (Ps. 51:17). He knew that when it was all said and done, integrity determined whether a man ultimately stood or fell. He stated, "I know, my God, that you test the heart and are pleased with integrity. All these things have I given willingly and with honest intent. And now I have seen with joy how willingly your people who are here have given to you" (1 Chron. 29:17).

The writer of the very first psalm in the biblical hymnbook hit the nail with his head when he said:

Blessed is the man
  who does not walk in the counsel of the wicked
or stand in the way of sinners
  or sit in the seat of mockers.
But his delight is in the law of the LORD,
  and on his law he meditates day and night.
He is like a tree planted by streams of water,
  which yields its fruit in season
and whose leaf does not wither.
  Whatever he does prospers. (Ps. 1:1–3)

He drove his point home in Psalm 101 with these profound words:

I will sing of your love and justice;
  to you, O LORD, I will sing praise.
I will be careful to lead a blameless life—
  when will you come to me?
I will walk in my house
  with blameless heart.
I will set before my eyes
  no vile thing.
The deeds of faithless men I hate;
  they will not cling to me. (vv. 1–3)

If we have integrity in our private lives, we'll be forced to take strong stands in our public lives. Strong stands will send our enemies scurrying deep into the catacombs of our private lives to find something that would discredit the moral stand we're taking in our public lives. They did it to Daniel (Dan. 6:4). They did it to William Wilberforce, the British parliamentarian, who

fought forty-five years to abolish the slave trade and emancipate the slaves. He committed his entire professional life to this cause. He endured the ridicule, hostility, and threats of those who capitalized on the capture and marketing of humans. Had he not understood truth, had he not embraced

convictions, he could never have gone the distance. His commitment to the sanctity of human life grew out of his relationship with the God who gives life.[3]

In Wilberforce's twilight years, after he paid so dearly for his convictions, public sentiment finally got behind his cause. It filtered its way into Parliament. Just before he died, England outlawed the slave trade.

Integrity helps the spirit stay strong. But we need to mix in one other quality with it in order to see our commitments stand up to the inevitable tests.

THE SECOND SUPPORT BEAM: ENDURANCE

Men who endure never forget the finish line. It was June of 1976. I had just graduated from Dallas Seminary, and my wife and I were back in Pennsylvania visiting my parents. The Kimmel Products Company manufactured office and school furniture. My parents' home was across the road from it. Both stood isolated out in the beautiful rolling hills of western Pennsylvania. The factory covered several acres of ground.

The fire started in the old barn that had been the original building where the Kimmel Products Company had its beginning. It was connected to the modern factory that surrounded it. We should have torn the barn down years before. We worried that it presented a fire risk. As it turned out, our fears were well founded. The fire started in the former hayloft just after noon. In a matter of minutes it engulfed the entire barn, and within a half hour, the fire owned every last square foot of the factory.

Ultimately, there was nothing any of us could do. We just sat back on the grass in front of our house—my mom and dad, my grandparents, my aunt and uncle, my brothers, sister, wife—and we watched. The firemen tried in vain. Some Amish farmers tried to fight it but were quickly sent running from the heat. And so we sat and watched as decades of sweat and determination burned down to the foundation in a couple of hours. At dusk, only a few isolated flames flickered.

Finally, Dad stood up, helped up Mom, and said, "Let's go get cleaned up for supper. We're going to need a good night's sleep. Because the sun is coming over that horizon tomorrow morning, just like it always has, and we're going to be there to meet it, just like we always have." Dad knew that the fire was not the finish line. But we weren't going to survive if we let it become the finish line for us. Within twenty-four hours, Plan B had been formulated. We all knew our assignments. And we moved on with our lives.

Men who endure crash through quitting points. It was October 20, 1968. Mexico City, Olympic Stadium, 7:00 P.M. The closing ceremonies had just been completed. The spectators and athletes, still warm from the euphoria of the celebration, were gathering their belongings to leave the stadium. Then the announcer asked them to remain in their seats. Down the boulevard came the whine of police sirens. From their vantage point, many in the stadium could see motorcycles with their flashing blue lights, encircling someone making his way toward the stadium. Whoever it was, he was moving slowly.

Everyone remained seated to see the last chapter of the Olympics take place. By the time the police escort got to the stadium, the public address announcer said that a final marathoner would be making his way into the arena and around the track to the finish line. Confusion was evident among the crowd. The last marathoner had come in hours ago. The medals had already been awarded. What had taken this man so long? But the first sight of the runner making his way out of the tunnel and onto the track told the whole story.

John Stephen Akhwari from Tanzania, covered with blood, hobbled into the light. He had taken a horrible fall early in the race, whacked his head, blown out his knee, and endured a trampling before he could get back to his feet. And there he was, 26 miles and 385 yards later, stumbling his way to the finish line.

The response of the crowd was so overwhelming, it was almost frightening. They encouraged Akhwari through the last few yards of his race with a thundering ovation that far exceeded the one given the man who, hours earlier, had come in first. When Akhwari crossed the finish line, he collapsed into the arms of the medical personnel who immediately whisked him off to the hospital.

The next day, Akhwari appeared before sports journalists to field their questions about his extraordinary feat. The first question was the one any of us would have asked. "Why, after sustaining the kinds of injuries you did, would you ever get up and proceed to the finish line, when there was no way that you could possibly place in the race?" John Stephen Akhwari said this: "My country did not send me seven thousand miles to start a race. They sent me seven thousand miles to finish one."

It's not enough to know where the finish line is; you have to also be prepared to crash through the quitting points you encounter on your way to it.

Men who endure surround themselves with conquerors rather than quitters. When I turned forty, I had a difficult time processing all that the milestone represented. It bothered me that there was a good chance that fewer years waited ahead of me than stood behind me. I wondered how well I would run the last major laps in this race called my life. My wife, Darcy, and I were out to dinner at a CoCo's restaurant. We had ordered our meals and were waiting in silence for them to arrive. She was looking around the restaurant seeing what everyone ordered while I, with pen in hand, worked steadily on a work of art on my napkin. When I finished it, I slid it across the table to her. She picked it up and saw that I had drawn a pretty good likeness of a casket. She knew I wasn't processing my fortieth birthday very well, and the rolling of her eyes and the shaking of her head made it clear that she felt I was losing perspective. Actually, I was trying to gain it.

I said, "Darcy, how many men does it take to carry one of these?"

She thought for a moment and then replied, "Six."

"Honey, if I died tonight, who would you call? Who would my pallbearers be?"

She named two friends right away. Then she named a third. Then she started filling in the remaining spots with my brothers. "No, no," I said. "They have to be there; they're my brothers. They may end up being my pallbearers, but for now, I want to see if you can name six men you could call who would drop whatever they are doing to come and drop me." I wanted to know who the men were that she felt I was pouring my life into enough that they would be the logical men to take me to my last earthly engagement.

You see, I wasn't concerned about dying; I was concerned about finishing. And I wanted to finish well. If I was going to finish well, I realized that it was essential that I keep the finish line clearly in sight, and that I wasn't going to make it there on my own.

By the way, if you died tonight, who would your pallbearers be? Who would your wife call? Who are the men that you are pouring your life into?

Hebrews 12:1–3 says it this way:

Since we are surrounded by such a great cloud of witnesses, let us throw off everything that hinders and the sin that so easily entangles, and let us run with perseverance the race marked out for us. Let us fix our eyes on Jesus, the author and perfecter of our faith, who for the joy set before him endured the cross, scorning its shame, and sat down at the right hand of the throne of God. Consider him who endured such opposition from sinful men, so that you will not grow weary and lose heart.

Paul summarized the point well: "Let us not grow weary while doing good, for in due season we shall reap if we do not lose heart" (Gal. 6:9 NKJV).

3. MEN OF HONOR
ARE *COMPASSIONATE*

We can have convictions and be men who stick by our commitments, but if we try to maintain these two dimensions of our lives without an overriding spirit of compassion, their ultimate effectiveness will be minimized. That's why we need to mix in this third essential for men who stand in the gap.

Let's define the term. I define *compassion* as "anticipating a person's needs in advance and doing the things that minimize potential harm and maximize potential benefit."

And we have to be prepared to show compassion at the times that are least convenient to us. If you picked any time in Jesus' life when he seemed to be justified in being a bit preoccupied and selfish, it would be those hours when he hung on the cross. But the biblical account shows that he assured the thief hanging next to him of his eternal security (Luke 23:39–43) and made sure his mother's earthly needs would be taken care of by a reliable friend (John 19:25–27), all while he was dying to redeem the very people who were putting him to death. That's compassion. Let me mention a few people to whom God calls us to show compassion.

We need to be compassionate to our parents. There are three ways that we can do this. First, we need to *forgive them* if they fell short of what we needed in parents. Too many men are held back from being the kind of men God wants them to be because they refuse to knock the chips off their shoulders in regard to their parents. As long as we carry files of rage and revenge around with us, we fall short of the character God has called us to. The Bible doesn't have exception clauses when it comes to forgiveness. It just says to forgive and let God worry about revenge (Rom. 12:16–19; Eph. 4:31).

Second, we need to *thank them.* They need to know that we appreciate all of their sacrifices when we were young that enabled us to get where we are today. I'm not so naive as to assume that everyone reading this book came from a great home. Maybe you feel that your parents really "short-sheeted" you emotionally. It still would enhance the healing process if you could communicate to them your genuine appreciation for the good things (regardless of how few or how minimal) they did that have enhanced you as an adult.

Third, we need to *assure them that we will be there for them in their old age.* They were there for us when we were unable to care for ourselves. The Scriptures tell us that we are to honor our fathers and mothers (Ex. 20:12; John 19:26–27; Eph. 6:2). This commandment was directed not just to small children but also to grown children.

We need to be compassionate to our wives. In the next chapter we'll go into detail on the many ways that God calls us to be compassionate to our wives. One way to prepare for that time is to think of the needs of your wife that God has called you to "anticipate in advance." How can you be used of God to bring the best out of her?

We need to be compassionate to our children. Officer Candidate School in God's army wouldn't be complete without a look at our role as fathers. Before you finish reading this book, I hope that God tattoos onto your heart the overwhelming magnitude of your calling as a dad. We'll spend an entire chapter on this subject and see how compassionate dads groom sons and daughters to survive and succeed in the future. It is our job to teach them how to win and lose at work and at play. Even if you don't have children, you can still be used in a powerful way to show compassion to nieces, nephews, and kids you encounter at church and in your neighborhood.

We need to be compassionate to our friends and fellow workers. Many people surround our lives. They need a little touch from the Savior each day in order to keep their chins up and stay in the battle. You and I are that touch. An encouraging word, a helping hand, a shoulder to cry on, or a wise answer to one of the many mysteries of life shows them that we care.

We need to be compassionate to our enemies. It sounds foolish, but it's biblical. Jesus declared,

> But I say to you, love your enemies, bless those who curse you, do good to those who hate you, and pray for those who spitefully use you and persecute you, that you may be sons of your Father in heaven; for He makes His sun rise on the evil and on the good, and sends rain on the just and on the unjust. (Matt. 5:44–45 NKJV)

One of the best ways to turn an enemy into a friend is to anticipate needs and do something that helps the person's life go a little more smoothly.

All compassion is, is love acted out. But what is love? We talk about it, read about it, go to movies about it, and sing about it. But if we were pinned down and forced to define it, what would we come up with? Let me offer a definition of love that can help you carry out your role as a compassionate man: *love* is "the commitment of my will to your needs and best interests, regardless of the cost."

You can take that definition to the bank. It's true, and it works. And when it becomes the essence of how you deal with the people you're called to love, spiritual and emotional stock values go up in everyone.

Men of honor are men who live with clearly defined convictions. They maintain their commitments, and they show compassion. There is one last characteristic of men who stand strong, stand tall, and stand alone.

4. MEN OF HONOR
ARE *COURAGEOUS*

Of all the abstract but vital ingredients needed to make a difference in life, I think courage is the one that is most often missing. Without it, however, we're toast. It doesn't matter how great we walk or how bold we talk at church or around our Christian friends. These venues don't represent the battlefield. It's easy to wax eloquent for the cause among allies. But Monday morning is coming. The pressures are waiting. It's when our faith is on trial, and our patience is tested to the max, that we show what kind of men we really are. That's why we must deliberately build courage into our lives.

The Bible tells us that God *expects* us to be courageous. He has *commanded* us to be. And in the process of telling us to be courageous, he tells us how, why, and what to expect. Look at Joshua 1:6–9 (NKJV):

> **Be strong and of good courage, for to this people you shall divide as an inheritance the land which I swore to their fathers to give them. Only be strong and very courageous, that you may observe to do according to all the law which Moses My servant commanded you; do not turn from it to the right hand or to the left, that you may prosper wherever you go. This Book of the Law shall not depart from your mouth, but you shall meditate in it day and night, that you may observe to do according to all that is written in it. For then you will make your way prosperous, and then you will have good success. Have I not commanded you? Be strong and of good courage; do not be afraid, nor be dismayed, for the LORD your God is with you wherever you go.**

Joshua was inspired by God to use the imperative mood when writing this counsel to us. In other words, it isn't a request. It's what God expects from us. Courage is nothing more than our faith and our hope with muscle behind them. It's the ability to do what we should do in any given situation. Or as John Wayne would say, "Courage is when you're scared to death, but you saddle up anyway."

You want to be courageous. Allow me to suggest the following ways:

Courageous men maintain healthy fears. Let me flesh out this concept a little bit. Most people are confused when it comes to the relationship between courage and fear. They're under the impression that courageous people are fearless. Wrong. Fools are fearless. I've sat for hours on end with retired Brigadier General Joe Foss. Joe can list many accomplishments on his résumé, such as being the governor of South Dakota or commissioner of the American Football League. But his greatest and most heroic accomplishments took place in the skies over Guadalcanal. He flew his F4F Grumman Wildcat into the teeth of the Japanese for several months during World War II. He was shot down four times, and each time he survived to fight again. When malaria finally grounded him for good, there were twenty-six Japanese flags painted on the fuselage of his plane.

For Joe's extraordinary bravery, FDR personally hung the Medal of Honor around his neck. Ask Joe whether he was ever scared, and he will just look at you sideways as if you're crazy, and then he will say, "Scared? Of course, I was scared. I've never been more scared in my life." So why did he keep going back to face the enemy? The answer was simple. He was afraid of other things that were greater than his fear of getting killed: the victory of the Japanese over the Allies, the possible loss of our freedom, the inevitable destruction of the dream our country was founded on, and the ultimate loss of the safety of our families. Those fears drove him to overcome the other fears waiting for him every time he turned his plane into the wind at Henderson Field and took off after the enemy.

So what you need, then, are healthy fears that overcome your unhealthy fears. Let me list some healthy fears that empower men like you and me to maintain a consistent pattern of courage in our lives:

- The fear of God. It gives you the keys to the door that leads to wisdom. (Ps. 111:10; Prov. 9:10).
- The fear of debt. It keeps you from falling into it. As long as you're spending more than you're taking in and owing more than the value of your assets, God's agenda for your life and your family must take a backseat to your creditors. One of the greatest gifts that you can give your family is a solvent financial position.
- The fear of disqualification. It empowers you to turn your back and flee from temptation. You need to be a man who fears the consequences of giving in to your urges. You need to fear the devastation that surrendering to the alluring shortcuts in life will have on your family, your reputation, and your relationship with God.
- The fear of squandering your God-given talents. God gifted every one of us in order to enhance what he is doing on the earth. The last thing you want to do is waste such a golden opportunity.
- The fear of shortchanging your kids. They are counting on you. You can't afford to be preoccupied when they are at such critical ages. You need to be motivated to courageously sacrifice for their best interests by, among other things, refusing to allow the devastation they would be forced to endure if you don't do your job.
- The fear of standing before God to give an account and having nothing to show for your efforts. As I said earlier, life is too short and eternity is too long to waste such an opportunity.

There is a second thing that you can do to enhance your ability to be courageous.

Courageous men make promises and keep them. You need to promise your wife your uncompromised faithfulness. She doesn't need to be worrying about whether or not you can be trusted. The marriage vows have to be nonnegotiable and authentic.

You need to promise your children your discretionary time and attention. When you come home from work at night and push the button in your car that raises the garage door, your kids' legs often appear like teeth as the door lifts up. They're waiting for their father. They need help with a math problem, they need help hitting a fastball, they need to wrestle, or they need to talk. At that very moment, when their needs are at their peak, your energies are at their daylong low. There is no time for a nap. Put the kids off until tomorrow and you'll regret it. When tomorrow comes and you finally have time for them, they will have long since moved into their own homes to raise your grandkids. It takes courage to suck it up and jump into the middle of it all with enthusiasm.

You need to promise your employer a good day's work. He paid for it. It takes courage to put out the sweat in the morning when you're still half asleep or in the dog hours of the afternoon. It takes courage to work down to the whistle when everyone else around you has emotionally shut down a half hour before quitting time. Real men don't coast. Real men don't make excuses. Real men work hard.

You need to mix a third ingredient into your recipe for a courageous heart.

Courageous men realize who is ultimately in control and trust him all the way. Frederick the Great was a scoffer of Christ. He had a great general, Von Zealand, who was a disciple of Jesus Christ. One day at a gathering, Frederick the Great was entertaining his guests by making coarse jokes about Jesus Christ. The whole assembly rolled in laughter. Except for Von Zealand. Finally, unable to stay silent any longer, General Von Zealand rose stiffly to his feet and faced the king.

"Sire," he said, "you know I have not feared death. I have fought and won thirty-eight battles for you. I am an old man; I shall soon have to go into the presence of One greater than you, the mighty God who saved me from my sin, the Lord Jesus Christ whom you are blaspheming. I salute you, sire, as an old man, who loves his Savior, on the edge of eternity."

After a long pause, Frederick the Great broke the silence with his trembling voice, "General Von Zealand, I beg your pardon. I beg your pardon! I beg your pardon!"

The party silently dispersed.[4]

There is an epitaph on a stone in the mausoleum beneath St. Paul's Cathedral in London. It's a two-line summary of a man named Lord Lawrence. Although the words are few, they say everything: "He feared man so little, because he feared God so much." When it comes to trusting in the God who has everything under control, I think that epitaph says it all.

GOD'S POSSE

It's "high noon." For most of us, it's now or never. God is looking for a few good men to take up his banner and his cause in their marriages, with their children, in the marketplace, and in their relationships with people they encounter in their day-to-day lives. There is a price tag. The stakes are high. But the payoff is beyond calculation. Are you willing to be one of God's good men?

Teddy Roosevelt put it this way: "Far better it is to dare mighty things, to win glorious triumphs, even though checkered by failure, than to take rank with those poor spirits who neither enjoy much nor suffer much because they live in the gray twilight that knows neither victory nor defeat."[5]

STUDY AND DISCUSSION QUESTIONS

UP FRONT AND PERSONAL

1. Can you recall a political or church leader giving a brave defense of a cowardly position? What else could he have done, and would it have changed anything?

2. Are you the leader in your home? Or have you abdicated that role, leaving it for your spouse to assume? What is the evidence for your answer?

3. How would your best friend describe your commitment to integrity and endurance?

FOR THE GROUP TO DISCUSS

1. Where is the Officer Candidate School for the officers in God's army?

2. The author says you are reading this book because you want to make a difference. Does that mean you must become a leader if you aren't one now? Can you act alone and still make a difference?

3. Complete this statement: "If there was one conviction in my life worth dying for, it would be _____."

4. How do your family members know they can count on you to make the right choices?

5. If your private life does not align with your public life, could there be consequences to pay? Give examples of prominent men of politics or the church whose public and private lives were at odds, and identify the ultimate outcome.

6. Discuss this statement: "Convictions determine whether you have a stand; integrity determines where you stand."

7. What are the two supporting crossbeams that give our commitments strength? Define them in one-sentence explanations.

8. What does it take to be a man of honor?

9. Discuss how compassion and forgiveness are linked.

10. Will showing compassion infringe on your need to appear

strong and manly in the eyes of your family and friends? How much "manly need" do you have?

11. Does God expect us to be courageous? Is this optional?

12. Define healthy fear. List several sources of unhealthy fear.

13. What are a few courageous promises we need to make? Why are they so hard to keep?

APPLYING GOD'S WORD

1. Read Proverbs 28:1. How hard is it for you to be like the lion?

2. Write down the name of a great man of God, biblical or modern day, and list his courageous qualities you admire.

CHAPTER 9

OFFICER CANDIDATE SCHOOL: A FEW GOOD HUSBANDS

If you're not sitting, you might want to. It will be easier to process the impact of these statistics I recently ran across. Did you know that 25 percent of all men kiss their wives good-bye when they leave their houses? However, 99 percent of all men kiss their houses good-bye when they leave their wives!

Something about that second statistic makes us want to pay closer attention to the first one. We made our vows until death us do part. If we're men of honor, then we're in it for the long haul. It's a hand-in-hand, side-by-side commitment to our brides. And when we take our cues from God, the love that we have for our wives is a present-tense illustration of God's love for his people. But life at street level has a bad habit of kicking the slats out of our commitments. It's a daily battle to maintain the freshness of our love toward our wives when we have to do it in an arena that is so utterly hostile to the sanctity of the marriage commitment.

The good news is that there is no ambiguity when it comes to what God expects of us. His Word is outspoken. And every command he gives us is in our best interest as well as the interest of the entire family.

If somebody came along and tore two chapters out of the Bible, 1 Peter 3 and Ephesians 5, and told you that these would be all the instruction you would receive from God on how to be a husband, these two passages would be all you need. They have so much help for us as husbands that if we did only what we found in them, we would be light-years ahead of some of the best husbands out there.

MAKING A MARRIAGE STRONG

Let's look at the 1 Peter passage first. "To sum up, let all be harmonious, sympathetic, brotherly, kindhearted, and humble in spirit; not returning evil for evil, or insult for insult, but giving a blessing instead; for you were called for the very purpose that you might inherit a blessing" (3:8–9 NASB). This passage gives great advice to everyone, but it is specifically directed to married couples. Peter listed five qualities that make a marriage strong. Marriages that go five for five are ready to take anything that life dishes out. Let's look at these qualities.

1. HARMONY

A useful way to clarify the meaning of a word is to look at its opposite. The opposite of harmony is discord. I played brass instruments in the orchestra all through high school and college. Before a concert, we would take our places on the stage and warm up our instruments. Approximately twenty minutes before the concert began, we would be sitting in place playing scales, parts of our music, or whatever we needed to do to warm up our lips and our instruments.

Just before it was time to start the concert, a signal would be given offstage to the first chair clarinetist. That's when he or she would stand up and play concert B flat. We would all be quiet for a second, listening to the note, and then we'd start playing the corresponding note on our instruments. String players would tighten or loosen strings to bring them into pitch. Brass players would move slides in or out. The goal was to be able to play the note as an orchestra in such a way that it sounded like one instrument. Once we were in tune, the conductor would walk onstage and lift his baton, and we'd make gorgeous music.

God's Word is concert B flat. Once we're in tune with it in marriage, we can make beautiful music as couples.

2. SYMPATHY

The opposite of sympathy is insensitivity. We tend to be insensitive when we fail to factor in the pressures that our wives have been under.

One of the better autobiographies I've read recently was General H. Norman Schwarzkopf's book, *It Doesn't Take a Hero*. During his first tour of duty in Vietnam, he was assigned as an adviser to the II Corps of the South Vietnamese Army (SVA). He fought with the Third Battalion in the Battle of Duc Co. Their reconnaissance had given them faulty intelligence reports on the size of the enemy's forces in the area. They were told to expect a couple of battalions; instead, they encountered two regiments!

The fighting was fierce, violent, and costly. They were separated from their supplies and from the protection of their bunkers. They fought the enemy, without relief, for ten days. They patched their wounded and piled up their dead. At night, a young South Vietnamese officer sneaked into the jungle to dig up wild turnip roots for the men to eat. Major Schwarzkopf ate the roots, fought side by side with the SVA, worked on their wounded, and helped carry out their dead. The putrefied bodies he loaded onto helicopters left a stench on him that wouldn't come off even after many washings.

Finally, the battle ended. The remnants of the Third Battalion assembled at the camp. They were hungry, filthy, and exhausted, and they stank. Suddenly the sky filled with helicopters. Once they landed, the area was crowded with reporters, cameramen, a general, and his staff. The high-ranking military officers strutted by Schwarzkopf and the filthy, hungry, and exhausted remnant of the Third Battalion—totally ignoring them. They staged a briefing for the press. The general and his staff waxed eloquent about a battle they had not fought.

When the briefing ended, the general approached Major Schwarzkopf with the cameras running. First, he recoiled from the stench. Gradually, he moved close enough to ask a couple of questions. Major Schwarzkopf was expecting comments such as, "Are your men all right? How many people did you lose?" or "Good job. We're proud of you." Instead there was an awkward silence, and then he asked, "How's the chow been?"

> The chow? For #!*, I'd been eating rice and salt and raw jungle turnips that Sergeant Hung had risked his life to get! I was so stunned that all I could say was, "Uh, fine, sir."
> "Have you been getting your mail regularly?"
> All my mail had been going to my headquarters in Saigon and I assumed it was okay. So I said, "Oh, yes, sir."
> "Good, good. Fine job, lad." Lad? And with that he walked off.[1]

The general, though the commanding officer, showed zero sympathy or sensitivity to the plight of his men. It's no wonder General Schwarzkopf went on to write, "At that moment I lost any respect I'd ever had for that general."[2]

You are the leader of your home. It is essential that the people you lead respect you. Respect is not demanded; it's earned. When you come home at night and trivialize the pressures your wife has been under at her job or with the kids, or get upset with her that things don't look as nice as you'd prefer, her desire to respond to your leadership drops several notches.

I know how this works. I've made this mistake. I'd come home from the office to find Darcy down on her knees in a heated debate with our six-year-old son, and she was losing. I'd say something foolish: "Don't argue with him. Just tell him what you want him to do, don't give him any other options, and then tell him to get to it, like this. . . ." And then I'd proceed to say something to my son that he would immediately obey.

Then I'd get that look from Darcy. She'd say, "You don't know what it's like. You're not around them all day long. They're relentless. They break down your defenses."

"Yeah, right, Darcy! They're just kids. You just have to let them know who's in charge." Words of a fool!

Saturday would come. Darcy would run errands while leaving me home with the four kids. They'd be in the corner huddled together, mumbling something about "fresh meat!" Within an hour, I'd be down on my knees eye to eye with my six year old, losing a debate with him!

A good husband ultimately learns sensitivity to his wife's plight.

3. BROTHERLINESS

The opposite of brotherliness is hostility. Siblings have rivalries. I had four brothers, and we got after each other quite often. But there was an invisible bond and an unstated, but very real, assumption that we were committed to one another as brothers.

Hostile people preoccupy themselves with their next conflict. They plot the destruction of the other person until their anger permeates every nuance of the relationship. When it comes to this kind of behavior permeating a marriage relationship, Peter said, "No way!" His advice was to treat each other with the commitment that you'd find between brothers.

4. KINDHEARTEDNESS

The opposite of kindheartedness is hard-heartedness. Hardhearted people are not people who fail to see another person's plight. They look right at it, they know full well that the other person can't solve the dilemma, they know they can, but they turn their backs on the person anyway.

Peter told us to have a heartfelt attitude of kindness toward your spouse. That means you see her need, and you do everything within your power to help her meet that need.

5. HUMILITY

The opposite of humility is pride. You know what is required to be humble. Paul taught in Philippians 2:3–4, "Do nothing out of selfish ambition or vain conceit, but in humility consider others better than yourselves. Each of you should look not only to your own interests, but also to the interests of others." He followed the admonition with the example of the Lord Jesus who, having seen our need, relinquished his royal privileges as King of kings and assumed a humble role as a servant and sacrifice to, and for, the human race. As you'll see, you have to be humble enough to be willing to die for your wife (Eph. 5:25).

You demonstrate these qualities by responding in God's way rather than your own selfish way to problems and challenges within your marriage. Peter explained that God's way to respond to problems and challenges is through giving and being a blessing. The selfish way to respond to problems and challenges is through evil and insults. Here's how he put it:

> **Let him who means to love life and see good days**
> **Refrain his tongue from evil and his lips from**
> **speaking guile.**
> **And let him turn away from evil and do good;**
> **Let him seek peace and pursue it.**
> **For the eyes of the LORD are upon the righteous,**
> **And His ears attend to their prayer,**
> **But the face of the LORD is against those who do evil.**
> (1 Peter 3:10–12 NASB)

This passage outlines the consequences for a man who fails to follow God's orders. Let's rehearse the orders one more time. You're to live in harmony with your wife, show her sympathy, brotherliness, kindheartedness, and humility. If you don't, the consequences to you personally are horrific. Peter said your failure will result in the following:

A joyless life. A life with God's face against you is a joyless life. Let's differentiate between joy and happiness for a second. Happiness is a result of external forces that we have no control over lining up in our favor. Which is why it is a waste of time pursuing it. Since we have no control over it, why not pursue the things we do, and then enjoy the happy moments life brings our way? Joy has more to do with contentment, and it *is* in our power. My pastor, Darryl Delhousaye, likes to define *joy* as "the absence of fear."

Your failure to respond in an understanding way to your wife will suck day-to-day joy out of you. And it allows you to be haunted by a lot of fears that you shouldn't have. I meet men who make $100,000 a year and are worried about what would happen if the flow of money stopped. Or they're worried about not having enough. They can't enjoy what they have because of all of the fears within them. Invariably, I find through interviewing them that they are disobeying one or more of these five commands toward their wives.

I meet people who are worried they are going to be involved in some kind of personal violence against them. They've never been attacked before. Other than the tabloid newscasts designed to prey on fears, nothing indicates that they need to be worried. But the reality still doesn't stop them from worrying.

We get a hint of what's going on in Leviticus. God outlined through Moses what would happen if people disobeyed his commandments. One of the consequences was that "you will flee even when no one is pursuing you" (26:17). In other words, paranoia. God causes us to be afraid of everything, even when the facts say we should be afraid of nothing. Obedience takes away unfounded fears and in the process gives us joy.

Hindered prayers. Peter said that your failure to treat your wife the way God wants you to treat her puts God in a position where he is not obligated to respond to your prayers. Have you ever prayed and felt that God wasn't listening? I have. Invariably, it happened at times in my life when I was neglecting Darcy's needs.

Broken fellowship with God. This consequence is obvious. A lack of fellowship with your wife brings about a lack of fellowship with the Lord. His attitude is, "I gave you your wife as a gift. If you treat my gift unkindly, then I'm taking it personally." God wants you to enjoy the gift that he has given you, take care of her, and ultimately present her back to him someday in better condition than you received her (Eph. 5:27).

Let's learn how this can be done. It's all in his marching orders to you as a husband.

MARCHING ORDERS!

God has given you clear and concise marching orders when it comes to your role as a husband. They are found in Ephesians 5:23–30.

MARCHING ORDER NO. 1: LEAD HER HUMBLY!

The first thing that Paul said was, "For the husband is head of the wife, as also Christ is head of the church; and He is the Savior of the body" (Eph. 5:23 NKJV). Let me mention several ways that you can be a humble leader.

A humble leader views his wife as an equal—not a subordinate. This passage is often misinterpreted in a military context using the idea of a hierarchical ranking system. Wrong! The apostle Paul said you're the "head." He used a physical metaphor, not a military one. He drew an analogy similar to the relationship between the heart and the lungs. If you had to pick one of the two organs to do without, which one would you pick? Obviously, you can't part with either. And the heart and the lungs work as a team. One cleans the blood while the other pumps it through the rest of the system. Your wife is to be viewed not as inferior or subordinate but as an equal who serves a different function in the relationship from the one you have.

A humble leader empowers his wife—never controls her. Let me define *control:* "Control, is when I leverage the strength of my personality or my position, against my wife's weaknesses, in order to get her to meet my selfish agenda."[3] You can see, when you define control this way, it would be easy to control your wife. Your size, your strength, your volume, or the amount of your paycheck can enable you to get what you want from your wife. But God said that you are to lead her as Christ leads his church.

No one can name a time when Christ *made* his church do anything. He never *made* his disciples do anything. He gave instruction that they sometimes followed and sometimes ignored (Matt. 21:2–6; 19:13–14). But their response never determined his commitment to them. In fact, it fueled him even more to go through with his plan to save them. The Ephesians passage reminds you that Christ led the church by first rescuing the church. You are to lead your wife in the same way—with humility that says to her, "Your needs come ahead of mine."

You can find an excellent guideline for this kind of attitude just a few pages beyond the Ephesians passage in your Bible; look in Philippians 2. Paul wrote that you're to have the same attitude toward others as Christ had toward you (vv. 5–7). His attitude ultimately showed itself through the action of being willing to become a bond servant and die for you. He put everything he had on the line for you. Skipping back to the Ephesians 5 passage, the unstated but clear advice is, "Go thou and do likewise."

A humble leader knows his wife's limits—and honors her. You can't expect from her the same things that you expect from yourself. You are to take into consideration what she is and what she isn't. The apostle Peter offered insight on this point: "Husbands, in the same way be considerate as you live with your wives, and treat them with respect as the weaker partner and as heirs with you of the gracious gift of life, so that nothing will hinder your prayers" (1 Peter 3:7). He referred to her as a "weaker vessel" (KJV). She was not termed the weaker vessel "for intellectual or moral weakness, but purely for physical reasons, which the husband must recognize with due consideration for marital happiness."[4] Another thing you need to understand is that this passage is not implying that if she is the weaker vessel, you are the stronger. It is implying that she is the weaker, and you're the "weak"! The next notch up from weaker is weak. In other words, you're both fragile in your own ways. She is more like an exquisite vase, and you're more like a Crock-Pot! A Crock-Pot will break if it hits the floor hard enough, but it's designed to endure more rough handling than a vase.

You honor someone when you recognize her inherent worth. Too often, your put-downs to your wife are insults to the very things about her that make her so valuable. For instance, you shouldn't begrudge these things:

- Her tears
- Her fatigue or need for more sleep
- Her inadequacies in the area of sports or mechanical things
- Her insecurities
- Her fears

My wife had all of our children by C-section. That type of delivery required her to stay in the hospital a little longer than usual in order to recover. One night I was going to the hospital to visit her. It was at the time the nurses were changing shifts. I parked my car on the back side of the hospital and walked across the street toward the maternity wing entrance. I saw a nurse whom Darcy and I had gotten to know over the past few days. She was coming out of the main doors and preparing to cross the street to her car. I called out to her by name and said, "Hello." Because she couldn't recognize me in the limited light, she was hesitant to say anything. When I asked, from a distance, how Darcy was doing, she realized who I was and approached me to talk. When she got up close, I could see that she had her pepper spray in one hand and her car keys protruding out between the fingers of her other hand (in the form of a fist). We visited, and then she went on to her car.

I stayed there and watched her until I knew she was safely inside her car. It dawned on me that I was crossing the street unarmed, unprepared for an ambush, and unconcerned about one too. The reason was simple: I wasn't a mugger's typical prey. Most people who assault others take into consideration what they're getting themselves into. Most likely, they wouldn't mess with a full-grown man because they might surmise that he would be inclined to not only defend himself but possibly destroy them in the process.

Your wife has fears directly related to being physically weaker that don't even cross your mind. As you humbly lead her, you are to keep this reality of her fears in mind.

A humble leader respects his wife's opinion—and esteems her. This requires that you not only seek out her insights but also be prepared to act upon them. She has the most to offer you because she has the most to lose if you lose. For 99 percent of married men, the most valuable adviser and confidante is his wife. One of the things that sets a wise leader apart from a foolish one is that a wise leader carefully listens to his best advisers.

TEN WAYS TO LEAD YOUR WIFE

1. Include her in your vision for the future.
2. Accept spiritual responsibility for the family.
3. Pray with her on a regular basis.

4. Seek financial consultation with her on all major financial decisions.
5. Initiate meaningful family traditions.
6. Initiate fun outings for the family on a regular basis.
7. Encourage her to grow as an individual (hobbies, sports, continuing education, etc.).
8. Take the initiative in establishing with your wife clear and well-reasoned convictions on issues such as alcohol, finances, child discipline, allowable movies and television, etc.
9. Join a small group of men who are dedicated to improving their skills as husbands and fathers.
10. Make your personal free time available to the needs and best interests of your family members.

MARCHING ORDER NO. 2: LOVE HER SACRIFICIALLY!

Husbands, love your wives, just as Christ also loved the church and gave Himself up for her; that He might sanctify her, having cleansed her by the washing of water with the word, that He might present to Himself the church in all her glory, having no spot or wrinkle or any such thing; but that she should be holy and blameless. (Eph. 5:25–27 NASB)

This passage teaches you that you are to sacrificially love your wife. That's how Christ loved the church. He loved her enough that he was willing to sacrifice his very life for her. Which brings up the first command from this passage.

A sacrificial lover should be willing to die for his wife. There is one simple litmus test that proves to your wife whether (if the opportunity came along) you'd be willing to die for her: Are you willing to live for her? How do you do that? At the end of this section, I'll give you ten suggestions.

A sacrificial lover doesn't subject his wife to the poison of comparison. A man gets up in the morning, nukes breakfast in the microwave, kisses his wife good-bye, and heads out the door. As he kisses her, he notices that she's looking her worst.

There are reasons for this. One of them has to do with the fact that she didn't take the mousse out of her hair the night before and therefore has a bad case of "bed head." Another reason she looks disheveled is that she didn't sleep through the night. Few women do. That's because God has equipped them with an internal satellite dish with which they monitor everything going on around them. Men sleep in comas. They're next to impossible to stir. Women, on the other hand, are up and down all night, checking on the kids, checking on the house, checking just to check!

So the last image this guy has of his wife is of her looking her worst. Then he passes a couple of billboards of women airbrushed to perfection. Next he passes through an outer office filled with unmarried women who look perfect. They look so perfect because all they had to do from the time they left the night before was to prepare to come back to work the next morning. They had time to go to the club and work out with Sheena and Cher. They could follow through on their *Buns of Steel* video and spend forty-five minutes on their Ab-Roller. This guy's poor wife got up that morning and put Jane Fonda on fast-forward to try to get in a few minutes of aerobics. The women in the office didn't have to do laundry for four other people, help with homework, read two little ones a story, and solve one of life's great mysteries for a teenager.

This guy slips through a cloud of Georgio perfume and makes his way to his private office. On the corner of his desk is a picture of his wife with their three children. He looks at his wife and then looks out his door at one of the women in the outer office. He looks at his wife again, then sniffs the perfume coming from just outside his office door. Then staring at the picture one last time, he makes a comparison and says something extremely foolish to his brain: "Boy, she sure isn't what she was like when I married her." You want to scream at him, "Hey, man! Look in the mirror! Gravity located you too! And besides, do you see those three kids in the picture with her? They once lived *inside* of her—three quarters of a year, each. That puts a lot of miles on a body. How would you look if you had some kid inside you skipping rope with his umbilical cord and kick-boxing your bladder? It makes your hair hurt just thinking about it!"

But guys who surrender to the comparison trap are notorious for abandoning the wife in the picture to chase one of the skirts in the outer office. And men are so clever that they've actually coined an expression to explain this behavior away. They call it "a midlife crisis." It sounds as if it's not their fault.

Malachi, the Old Testament prophet, spoke about this. He talked about men complaining about the fact that God didn't seem to pay attention to them anymore (once again, a reference to prayers being ignored). They wanted to know why. Listen to what he said:

> You ask, "Why?" It is because the LORD is acting as the witness between you and the wife of your youth, because you have broken faith with her, though she is your partner, the wife of your marriage covenant. Has not the LORD made them one? In flesh and spirit they are his. And why one? Because he was seeking godly offspring. So guard yourself in your spirit, and do not break faith with the wife of your youth. (Mal. 2:14–15)

What about men who have already divorced the wife of their youth and have remarried? Are they doomed to a life of fruitless praying and lack of blessing? I think there are two things they can do to minimize God's disappointment.

First, admit that they've sinned in divorcing their wives, regardless of the circumstances. They need to admit it to God, to themselves, and—if they have the guts—to the wife of their youth.

Second, make sure that they are taking care of the needs of the wife of their youth. Most women who are left behind by their husbands move to poverty level. I heard a census report on my car radio one afternoon that said the fastest way for women and their children to find themselves in poverty is by experiencing a divorce. Although the statistics are correct, the action isn't right.

You may not be able to go back and marry the wife of your youth. But you can make sure that she is at least adequately cared for. It may sound ridiculous, and I know it's impractical, but you must be certain that you're honoring God by doing the best you can to rectify all of the mistakes you've made with and/or against people.

A sacrificial lover honors his wife's uniquenesses—and encourages them. About a decade ago, the big rage among women was to decorate T-shirts. To me, there are fewer things more frightening than a woman with a glue gun! Darcy decided she wanted to try her hand at designing and decorating a few T-shirts. Her first attempts were "interesting," to say the least. When she modeled them for me, I had a difficult time voicing approval for her efforts. In my heart, I felt that she didn't have the gift and was afraid that she'd never find out.

But a funny thing happened in the midst of splatter paint, sequins, and ribbons—she got good at what she was doing. In fact, she got great. She made beautiful outfits for her and the girls, and she saved us a lot of money in the process. If I had put down her efforts at the beginning, she would have given up early and never been able to discover her hidden talents.

While we're on the subject, let me mention something about the perfectionist husband—he kills his wife's spirit. No matter how hard she tries, a perfectionist husband sees only her inadequacies, shortcomings, and mistakes. After years of listening to that kind of criticism, the spirit of a woman eventually shrivels up and dies. Ephesians 5:27 says that you are to present your wife to God in all her glory. The word translated "in all her glory" has to do with a brilliance in purity, a radiance.[5]

Let me ask you a question. Does your wife light up a room? When she walks into church on Sunday, does she radiate? The Bible says that the answer to that question is pretty much determined by *you*. You determine the wattage of your wife! Right now, this moment, is a great time to evaluate how you're doing and to make a strategy to increase your wife's wattage!

A sacrificial lover learns what his wife's greatest needs are—and puts them above his own. That's love in action. As I said earlier in the book, love is the commitment of my will to your needs and best interests, regardless of the cost. Love is nothing without sacrifice. There is no such thing as free love. Love is precious and priceless. Look over the following list and see if there are some ways in which you can increase your commitment to love your wife sacrificially.

TEN WAYS TO LOVE YOUR WIFE

1. Assume responsibility for your actions and be quick to say, "I'm sorry," and "Forgive me."
2. Follow through on commitments you make to your wife.
3. Frequently tell her what you like about her (be specific).
4. Provide the finances for the family's basic living expenses.
5. Go over the upcoming week with your wife, and clarify your schedule as well as anticipate pressure points.
6. Praise her in public.
7. Remember her on key holidays and occasions (birthday, anniversary).
8. Give her time to be by herself.
9. Encourage her to cultivate deep and supportive friendships.
10. Take her to a Christian marriage conference or retreat every two to three years.

MARCHING ORDER NO. 3: CARE FOR HER ENTHUSIASTICALLY!

So husbands ought also to love their own wives as their own bodies. He who loves his own wife loves himself; for no one ever hated his own flesh, but nourishes and cherishes it, just as Christ also does the church, because we are members of His body. (Eph. 5:28–30 NASB)

You have to remember only two words if you want to care for your wife enthusiastically: *protect* and *provide*.

An enthusiastic caregiver protects his wife. You care for your wife by creating a secure home environment. You want to make sure that the house and her car are always maintained for safety. This is more than just keeping everything in working order. You don't want things around her that would cause her insecurity. That's why we'd all do our wives a favor by throwing the swimsuit edition of *Sports Illustrated* in the trash without looking through it first. Don't bring home movies to watch that would make her feel afraid, cheap, or insecure. And you need to protect her from the kids. Children should never think that they can talk disrespectfully to their mother. That won't stop them from trying, but how you respond to them will have a lot to do with whether they try it again.

Let me suggest something for you. The next time one of your kids sasses or talks back to your wife, instead of saying, "Don't talk to your mother that way," try this. Get in between your child and your wife, get eye level, and say, "Don't talk to my *wife* that way. Nobody talks to my wife that way. You talk to my wife that way, and you're going to end up messing with me. Now figure out how to voice your disagreement or frustration to her with respect." You'll be amazed at the effect.

God can use your protective attitude toward your wife to also click a strategic thought into your daughter's brain. In the back of her mind she'll be thinking, *I've got to get one like this when I get married!* Your son will be thinking, *I've got to remember to do this when I'm married with children.* But keep in mind that this will work only if you make it a habit of never speaking disrespectfully to her when you're frustrated or angry with her. You have to put your sermon into practice. If you wonder how to deal with conflict in a proper way with your wife, check out Ephesians 4:17–32. It gives excellent guidelines for how to fight fair. It's a passage well worth studying.

Another way that you can protect your wife is by handling money wisely. Specifically, you need to *save* money. One of the best reasons to save money is that it forces you to exercise discipline in just about every area of your life. You are a steward of money for God. It's all *his.* You just take care of it for him. By handling your money wisely, you take away a lot of your wife's fears when unforeseen things happen, such as getting laid off or fired, or having a major appliance break down. By saving money, you're not putting confidence in your money. You're putting confidence in God. A savings account is a lot like a seat belt. You might pray and ask God to protect you on a trip. You still put on a seat belt because that might be the thing he uses to protect you. God wants you to use your head. He wants you to live a balanced, careful life. Saving money and *staying out of debt* are excellent ways to demonstrate this quality to your wife.

An enthusiastic caregiver provides for his wife's needs. You can provide for your wife in several ways:

- By considering it a privilege to work and provide financial resources for the family. Do you whine about your job? Do you complain about having to go to work? Every time you do that you're making a statement about how you view your family. Every job has things about it that you don't enjoy. And you may be in a job that is not suited for you. But if it is providing a paycheck during the time that you're looking for a job that is suited for you, you should be thankful for it. You should approach work as one of the biggest ministries that you can have to your family.

- By maintaining a standard of living that frees her up to provide time and attention to meeting the family's physical and emotional needs. A lot of men force their wives into the work arena in order to raise the standard of living. They want certain perks and benefits that they can't acquire on their salary. Or they've allowed the family budget to run at a deficit and have no choice but to put their wives out into the work arena. Either way, there is a significant and painful price that must be paid by the family—especially by the kids. Kids don't do well when they are forced to raise themselves. If we let them be baby-sat by MTV or *Beavis and Butthead,* we shouldn't be surprised that they turn out as children without strong inner convictions. Life might be expensive, but eternity is even more so. Most women would love the opportunity to pour their lives into the job of grooming their kids for the future. It can't be done well if they're doing it part-time. You need to do everything within your power to scale the financial lifestyle of your family to the level of your personal income.

- By tenderly and patiently meeting her sexual needs. When it comes to your sexual relationship with your wife, there are two extremes to avoid: demanding and defrauding. God hasn't wired men and women the same when it comes to sex. For most men, it's their number one need. For many women, lots of things would take priority over it (such as ironing). It takes the average man 2.3 minutes to climax. It takes the average woman 13 minutes. You could probably read a phone book in 13 minutes. That's why you need to be patient, sensitive, and understanding.

Most men that I talk to wish they had a better sexual relationship with their wives. They wish that they had sex more often, and that when they had sex, their wives would really get into it and enjoy themselves. Let me review how you can have your sexual dream become a reality:

1. Live in harmony with her.
2. Be sympathetic to her.
3. Treat her with brotherly kindness.
4. Be kindhearted toward her.
5. Show humility toward her.
6. Lead her humbly.
7. Love her sacrificially.
8. Care for her enthusiastically.

God has called on you to love, lead, and care for your wife. He has asked her to submit to you. There is no place in the Bible where you will find God giving you permission to make her submit. It's not in there. Whether she submits to your leadership isn't any of your business. It's between her and God. My wife has found submission to be a fairly easy thing to do. I think it's because of how she defines submission. Darcy says that _submission_ is "ducking, so God can hit your husband!" Let's be men who don't give God a reason to have to nail us.

Before you close this chapter, look over the following list and pick out some specific ways you can care for your wife enthusiastically.

TEN WAYS TO CARE FOR YOUR WIFE

1. Keep your family out of debt.
2. Draw up a will and have a well-conceived plan for the children in the event of your death.
3. Make sure she gets adequate rest.
4. Discuss household responsibilities with her and make sure they are fairly distributed.

5. Be sensitive to the changes that she goes through emotionally and physically.
6. Work closely with the children in providing practical instruction about life.
7. Give your wife and children access to the interior of your life (emotions).
8. Make sure her car is maintained and safe.
9. Protect her from verbal, emotional, or physical attacks from anyone (including the children).
10. Give her daily and generous hugs, kisses, and "I love you's."[6]

STUDY AND DISCUSSION QUESTIONS

UP FRONT AND PERSONAL

1. The author has described five qualities that make a marriage strong. Reread them; then rank yourself on a scale of 1 to 5 (with 1 being "ideal" and 5 being "need work") on how well you personify the qualities. What steps can you take to improve any ranking higher than 3?

2. Are you humble enough to be a great husband? A great father? Read Ephesians 5:23–30.

3. Is it easy for you to subjugate your needs to those of your wife? Describe what makes it easy or hard.

FOR THE GROUP TO DISCUSS

1. Make a statement about the relationship between humility and greatness. Could you use Abraham Lincoln, Winston Churchill, or Jesus Christ to illustrate?

2. Explain the difference between joy and happiness. Is one more spiritual, or more physical, than the other?

3. Is a wife's role totally subordinated to the husband's? What does the Bible say about this issue?

4. What have you learned about the limits of your spouse, and do you honor and appreciate them? How do you do this?

5. Just what is it that a sacrificial lover is sacrificing?

6. If divorce occurs, how can a man still honor an ex-wife? Is there a need to do this?

7. What would be the value of you and your wife attending a Christian marriage conference? Should people with healthy marriages go to such conferences? Why or why not?

8. List two traits of an enthusiastic, caregiving husband.

9. Could a poor sexual relationship sabotage a marriage? How?

10. List five ways to care for your wife that are not financial. How are you doing with them?

APPLYING GOD'S WORD

1. Ask your spouse if you have honored her as a wife. If the answer is yes, celebrate. If the answer is no, sometimes, or maybe, ask her forgiveness.

2. Read Ephesians 5:28–30. How are you conforming to this standard of a husband's love?

CHAPTER 10

OFFICER CANDIDATE SCHOOL: A FEW GOOD DADS

When a five-star general gives you a peek into the inner recesses of his heart, most soldiers perk up and take notes. Listen to these sober thoughts from one of America's most celebrated warriors, General Douglas MacArthur:

> By profession I am a soldier and take pride in that fact. But I am prouder—infinitely prouder—to be a father. A soldier destroys in order to build; the father only builds, never destroys. The one has the potentiality of death; the other embodies creation and life. And while the hordes of death are mighty, the battalions of life are mightier still. It is my hope that my son, when I am gone, will remember me not from the battle but in the home repeating with him our simple daily prayer, "Our father, Who art in heaven. . . ."[1]

General MacArthur's words have a powerful and timeless ring to them. An officer and a gentleman with a circle of five stars on his epaulets is lifting his hand to his forehead and snapping a crisp salute to the position of "father." It's not every day you can get a man of his stature to see, let alone admit, this truth. But I have to take exception with one point that General MacArthur makes. He says, "The father only builds, never destroys." Actually, a father is quite capable of destroying. He has the highest potential for good *or* evil of just about any other person in the child's life. Dads write a great deal of the script their children will be reading from as they play out the rest of their lives. It's crucial that dads write carefully.

Actor Burt Reynolds has had his share of problems as an adult. In a cover story in *Parade* magazine, entitled "What Love Means to Me," Burt appeared with his then wife, Loni Anderson. He opened up his story with this statement:

> My dad was the chief of police, and when he came into a room, all the light and air went out of it. . . . There's a saying in the South: "No man is a man until his father tells him he is." It means that someday when you're 30 or 40, grown up, this man—whom you respect and love and want to love you—puts his arms around you and says, "You know, you're a man now, and you don't have to do crazy things and get into fist-fights and all that to defend the honor of men. You don't have to prove anything. You're a man, and I love you." We never hugged, we never kissed, we never said, "I love you." No, we never cried. . . . So what happened was that I was desperately looking for someone who'd say, "You're grown up, and I approve and love you. And you don't have to do these things anymore." I was lost inside. I couldn't connect. I was incomplete. I didn't know then what I needed to know.[2]

Many men feel like Burt Reynolds. They talk about being lost inside, unable to connect, incomplete, not knowing what they need to know. Mr. Reynolds's generation is being stalked by a generation that is struggling with a more sophisticated version of the same core problems. Too many of them are adrift, lost, searching. Which increases my concern for the generation they are raising. You know, the generation that is playing Nintendo in the family room or listening to her Walkman as she washes her dad's car. Too many of these kids are being raised by a group of dads who suffered the consequences of another generation's search for moral absolutes. Former Secretary of the Navy James Webb, a father of four, put it this way:

> I fear that the greatest legacy of the babyboom generation will be that although it asked all the right questions, in the early years of its adulthood, it resolved nothing. Raised by parents whose sacrifices during the Great Depression and World War II purchased for us the luxury of being able to question, we all understood the standards from which some of us were choosing to deviate. But lacking unity, riven by disagreement on every major issue and most minor ones, we have, perhaps unwittingly, encouraged our children to believe that there are no touchstones, no true answers, no commitments worthy of sacrifice. Our children have been treated to grand debate and in many cases have grown up under the false illusion that there are no firm principles. That for every cause there is a counter-cause. For every reason to fight there is a reason to run. For every yin there is a yang.[3]

A generation without a moral compass has left us reeling as a nation. The responsibility for transferring the value system of a people falls primarily on the fathers of our nation's children. When we neglect that responsibility in a wholesale way, we force God to take action against our nation. We've seen our country struggle through a lot of economic ups and downs. And one senses a pervasive discontentment, regardless of whether the Dow Jones is moving up or down.

Pundits of right and wrong wax eloquent about possible solutions. And even when they don't, we hear the American people demand them nonetheless. I hear people screaming for solutions to our problems from the halls of government. Washington can't solve our problems. I hear people screaming for more education to solve our problems. Education is only as effective as the material it has to work with. If the teachers were raised in an environment that did not assume moral absolutes, and the kids are coming from homes where parents threw the moral compass overboard, we can pour all of the money we want into fixing our problems through education, and we'll create little more than a vast financial sinkhole.

The politicians, the educators, and anyone else who believes these two hold the prescription for our national ills have missed the point. There's a simple explanation for why we are struggling as a nation, and the explanation holds the key to the solution.

Malachi prophesied to an anemic and apathetic nation of Israel, about one hundred years after they had returned from captivity in Babylon. They were proving the most important lesson a person can ever learn from history, and that is, *people seldom learn from history*. We ignore its hard-earned lessons and then are forced to repeat them over and over again.

Let me do a little biblical geography to put this small, but potent book of the Bible into context. Malachi is the last book of the Old Testament. Its fourth chapter is the last chapter of the Old Testament. Verses 5 and 6 are the last two verses of the Old Testament. If any verses serve as hinge verses between two great theological paradigms, these verses do:

> **Behold, I will send you Elijah the prophet**
> **Before the coming of the great and dreadful day of**
> **the LORD.**
> **And he will turn**
> **The hearts of the fathers to the children,**
> **And the hearts of the children to their fathers,**
> **Lest I come and strike the earth**
> **with a curse.** (Mal. 4:5–6 NKJV)

Who does "he" refer to in verse 6? Jesus told us in Matthew 11:11–15. He said that Malachi was referring to his cousin, John the Baptist. In verse 14, he said, "And if you are willing to accept it, he is the Elijah who was to come."

But what was the purpose of John the Baptist? He was to prepare the people to receive their Messiah. He was the trumpet flourish announcing the arrival of their King. So Malachi was saying that Jesus, through the announcement of John the Baptist, was coming to restore the relationship between fathers and their children. But he said something else: if fathers ignore Jesus and the instructions he gives us as fathers, God will sour

our personal economy. If we do it as a nation, he'll sour our national economy.

I believe with all my heart that the greatest hope for our nation is not in our local churches, but in our domestic churches—*the home* under the pastoral leadership of a father committed to Christ. And as long as we, as a nation, ignore this priority, then we, as a nation, will struggle with a fickle economy, paranoia in the marketplace, and unrest in our homes.

We cannot think for a second that we can neglect our roles at home and then assume that God will wink at our negligence and do nothing. We've already seen the consequences. Rev. Jesse Jackson put it this way: "Many of us allow our children to eat junk, watch junk, listen to junk, talk junk, play with junk, and then we're surprised when they turn out to be social junkies."[4]

The office of father is a *sacred trust*. You want to assume that trust and carry it out to and for God's glory. For you to do it well you must do at least three things for your children: (1) administrate their childhood, (2) advance their confidence in God, and (3) be a person they can admire. Let's look at these three parts of the job description one at a time, and learn some specific ways to carry them out.

1. ADMINISTRATE THEIR CHILDHOOD

First of all, let's make sure we're on the same page when it comes to assessing the degree of difficulty of your role as a parent. I'm not inclined to pay much attention to men who whine about their responsibility as a dad when they have only one child. If you have only one child, you and your wife can double-team him. If you have two children, you have to play man-to-man defense. Three kids: zone defense. And sometimes, when your wife is running errands and has left you home with the kids, your kids flood your zone! If you have four or more kids, it's a "prevent" defense. You say, "Honey, let them have the short one. Just don't let them get behind us for the bomb!"[5]

Whether you're in a double-team, man-to-man, zone, or "prevent" defense, you need to know what your job is and have a workable plan to carry it out if you are to administrate your children's lives. Let's start by defining the role of *administrator*.

An administrator is a person who provides an environment, materials, and direction needed to bring the best out of another person. If you wanted to use a marketplace analogy, your job as a father is to raise the stock value of your children. You need to be a value-added dad. How do you do this? Let me suggest some ways.

First, administrate your children by keeping them under control, but don't control them. Let me repeat the definition of control that we went over earlier: control is when I leverage the strength of my personality or position against your weaknesses, in order to get you to meet my selfish agenda. When you want them to score touchdowns *for you,* strike out batters *for you,* hit home runs *for you,* make straight A's *for you,* dress to *your tastes,* or submit to *your taste* in music, you are controlling them.[6] If you made a pattern of that, the Bible says that you wouldn't be qualified to be an elder of a church because an elder is to keep his children "under control."

You can read it for yourself in 1 Timothy 3:4 (the passage that outlines the qualifications for an elder): "He must be one who manages his own household well, keeping his children under control with all dignity" (NASB). The word *control,* in this context, has to do with subjection of obedience, but it is preceded by another word that clarifies its meaning as "under control."[7] Had Paul left out the preposition, it would have read, "He must be one who manages his own household by controlling his children." But he would have had to leave out the concept of "managing well, and doing it with the children's dignity in mind," because excessive control is the worst way to manage anybody. It demeans one's spirit rather than builds up one's dignity.

When you want your children to do things your way, see it your way, be it your way, say it your way, you are attacking their dignity. On the other hand, when you keep them under control, you set very clear moral guidelines and help them maintain the guidelines by blessing them when they stay inside them and letting them face the consequences when they step outside. Your job is to teach them to obey you while keeping their uniqueness and individuality intact. You want to guard their uniquenesses and give them a sense that they are highly honored for the contributions they make.

Take firstborns, for instance. They can build a lot of resentment toward their parents when they're treated like little more than a live-in nanny. They get old enough to watch the other kids, and the parents take off and don't look back. Sometimes it is fair and legitimate to expect the older child to watch the others (when you're running family errands, shopping for groceries, visiting the doctor, etc.), but other times, when you're going out or doing something personal (playing golf, going to a game, etc.), you should treat him with dignity and worth by paying him to baby-sit. And you need to pay him the going rate. Otherwise your neighbors will hire him out from under you!

Another way that you can guard your children's dignity is to provide them with an adequate outlet for their anger. Otherwise they'll be like pressure cookers without a release valve. Eventually, they're going to explode. Set special times during the month (maybe one-on-one at a yogurt shop with a friendly attitude) when they are allowed to ventilate their frustrations toward you. This keeps them from carrying anxious thoughts that can turn into bitter hearts. You need to allow them to tell you how you're frustrating them. But when you do this, it is crucial that you don't defend yourself. Otherwise they won't bother being honest. It's no surprise that you frustrate your kids, so you shouldn't hesitate to create a way to help them let off steam in an honoring way.

Second, administrate your children from a position of total dependence on God. The Scripture advises,

> By wisdom a house is built,
> And by understanding it is established;
> And by knowledge the rooms are filled
> With all precious and pleasant riches. (Prov. 24:3–4 NASB)

Third, administrate your children from a position of wisdom. Once again, let's see what the Scripture says on the subject: "The fear of the LORD is the beginning of wisdom, / And the knowledge of the Holy One is understanding" (Prov. 9:10 NASB). The profound lesson in this verse is that if you don't fear God, it is impossible to be wise. It also teaches that merely fearing God doesn't make you wise. But it gives you the keys to the door through which you go to obtain wisdom. Wisdom is gained by going through the process of fearing God year after year. One more verse on this principle: "My son, pay attention to my wisdom, listen well to my words of insight" (Prov. 5:1). If you want your children to learn wisdom from you, it assumes that *you* fear the Lord and trust in him each day.

Fourth, administrate your children from a position of understanding. A key verse here is Colossians 3:21: "Fathers, do not exasperate your children, that they may not lose heart" (NASB). If you did some groundwork in a Greek lexicon, you would find that the word used for "exasperate" literally means to "do something to cause them to resent you." You resent people who have authority over you but don't go out of their way to know where you're coming from when they're passing out orders.

Let me share something with you that comes from the drill sergeant's handbook. When it comes to the task of administrating our children, we need to take into consideration their *maturity* and their *ability* every time we assign them a duty or responsibility. If their maturity or ability is *low*, we need to *direct* them. We do this by telling them or showing them how to do something. If their maturity or ability is *moderate*, we need to *develop* them. We do this by asking them questions: "How do you think we should do this?" or "How have you done this in the past?" If their ability or maturity is *high*, we need to *delegate* the task to them and let them do it their way.[8]

You can see how exasperating it can be to a child if you delegate to him a task that he has no ability or maturity to carry out. It is equally exasperating to instruct a kid on how to do something she is mature enough and able to do. You may have five things you have assigned for your child to accomplish on a Saturday. He may need direction on two of them, development on one, and delegation on the other two. It is impossible to know where your children are on these different levels *if you're not involved in their lives*. Therefore, to administrate with understanding, you must be an ongoing student of your children. That takes major commitments of time.

Fifth, administrate your children from a position of knowledge. The Scripture urges, "Know well the condition of your flocks, / And pay attention to your herds" (Prov. 27:23 NASB). If knowledge of your children is crucial to being an effective administrator, then let me ask you a handful of questions:

- Who are your children's teachers?
- Have you ever met them?
- Who are your children's closest friends?
- Have you met those children's parents?
- Have you met the kids your children are dating?
- What kinds of homes are they from?

If you're managing a position in a factory, you need to know what you're making, what the resources are, the inventory, and the personnel. That's a simple template to use when administrating your children's childhood too.

One final topic before leaving this subject of administrating your children's childhood from a position of knowledge. Do you have cable in your home? Do you get MTV? Do your children watch it without you watching it with them? One of the popular shows on MTV is the now famous *Beavis and Butthead*. Do you know what's on this show? Let me quote Bob DeMoss of Focus on the Family:

This daily half-hour "cartoon" combines ridiculous and vulgar "adventures" with clips of the two idiots (after whom the show is named) sitting on the sofa babbling about music videos (mostly heavy metal) which play on the screen. Whether mocking the Challenger disaster or mooning *The Brady Bunch*, these two delinquents take television to an all-time low.

Beavis and Butthead's conversation resorts to scatological name-calling and comments about erections, urination, sadomasochism, mucous, flagellation, vomiting, and masturbation. . . .

The boys show disrespect for all authority. Their exploits also include stealing and destroying property, verbally assaulting a schoolmate ("Do you get periods?") and voyeurism (leering at girls in music videos, peering into a van at a couple having sex, and so on). . . .

In essence, this MTV feature presents two juvenile media junkies left to follow their own standards of morality and conduct—which, in some ways, probably mirror the values of the executives at MTV who program such twaddle.[9]

The first thing you've learned about your job as a dad is that you are to administrate your children's childhood carefully. You can't do it without making the effort to be involved in their day-to-day lives. Let's look at your second major responsibility as a father.

2. ADVANCE THEIR CONFIDENCE IN GOD

Let's start out learning about this principle by looking at a key passage of Scripture: "Shepherd the flock of God among you, exercising oversight not under compulsion, but voluntarily, according to the will of God; and not for sordid gain, but with eagerness; nor yet as lording it over those allotted to your charge, but proving to be examples to the flock" (1 Peter 5:2–3 NASB).

This passage is directed at the leaders of the church. But a family really is just the smallest form of the church. Pope John Paul II calls it "the church in miniature" (*Ecclesia domestica*).[10] Therefore, a legitimate and direct application of this passage is to the role that you play as overseer, or father, of your children. Let me suggest several ways that you can make this passage of Scripture a reality in your home.

First, you advance your children's view of their worth to God and you by considering it a privilege to care for them (v. 2, "voluntarily"). They need to see your work as something you consider a privilege to do for the family. Clue your wife in on this, and let her help you communicate this to your kids. A lot of fathers feel guilty because of the time they have to spend working. Obviously, you can spend too much time at work. But assuming that your hours are within reason, your kids need to view your time away from them as just as important as your time with them. They need to know that you are grateful to be able to go to work to make money to provide for them.

Second, you advance your children's view of themselves in God's eyes by making them a priority (v. 2, "eagerness"). You do this by spending time with them. You can't spend time with them if you're not willing to put your discretionary time up for grabs. You may have to wait until they're out on their own to take those strokes off your handicap, catch that monster bass, or kill that trophy deer. You may have to develop the 1990s art of what I call sound-bite parenting. You don't have a lot of time each day. But if you use it wisely, you'd be amazed how effective you can be in their lives.

Here are some tips:

- Try to grab the first few moments and the last few moments of their day. Give them a cheerful wake-up greeting, and be available at bedtime to help with baths, pajamas, and reading stories. Listen to them talk out their problems; share prayers and kisses.
- Date your daughters and form a Breakfast Club with your sons. These one-on-one times will be some of the most precious memories they have of you.
- Religiously eat dinner together—and turn the television off. Studies have shown that the top students in America come from families that eat dinner together.[11] So you'll not only be building a strong relationship with your children, but you'll be helping to raise their grade point average at the same time.

Third, you advance your children's view of themselves in God's eyes by maintaining a life of integrity (v. 3, "example"). Psalm 101:2–3 puts it this way:

> I will be careful to lead a blameless life—
>   when will you come to me?
> I will walk in my house
>   with blameless heart.

> I will set before my eyes
>   no vile thing.

The psalmist reminded us of the priority of an upright and moral life at home. Proverbs 20:7 reinforces this: "A righteous man who walks in his integrity— / How blessed are his sons after him" (NASB). In other words, God goes out of his way to honor the efforts of righteous men by blessing their children.

Fourth, you advance your children's view of themselves in God's eyes by meeting their personal needs (v. 2, "shepherd"). Consider some specific ways to do this:

- Teach them a biblical view of sex before the world gets ahold of them.
- Have fire drills and teach them how to respond to emergencies.
- Teach them how to deal with bullies.
- Teach them how to deal with profanity, especially when it starts creeping into their vocabulary.
- Teach them modesty.
- Teach them how to choose movies and music in a godly way.

Fifth, you advance your children's view of themselves in God's eyes by telling them and showing them that you love them. The sky's the limit here, but there is one specific thing that you should do to your kids that will directly affect their sense of security—show them affection. Holding, hugging, and kissing your children—from day one, and regardless of age—give them a sense of acceptance that will minister to them when they are in hostile environments. You must give your daughters godly, righteous affections. It's the best way to keep them from climbing into the backseat looking for love in all the wrong places.

You may have sons who are self-conscious about their father hugging them. One alternative is wrestling with them. Clear the furniture and turn the family room into "Hulkamania."

The reason all of these things I've listed advance the way your children view themselves in God's eyes is that, as their earthly father, you can be an illustration of their heavenly Father. Their heavenly Father considers it a privilege to care for them, makes them a priority, holds a position of integrity, meets their personal needs, and loves them supremely. It's so much easier for them to believe all of this when they see these things illustrated by their earthly dad.

So far, you've seen that you need to administrate your kids' childhood and advance the way they view themselves in God's eyes. There's one final way that you can bring the best out of your children.

3. GIVE THEM A GOOD EXAMPLE TO FOLLOW

If you want them following your example, you must first model God's truth in your life. The psalmist declared, "So he shepherded them according to the integrity of his heart, / And guided them with his skillful hands" (Ps. 78:72 NASB). You are to speak truth and live truth around them, and you are to admit wrong when you do untruthful or unrighteous acts. There is nothing strong about a man who doesn't admit his faults and his mistakes to his kids. In fact, it's just the opposite. There's something fundamentally weak and pathetic about a man who would behave that way. Statements such as, "I'm sorry," and "I was wrong, please forgive me," are powerful builders of confidence in kids.

Second, you must realize that you're leaving a legacy. You don't have any choice about whether you do or not. You do have a choice about what kind. My favorite kind of legacy is the one that lasts forever.

The psalmist gave us some great teaching on this subject. These next few verses are taught in Sunday school and synagogues. They make sense to Gentile and Jew alike:

> For He established a testimony in Jacob,
> And appointed a law in Israel,
> Which He commanded our fathers,

> That they should teach them to their children,
> That the generation to come might know, even the children
>   yet to be born,
> That they may arise and tell them to their children,
> That they should put their confidence in God,
> And not forget the works of God,
> But keep His commandments. (Ps. 78:5–7 NASB)

This passage clearly teaches that what you are doing in your home affects your great-great-great-grandchildren. There are children yet to be born to people who will never know that you ever existed, yet will be affected by how you lived. It would probably floor you to know how many generations are affected by your life. Would you believe a thousand? That's exactly what God's Word says: "Therefore know that the LORD your God, He is God, the faithful God who keeps covenant and mercy for a thousand generations with those who love Him and keep His commandments" (Deut. 7:9 NKJV).

You can view your life as a parent as though you're in a relay race. If you've ever run relay races, you know that the most important part of the race is the transfer of the baton. You can run at a blurring speed, but if you drop the baton, an inferior team can beat you. God's truth and God's Spirit represent the baton you want to hand off in the relay from one generation to the next. You can't afford to leave legacies of shame, anger, regret, disappointment, bitterness, or absenteeism. You need to be present, accounted for, and ready to take your stand for your children.

Third, you must diligently use daily opportunities to equip your children for righteous and godly living. When an NC-17 movie is booked at the mall theater, take one of your kids with you as you go to talk with the manager about it. Show him a kind but bold father respectfully voicing his concerns about the dilemma a movie like this poses to kids who happen to be at the complex viewing other movies. You may not expect the manager to change the movie venue. In most cases, he'll say that the decision is out of his control. But at least your voice will be heard and your child will watch how a righteous man deals with community problems.

When you return the grocery cart to the corral instead of leaving it to block a parking place or be struck by a car, you teach your children how to protect other people's property and show kindness to other people.

When you clean up your mess at Burger King, you remind your kids that there are other people in the world—that each of us is not the center of the universe.

When you voice concerns about a politician in a way that still respects that person's dignity and the dignity of the office, you prepare your kids for confronting people who rise up against their values in the future.

When you occasionally pull your son aside before he goes out on a date and remind him of his responsibility to his girl-friend's father and mother, to her, to her future husband, to himself, and to you and his mother, you help him incorporate his faith into real time.

God's Word is outspoken on this subject: "And these words, which I am commanding you today, shall be on your heart; and you shall teach them diligently to your sons and shall talk of them when you sit in your house and when you walk by the way and when you lie down and when you rise up" (Deut. 6:6–9 NASB).

Although this passage leaves room for formal teaching times in the Bible, I think that it refers more to the opportunities that come up in the day-to-day comings and goings of children.

You don't have to be preachy. You simply have to let God's Word get sprinkled into your victories and defeats in such a way that your kids can see how it can work in their lives. That's why you need to spend time with them. And even if you work long hours, you can still capture the time you do have with them wisely.

Fourth, you must institute formal teaching times to instruct them. Sunday school, church, children's church, and youth group are the standard ways. You negate much of what the church is trying to teach the kids if you aren't in church, too, growing in God's Word. And then you need to use some regular opportunities to teach God's Word. Prayer at meals and bedtime is one way. Pick a night of the week to teach a prin-ciple at dinner. Teaching the kids how to use concordances, commentaries, and Bible dictionaries also helps you leave a clear path for your kids to follow. It enables you to teach them how to be students of the Word.

Proverbs 4:1–2 begins a passage in which a father gives his son some strong teaching about the traps that he will encounter in the world. His formal teaching of his son is designed to save that boy a trip to the wrong side of the tracks. Solomon wrote:

> **Hear, O sons, the instruction of a father,**
> **And give attention that you may gain understanding,**
> **For I give you sound teaching;**
> **Do not abandon my instruction.** (NASB)

YOU CAN DO IT!

A good father wants to carefully administrate his children's childhood, advance their view of themselves in God's eyes, and give them a great example to emulate. It's a tall order, but with the Lord's help, it is an achievable goal.

These three mandates for a dad look good on paper, but they become quite a challenge when we consider them next to the demands we receive from the marketplace. Companies are downsizing. They're increasing our workloads without increasing our paychecks. We are working long hours and coming home exhausted. How can you be a success in the marketplace and still get decent grades as a dad? Let me make a few suggestions.

1. Don't let the world define success for you. When it defines success, it usually adds up to a hood ornament, a title, the name on your watch, the label in your garment, or your address. There's nothing wrong with any of these things unless you let them become the sum total of who you are.

My wife and I found that redefining success in a way that aligns with our biblical responsibilities helped us make wiser decisions when the marketplace and our role as parents seemed to be on a collision course. Here's how we defined it: *success* is "the conscientious stewarding of the next generation." When hard choices about promotions, relocation, second jobs, or overtime came along, we simply submitted those questions to this definition. Life got a lot less complicated.

2. Realize that you're the moral high-water mark for your kids. You may be the only person in their lives they are expecting to show them the way. You'll make mistakes and let them down a few times. They don't expect you to be perfect, but they do expect you to fall in the right area code on the issues that matter most.

3. Realize that you must be courageous and tenacious if you want to finish the task God has set before you. Courage is the determination to do the right thing, no matter what the cost. Your biggest enemy will be fatigue. That's why you have to commit to pacing yourself and getting to bed at decent hours. Otherwise, fatigue will set your agenda.

4. The last thing you need to be reminded is that your children are worth all of your efforts. *It's never too early; it's never too late.*

DANCING IDIOTS!

I was reminded just how briefly the window of opportunity to affect our kids is open. It happened early one Saturday morning when I was still deep in sleep. A little hand was shaking me awake, and a little voice was whispering in my ear, "Daddy, it's time to get up to go on our date." At first it all blended into the backdrop of the particular dream I was experiencing. But the little hand kept shaking me, and the little voice kept beckoning me, "Daddy! Wake up! It's time for our date."

When my brain finally lifted me enough out of slumber to figure out what was going on, I realized that my daughter, Shiloh, was standing next to my bed in the dark, and for some reason, she was under the impression that I was supposed to be awake. A few seconds into consciousness, and the pieces started to fall into place. The night before, I had promised Shiloh that I would take her out on a breakfast date. That explained why she was standing beside my bed. But it was dark.

I looked at the clock. It was about fifteen minutes before

dawn. "Shiloh, it's still real early. The sun isn't up yet. Go back to bed and sleep for another hour, then we can go."

"But, Daddy," she replied, "I already got dressed just for you [she had on a mismatched outfit]. And I did my hair . . . just for you [it was snarled and knotted]."

She was ready to walk out the door, and there was no way she would ever be able to go back to sleep. I knew where she wanted to go was open, because it's open twenty-four hours a day, every day, including Christmas. It was a Circle K. If you don't have any of these in your area, just picture a 7-Eleven. They're similar.

I figured I was getting off cheaply on the breakfast tab, and the thought of a good cup of coffee in my hands made my brain perk up a few notches. In a few minutes we were pulling the car out of the garage and making our way through the predawn quiet to the nearest Circle K.

For her breakfast, she chose a couple of doughnuts and a bottle of juice. I chose a sixteen-ounce cup of regular coffee with some hazelnut-flavored creamer. We paid for our stuff and went outside to sit on the curb on the side of the Circle K—next to the Dumpster. Don't overreact! Everything was safe and sanitary.

Since it was her date, I let her set the agenda. Shiloh wanted to talk about the *Sleeping Beauty* video that her mom had purchased for her a few weeks before. She used a lot of hand motions to tell me the highs and lows of the story. Finally, I said, "Shiloh, what's your favorite part?"

"Dad," she said, "I love the part at the end when the handsome prince and Sleeping Beauty dance together in the castle." When I pictured that scene in my head (I, too, had watched the video), I admitted, "That's my favorite part too."

I don't know what provoked me to do what I did next, but I decided to reenact the scene. I put the lids back on our drinks, I put her doughnuts back in the bag, and then I picked up Shiloh and started waltzing her around in a small circle, singing the words to the song, "I know you, I waltzed with you once upon a dream."

But as I held my little four year old close and spun her around, I noticed that there was a field next to the Circle K, and across the field were some homes. There were some lights on in the kitchens of those homes. As I danced with my little girl and looked off at those lights in those homes, the thought crossed my mind, *There's a good chance that a guy is sitting at his breakfast table, stirring his coffee, looking out the window, and calling his wife: "Honey! Look! There's an idiot over at the Circle K, dancing with a little girl next to a Dumpster!"* But another thought crossed my mind at the same time that in a very brief period of time, some young man is going to walk up to me, tap me on the shoulder, and say, *"Mr. Kimmel, may I cut in?"* And he is going to waltz my girl out of my life for good. I decided that I'm going to grab every chance I can to be with my kids, because they're not at home long.

In Latin the term is *carpe diem,* "seize the day." It's easier to do when you carefully administrate their childhood, enhance their confidence in God, and give them a good example to follow.

An Old Soldier's Prayer

Build me a son, O Lord, who will be strong enough to know when he is weak, and brave enough to face himself when he is afraid; one who will be proud and unbending in honest defeat, and humble and gentle in victory.

Build me a son whose wishes will not take the place of deeds; a son who will know Thee . . . and that to know himself is the foundation stone of knowledge.

Build me a son whose heart will be clear, whose goal will be high, a son who will master himself before he seeks to master other men; one who will reach into the future, yet never forget the past.

And after all these things are his, add, I pray, enough of a sense of humor, so that he may always be serious, yet never take himself too seriously. Give him humility, so that he may always remember the simplicity of true greatness, the open mind of true wisdom, and the meekness of true strength.

Then I, his father, will dare to whisper, "I have not lived in vain."[12]

STUDY AND DISCUSSION QUESTIONS

Up Front and Personal

1. Are you a person your kids admire? How do you know?

2. This exercise takes some work but may reveal a hidden truth about the relationship between you and your children. First, estimate how much time you spend with your children each week. Include in your estimate things such as reading to them, helping them with homework, playing games, and just talking. Then find a weekly calendar and every night for a week note in the calendar every minute you actually spent interacting with each child that day. Include things like reading to them, helping with homework, playing games or just talking. At the end of the week, add up the time. How does the total compare with your estimate? Are any adjustments needed in your "quality time" schedule?

For the Group to Discuss

1. Why do you think so many men abdicate care of their children to their wives? Does this lack of involvement diminish a man's stature as authority figure in the household?

2. Is the permissive "do your own thing" credo of the baby boomer generation still something to be concerned about now that most of them are adults with their own families?

3. What does the author mean when he says a child must be "administrated"?

4. Define what or who the administrator is. Is this a male or female role?

5. Give three examples of controlling a child with dignity and three without it.

6. Read aloud Colossians 3:21. When your child is exasperated with you, is it usually because of a position you have taken or because he resents your authority over him? If the latter, what can you do about it?

7. List twice in the last seven days you have delegated a task to a child. What were your actual words? Did they show confidence in his or her ability to carry out the task?

8. Do you agree or disagree with the statement "It's not worth

my time to check what my kids see on TV because they'll watch what they please when I'm not around"? State the basis for your answer.

9. Ask your kids if they think your work (job) is important to the family and why. Ask them what you do at work. If necessary, explain the value of your work to your kids.

10. Complete this sentence: "If I didn't have to work so much, I would _____."

11. How do you communicate to your kids that it is a privilege to be their dad? Explain.

12. List three ways you are a living example for your children. What is the longer-term message of each example?

13. Do you live by the world's view of success or your own? How do they differ?

APPLYING GOD'S WORD

1. Read Proverbs 22:6. Do you feel a spiritual obligation to carry this out?

2. Have you ever held a family meeting where things important to every member are discussed and decisions made? If not, pick a time and try holding one every week. Let members bring up things important to them.

CHAPTER 11

EXPANDING THE RANKS

You're coming home from work, listening to talk radio, and paying little attention to traffic around you when *Boom!*—two cars ahead of you—a tire has exploded on the front of a station wagon. It swerves left into oncoming traffic. A delivery truck coming the opposite direction cuts to its left to avoid hitting the station wagon and plows head-on into the car directly in front of you. You break to the right and manage to miss them both, but fragments from their impact spray over your car as you blur by them.

You jump from your car to try to help. Others are immediately there to assist also. The car that struck the delivery truck had three young women coming home from their afternoon classes at the university. One is dead, one is bleeding badly but will survive if she can get help, and the third is dying from internal injuries. A doctor in one of the cars that stopped does a quick examination of the dying young woman and then leaves her to go over and work on the one who still has a chance.

You ask him what should be done for the other one. He tells you in hushed tones to do your best to make her comfortable, but he doesn't think she'll be alive by the time the ambulances arrive. So you go over to the young woman. She's conscious but quiet. You try to say a few reassuring words to her as you hold her hand and pat her arm. She looks up at you and says, "I'm scared I'm going to die. I don't know what will happen to my soul if I do. I'm so afraid. Can you help me, please?" And then she starts to whimper.

You've got exactly six minutes.

GOD WITH SKIN ON

How would you do in this situation? Would you know what to say? Would you be able to choose between what is important and what is extraneous and move the young woman to a point where she could put her faith in Christ? For some people, you are the closest thing they can find to God with skin on. You know the Savior. You've exercised the faith needed to pass from death unto life. Now God wants you to be prepared to help others through the same process of faith that can help them gain confidence in Christ's work on the cross for them.

Imagine how horrible you would feel if you were looking down at a young woman tethered to this earth by a few fleeting minutes of life and you didn't know what to say. You don't need to be awkward or intimidated by a scene like this. And although I hope it never happens to you (or to her), I would want you to be able to move her through the six minutes with poise and confidence. You can. You just need a working knowledge of the plan of salvation. And that is exactly what you're going to have by the end of this chapter.

EVANGELISM 101

In the scenario we have been talking about, you wouldn't have the luxury of being able to do a background study on the young woman. You wouldn't be able to pull out a Bible and show her around the Word. It wouldn't be physically feasible. You'd need to have the Scriptures deeply embedded in your memory and know which ones to choose to help her through to a point where she could exercise faith in Christ. To do this requires that you have an understanding of the plan of salvation and the poise to know which parts to emphasize for her.

There are many ways to develop God's plan of salvation from the Scriptures. A popular one is called the Roman Road. It uses verses taken strictly from the book of Romans to outline the gospel. It's very effective. The only problem is that it rules out using so many other great passages throughout the Bible. The Four Spiritual Laws, which was developed by Bill Bright and taught extensively by the people of Campus Crusade for Christ, is another excellent method of giving people the gospel. I'd highly recommend it. Some benefits of using the Four Spiritual Laws are that they are self-contained in a little pamphlet, you can read through them with the person you are sharing the gospel with, and then you can leave it with the person. There is usually a supply of the Four Spiritual Laws at any Christian bookstore.

In this chapter, I want to show you a way of sharing your faith that requires only two things: that you know how to read, and that you remember to look in the first blank page of your Bible! It's a simple method that allows you to use your Bible as a reference point and walk the person you're sharing with through a series of verses that develop the gospel. This method lets the people see the verses in the context of the whole Bible. It also enables you to get familiar enough with the verses so that you can etch them into your memory. This is the method that I was shown when I was sixteen years old. It's been a reliable friend to me ever since.

IT'S ALL IN YOUR BIBLE

To get the most out of this chapter, get your Bible and keep it beside you as we walk through these verses. (I'll be using the New International Version.) You can mark your Bible as you go.

Bibles usually have a few blank pages in the front. At the top of the first blank page, write the reference *Matthew 18:3*. Next, turn to it in your Bible. If you aren't that familiar with the books of the Bible, use the table of contents to find out where the book of Matthew begins. Once you find the verse, underline it so that it stands out, and then go back to the first page in your Bible and put the page number of Matthew 18:3 in parentheses beside the reference. Matthew 18:3 says: "And he said: 'I tell you the truth, unless you change and become like little children, you will never enter the kingdom of heaven.'"

The first thing you want the person to whom you are witnessing to see is that there is an attitude that makes it easier for a person to come to faith in Christ. Jesus said that we need to become like children. What's the big deal about children? Children are quicker to trust. They don't bring the suspicions to the table that many sophisticated adults do. Jesus was saying that we want to exercise trust in God from the outset that will enable us to receive the other verses that you're going to look at.

SHOWING THEM THE LOVE

Now you're ready for a second reference. In the margin of your Bible, next to Matthew 18:3, write the reference *John 3:16*. After you've looked it up in your Bible, underline it, and then go back and put its page number in parentheses under the reference you wrote next to Matthew 18:3.

John 3:16 is a famous verse. You might want to remind the person you're sharing with that this reference is often held up in the end zone during a field goal or extra point. It says, "For God so loved the world that he gave his one and only Son, that whoever believes in him shall not perish but have eternal life."

This verse perfectly capsulizes the work of God on our behalf. It contains several elements of the gospel: God loves us; he gave us the gift of his Son; if we put our faith in him, we get eternal life. You want to emphasize the first statement, "God loves you." You want the person to see written out in the Bible what most people already assume: God is a loving God, and he cares for us very much.

SHOWING THEM THE PROBLEM

If God is loving, then why is it that the average person doesn't seem to experience his love on a regular basis? That's where *Romans 3:23* comes in. Write Romans 3:23 in the margin of your Bible next to John 3:16. After you've looked it up and underlined it, come back to John 3:16 and write the page number of Romans 3:23 under its reference.

Each step of the gospel is important. This step, however, is the one where blinders drop off the eyes of the person you are sharing the gospel with. Let's look at Romans 3:23: "For all have sinned and fall short of the glory of God."

This verse challenges conventional wisdom. It blows wide open the door to the question of why the person needs Christ. If you took a microphone and camera down to street level in any town and asked the following questions, you could predict the answers.

"If there is a God, do you think he is a loving God?" Most people would say "Yes."

"If there is a heaven, do you think you will go there when you die?" Most people would say, "Yes."

"Why do you think you will get to go to heaven?" Most people would say, "Because I've lived a good life."

They are falling into the same theological trap that most people fall into. It is the false assumption that God grades on the curve. It assumes that some balancing scales await us when we die. Our good works are put on one side, and our bad works are put on the other. Whichever way the scales tip determines our destiny. This is the core assumption of all great religions of the world, except one. Christianity is that exception. It teaches that God reaches out to us in a specific way that is not tied up in our works. It's a take-it-or-leave-it proposition.

It is essential that the person you are talking to understands that there is absolutely no way he can get to heaven on his own. He might say, "But God is love, and his love will look past my sin." He is forgetting that God is holy and just. Since he is, he cannot allow sin to go unpunished. God's holiness demands that a person pay for his sin.

Or he might respond, "But I'm a good person. God isn't going to condemn me to hell just because I trip up every once in a while." Once again, the person is embracing the love of God without factoring in the requirements of his holiness. God cannot allow sin to go unpunished. His justice must be satisfied. And because a man is held responsible for his actions, the effect on a good person is the same as on an evil person when it comes to death; neither makes it to God on his own.

Here's a vivid way to illustrate this point. Suppose we all assemble on the beach in Malibu, California. About two thousand miles out in the Pacific Ocean are the islands of Hawaii. But let's say that we've rearranged some things and that Hawaii is now heaven. We're going to get from California to Hawaii by swimming. You say, "No human being can swim from California to Hawaii." We know that. But let's say that for the sake of our illustration, the distance you swim is based not on how good a swimmer you are, but on how good a *person* you are. You see where this illustration is going. People believe that they can get into heaven on their own merit. Let's just see.

Someone fires a starting gun, and everyone races down to the beach to start the righteous swim to Hawaii. Saddam Hussein trips and falls just shy of the surf, and water starts running over his head as he sucks it into his nostrils. He runs out of good works before he even gets completely into the water. The rest race past him and move on into the surf and out beyond the breakers. Some people get . . .

- a hundred yards before they drown.
- a mile before they drown.
- ten miles before they drown.
- a hundred miles before they drown.
- a thousand miles before they drown.
- near enough to see the silhouettes of the islands before they drown.
- near enough to hear the breakers on the shore before they drown.
- near enough that they are just about ready to walk up onto the shore before they drown!

But here's the vital point: *nobody walks up onto the beach!*

So whether you drown in the surf in Malibu or in the surf at Waikiki is a moot point. You don't make it!

God saw the dilemma we were in. He loved us and wanted to be able to enjoy our fellowship forever in heaven. But his holiness and pure righteousness could not allow our sin to go unpunished. Divine justice had to be satisfied (Heb. 9:22). So somewhere within the infinite mind of God, a solution to our dilemma was reached. Although God could not permit our sin to go unpunished, he would accept a worthy substitute on our behalf. That was where Jesus came into the picture. God's only Son took on human form by being born to a virgin. The virgin birth meant that he did not inherit a sinful nature from his father (1 Cor. 15:20–22). Since Jesus was perfect, he didn't have to die for his own sin; therefore, he could qualify to die for our sin. God the Father punished his perfect Son in our place.

Which brings up the next passage: *Ephesians 2:8–9*. Write it in the margin next to Romans 3:23, then look it up, underline it, and place the page number beneath the reference.

SHOWING THEM THE HOPE

Ephesians 2:8–9 says, "For it is by grace you have been saved, through faith—and this not from yourselves, it is the gift of God—not by works, so that no one can boast." God saw our need and knew our dilemma. In his infinite love, he gave us a gift. That's what grace is, when we distill it down to its bottom line. It's something we don't deserve given to us by someone who loves us more than we could ever quantify. So much so that he was willing to punish his Son in our place.

I didn't appreciate the magnitude of my sin or of God's love for me until I became a father. I have two sons. I would not sacrifice my sons' lives for my best friend, let alone my enemies. But that's exactly what God did (Rom. 5:8). But if it came down to a scenario where one of my sons was to be sacrificed, I wouldn't hesitate to change places with him. There isn't a decent father out there who wouldn't do the same thing.

So why didn't the heavenly Father give up his life in order to spare his Son's life? Once again, it took becoming a father to see the answer to this question. You see, it took the ultimate sacrifice to buy us from our sin. Let me ask you a question: Which would be harder, to give your life in place of your son's, or to stand by and watch cruel hands destroy your son and do nothing to intervene? That's how much our sin cost God! It required the ultimate sacrifice.

God supremely loves us. Jesus willingly gave up his life to rescue us from our sin and shame. The next verse you can take the person to is *Romans 6:23* (write it next to Eph. 2:8–9, look it up, underline it, and reference back the page number). This verse says, "For the wages of sin is death, but the gift of God is eternal life in Christ Jesus our Lord." A wage is something we earn. A gift is something we accept from the gift giver. We deserve to die for our sins, but God chose instead to satisfy his righteous judgment through his Son.

Next to Romans 6:23 you want to write *John 1:12* and then do the same things you've done with each of the other verses.

John 1:12 says, "Yet to all who received him, to those who believed in his name, he gave the right to become children of God." This verse teaches us several things. The two things you want to point out here are that we are to receive Jesus and that he is the only way to be saved.

You will run into conflict with some people at this point. On the first point, you may get some flak from certain students of the Bible. They bristle when you use the expression "receiving Christ." They argue that the expression isn't used in the Bible. I suggest they read John 1:12 again. Their second argument is that receiving Christ is a form of works on our part and the Bible explicitly states that salvation is a gift of God and not a result of works (as we saw in Eph. 2:8–9). The "works" in that context are good works, or works that deserve merit.

Receiving Christ is not a good work. It's on the same par as an act of desperation by a drowning person. If someone risked his life to rescue me, I wouldn't go around boasting that "he couldn't have done it without me. I held on so tight and made it easy for him to pull me to shore!" I'd be grateful for his efforts and recognize that in the context of a rescue, the person being rescued has no bragging rights.

Unfortunately, the splitting of theological hairs at this point trips up a lot of people. God has not made all of this that complicated. You're lost before he saves you; you're found afterward. You neither know him nor love him before you become a Christian; you do both afterward. It's a lot easier here if you keep everything simple.

The second problem I mentioned with this verse is that some people might find salvation by Christ alone to come across as a bit narrow and exclusive. It is.

What I find amazing is that people react negatively to the narrowness of the plan of salvation while at the same time submitting, without hesitation, to narrow options in other areas all day long. We drive on the right side of the road (in America), and we land airplanes on narrow runways. If the pilot tells the tower that he wants to land on the freeway, they always discourage him from doing it. It's not designed for it. People will get killed. Life is barely more than a series of exclusive choices.

I think we need to ask ourselves the logical question: If there was some other way for people to save themselves, why would God allow his Son to be killed? If we could make it on our own merits, then God would have left us to our own merits. But he knew there was no other way.

GIVING THEM THE OPPORTUNITY

Now you want to explain the last major point of salvation to the person to whom you are witnessing. At this strategic point each person must individually receive Christ by faith. This can be done by asking Jesus to come into one's heart. It's done by believing that Jesus is who he says he is and he did what he said he could do. Most people need help in praying. I'd suggest that you take the following prayer, type it out, and tape it in the back of your Bible. That way you'll have help remembering it, and the person you are witnessing to can follow along with you as you pray him through it.

You might want to show him the prayer and say something like, "This is a suggested prayer. It's not magical. It's just words on a page. But if you mean it in your heart as you pray it to God, he hears it, forgives you, comes into your heart, and gives you eternal life." You want to ask him if he'd like to follow along with you as you read the prayer and repeat it to God after you. If he says, "No," then thank him for giving you the opportunity to show him a few verses from the Bible, and be prepared to shift gears to another subject. It is absolutely unnecessary to coerce anyone to a point of salvation. You don't need to jam Jesus down anyone's throat. He'll reach the person on his own time. If you violate this principle, you usurp the power of the Holy Spirit.

But if he says, "Yes, I'd like to pray this prayer with you," then read him through it one phrase at a time. Pause after each phrase, and give him time to say it. If he is repeating it silently in his heart (as he might do if you were sharing the gospel with a large group of people), then pause long enough to repeat in your head the phrase you have just said. That way he won't feel rushed through it.

Some people might question that it all seems so easy. It doesn't require money, and it doesn't require much intellect. Point out to them that they are correct in their observation. The simplicity of it all sometimes trips up people. But mention to them that if it required money, then only the rich people would get to have Jesus. If it required intellect, then only the smart people would get to have Jesus. Jesus put everything on the bottom shelf so anyone could have him. People's pride sometimes wants to get in the way, but you want to encourage them to not let their pride block them from receiving the greatest gift that could ever be given to a person.

Once the person decides he wants to pray a prayer of repentance and salvation, then pray him through a prayer that goes something like this:

> *Dear Jesus, I need you. I know that I'm a sinner, and because of my sin, I'm lost. I know now that you love me, and you gave yourself for me. And so I want to ask you to forgive me of my sin, come into my heart, and make my life new. Thank you. In Jesus' name, amen.*

When he finishes praying the prayer with you, be quiet for a few seconds, and then tell him that as a result of his faith in Christ, he has just been forgiven of his sins and has received the gift of eternal life. Remind him that eternal life is not something he gets when he dies, but something he has right now.

He may mention that he doesn't feel any different. Tell him that it is quite normal not to feel different. What he did is an act of faith based on truth. It doesn't require an emotional response to be valid. In due time the emotions will catch up with the decision that he just made.

For some, however, giving their lives to Jesus is accompanied by a major show of emotions. Tears of joy often stream down their faces. That, too, is normal.

The last passage you want to show him is *1 John 5:13–15*. This is the last reference that you'll need to write in your Bible. It will go next to John 1:12. Go through the same procedure you used with the other verses. The purpose of showing him this passage in 1 John is to give him confidence in the decision he has just made. First John 5:13–15 says,

I write these things to you who believe in the name of the Son of God so that you may know that you have eternal life. This

is the confidence we have in approaching God: that if we ask anything according to his will, he hears us. And if we know that he hears us—whatever we ask—we know that we have what we asked of him.

These verses assure him that his prayers have been heard and answered. God wants him to know that he can count on God to save him and set him free.

POISED EVANGELISM

When God gives you the privilege to lead someone to a point of salvation, it is an awesome thrill. You want to do cartwheels and back flips because of the joy you feel in your heart. That's great. But there is often a temptation to want to bring him up to speed on all the ins and outs of theology and the Christian life. You need to discipline yourself to hold back at this point. If you start downloading all kinds of information about this new family of God he has just joined, it could overwhelm him. It also clouds the work of the Holy Spirit in salvation.

Let him savor his decision. The only thing I would suggest you mention to him is that his new faith grows when he prays and studies the Bible. You can help him on both issues as you talk at a future date. Therefore, you want to make an appointment with him to go over some ways to pray effectively and to get the most out of the Bible. That's when you could talk to him about the power and positive influence a good church could have on him.

If you won't be able to see him again, you need to get his address and telephone number so that you can write him with follow-up encouragement and then get his permission to pass his name along to a reliable person in his area who could nurture him in his faith. When in doubt, call Campus Crusade for Christ's headquarters in Orlando, Florida (1-800-827-2788), and ask them for the name of someone in the person's area who could invite him to a Bible study or do some follow-up with him.

LET'S REVIEW

To prepare your Bible with the plan of salvation, you want to write a verse reference at the top of the first blank page in your Bible. If you are new at finding your way around the Bible, you can also put the page number in parentheses with it. Then you want to write the next reference beside the one you just turned to. This keeps up until you're through the seven references I've suggested: Matthew 18:3; John 3:16; Romans 3:23; Ephesians 2:8–9; Romans 6:23; John 1:12; and 1 John 5:13–15.

You may want to substitute other verses. That's fine. Lots of great verses in the Scripture present Jesus' wonderful plan of redemption.

Copying the prayer of redemption was also one of the suggestions made. That way, you can have everything you need contained within the cover of your Bible, and until you know how to get around on your own, you have a simple map to lead you through.

BEING A BOLD WITNESS

God wants you to be ready to give an answer to the hope that is within you (1 Peter 3:15). He wants you to testify boldly and without shame (Rom. 1:16). Once you have taken people through the plan of salvation, you will feel more comfortable with it. You should commit the Scriptures to memory as soon as you can and memorize the logical sequence of the prayer. Then if you get a chance to witness, but you don't have your Bible handy, you'll do just fine. Putting all of this in your heart just might come in handy if you happen upon a terrible accident and need to help a young woman about to meet her Maker. Or it could help you if you happen to find yourself face-to-face with someone like Marilyn Monroe.

THE BLONDE BOMBSHELL

Albie Pearson was one of the littlest men to ever play professional baseball. But he compensated for his five-foot-five-inch stature by swinging a mighty bat. In fact, he hit a grand-slam home run in his first at-bat in the major leagues. I remember it. I was in the backyard of our home in Maryland. I was painting some pipes for my dad and had the Orioles game on the radio. They introduced Albie Pearson late in the game. He had just been brought up from the minors and was called on to make his debut with the bases loaded. The announcer made a few comments about how short he was, but the crowd, including the announcer, jumped to their feet when Pearson smacked a pitch out of the park. It was a great start for a great ballplayer.

Albie Pearson was not just a great ballplayer with a diminutive silhouette; he was also a Christian. He made his faith plain to his fellow players as well as the press. As a result of his bold witness, they dubbed him "The Little Angel." He took it in stride and kept up his witness.

Albie Pearson's career with Baltimore was short-lived. It looked as if his entire career would be the same. But Albie got a reprieve when the American League expanded its roster of teams. The league needed some players to fill positions. A lot of the men who were on the back side of their careers got a new lease on the game. The expansion teams needed some veteran experience. Albie Pearson was picked up by the Los Angeles Angels. They were ultimately renamed the California Angels. So "The Littlest Angel" was playing for the Los Angeles Angels.

Besides being a great ballplayer, Albie Pearson was a great spokesperson. That's what caused the March of Dimes to select him as the cochairperson of the annual drive. The other cochairperson was Marilyn Monroe.

Albie Pearson had seen Marilyn Monroe when she accompanied her former husband, Joe DiMaggio, to the stadium. DiMaggio used to love to come down and watch the game, and he often brought her along. But even though he had seen her sitting in Joe DiMaggio's box seats, Albie had never personally met her.

Albie's picture appeared with Marilyn Monroe's on all the promotional posters and pamphlets for the March of Dimes drive. But even though they were cochairpersons, they were never assigned to the same promotional venue together.

One Saturday night game, however, a plaque was to be given to a mayor of one of the towns in the Los Angeles area. Marilyn Monroe was to appear with Albie Pearson at the ceremony at home plate just before the game. Usually, Albie Pearson would have gone back to the locker room after he took infield practice. But for some unknown reason, he had stayed behind in the dugout to watch the stadium fill up with fans. He wasn't waiting for Marilyn Monroe because she wasn't scheduled to appear until just before the ceremony.

But as he was standing in the dugout, the door burst open on the other end and in stumbled none other than Marilyn Monroe. She was alone. Apparently, she had gotten turned around and happened into the dugout by mistake.

Albie Pearson said that as he looked on the famous starlet, the powerful figure who had lit up the silver screen for so many years, he saw a hollow, sunken face with the saddest eyes he had ever seen. Immediately, he heard a voice inside him say, "Tell her about me." Albie Pearson, by his own admission, had been sliding away from his responsibilities to Christ. So he walked over to her and chose instead to exchange small talk with her.

They kept it up until her entourage located her, the dugout filled up with people, and the stadium filled up with fans. It was time for the ceremony. When the announcer introduced Marilyn Monroe, Albie Pearson said that she went through a complete transformation. She pushed up her famous chest, lit up her dazzling eyes, and shook her bottom as she climbed up the stairs and walked onto the field to the applause and catcalls of the fans. Albie was also introduced along with the rest of the dignitaries. He was standing a little bit behind Marilyn Monroe with her platinum hair just a few feet from him. Again he heard a voice inside him say, "Tell her about me!"

When the ceremony was over, Albie followed Marilyn Monroe to the dugout. When she got to the bottom of the two stairs into the dugout, she swung around and said to him, "Do you have something to tell me?" Albie Pearson was flustered by the question and simply said, "No, I don't have anything to tell you."

A couple of days later, Albie Pearson's wife came into the bedroom, opened up the blinds to let in the early morning light, and threw the *L.A. Times* onto his chest. He picked it up and stared at the bold headlines: MARILYN MONROE DEAD BY SUICIDE AT 36.

Albie Pearson said that he jumped out of bed, fell on his knees, and begged God to forgive him. He pleaded with God to give him another chance and promised him that he would never again pass up an opportunity to tell a person about him. He has not reneged on his promise.[1]

Let's make sure we never miss an opportunity either.

STUDY AND DISCUSSION QUESTIONS

UP FRONT AND PERSONAL

1. Are you saved according to the instruction in Romans 10:9–10? If not, what's holding you back?

2. Have you established a Christian library in your home and stocked it with Christ-centered books? Will you?

3. What are you doing to help carry out the Great Commission of Matthew 28:19–20?

FOR THE GROUP TO DISCUSS

1. How do you become a little child as presented in Matthew 18:3?

2. Does salvation come by our good works, or good works by our salvation?

3. If you asked your family members whether they were going to heaven, what would they say? Do their reasons agree with John 5:24?

4. If the wages of sin is death, what are the wages of a godly life?

5. Have you ever borne personal witness of Jesus Christ? Why did you do it, and how did you feel afterward?

6. Practice the brief "sinner's prayer." Say it over and over so that you will not be short of words when you have the opportunity to lead a soul to the Lord.

7. What should you do if a person is indifferent, even hostile, to your message of salvation for him?

8. Do you have it in your heart to testify boldly and without shame? Discuss Romans 1:16.

APPLYING GOD'S WORD

1. Volunteer for something outside your comfort level. Donate some time to a homeless shelter, visit people who are hospitalized or cannot leave their homes, or help with a prison ministry. Do this to bring out the good works in you made possible by your salvation.

CHAPTER 12

DRESS PARADE

July 4, 1971. Washington, D.C. On the Mall, facing the Lincoln Memorial. Approximately 8:30 in the evening. It was supposed to be a big birthday bash for America. We were 195 years old. The population of the District doubled that evening as families from a four-state area converged on the nation's capital for the party.

My date for the evening would one day become my sister-in-law. It was probably a good thing she was with me that night. Of the two girls in my wife's family, her sister is, without debate, the more daring. She'd need to be before the night was over.

The U.S. Marine Band had started things off with some traditional patriotic tunes and popular Sousa marches. Tens of thousands of people jockeyed for position on the green belt between the Washington Monument and the Reflecting Pool. Off to our right, a few columns from different branches of the armed services marched in from Pennsylvania Avenue as a detachment from the National Guard fired off a twenty-one-gun salute somewhere near the Jefferson Memorial.

The Stars and Stripes led the grand review flanked by flags from each state in the Union. They formed in the small patch of grass that had been cordoned off in front of the massive stage built for the occasion. After the flags were placed in their sleeves and some senator made a few opening remarks, the crowd grew hushed as the Marine Silent Drill Team quietly marched in from behind the huge curtains and took center stage. For several minutes, thousands of Americans watched with their mouths agape as the team performed flawless maneuvers with their rifles and bayonets.

With their last flourish and the thundering applause of the crowd the marines silently slipped off stage right. And as they did, the band picked up the opening measures of one of the most familiar theme songs in modern America: "Thanks for the Memories." The curtains parted slowly as Bob Hope sauntered out carrying a 3 wood. He was the main reason most of the people had put up with all the hassles you face trying to find a parking place in Washington, D.C., on a holiday weekend. He and his cronies, Bing Crosby, Jack Benny, Dean Martin, and the Gold Diggers, were the main headliners for the evening. They probably did a nice job and had some funny lines. I wouldn't know. From about fifteen minutes into the show I was preoccupied with other more pressing matters.

My date and I were locked inside a sea of people. From our vantage point, Bob Hope looked like a gnat. But lacking a quality vantage point was a nonissue at that stage of our evening. The bigger problem we faced was the row of riot police standing directly in front of us and stretching to our left and right for the width of the Mall. I shouldn't say that they were our problem. Why they were there was our problem.

America was being overwhelmed by a lot of conflicting attitudes that had thrown a wet blanket over the entire celebration. Depending on the people you talked to, it was cynicism, apathy, indifference, or hostility. We were right in the middle of the Watergate mess, the powers that be had given up on any type of victory in Vietnam, the death count in Southeast Asia had risen too high for most Americans' tolerance levels, and the unbridled freedoms of the 1960s had built a gap between two generations that enslaved them both. Those frustrations had fueled a lot of anti-American sentiments among a large number of dissidents. And they had showed up at the rally intent on upstaging it.

They succeeded. I saw the first object about the time Bob Hope finished his monologue. It was a sixteen-ounce RC bottle thrown from somewhere off to the edge of the crowd. It cracked into the head of an unsuspecting celebrant and marked the beginning of the bombardment that would continue for another forty-five minutes. At first I thought it was just some random act of stupidity until one of the riot police told me that the organizers of the demonstrators brought in cases of empty bottles for that very purpose. "Because of their weight and shape, you can really lob them a long way," he said matter-of-factly. So instead of watching the show, I spent most of my time watching for incoming objects so my date and I wouldn't be sent home on stretchers. Besides bottles, an occasional brick or rock flew by.

Few people in the back half of the crowd were watching the show. When I asked why the cops didn't do something about it, I was told that catching the people doing it was virtually impossible. They were dispersed throughout the fringe of the crowd, and once they threw their volley of bottles or rocks, they'd simply blend in with everyone around them. So we were stuck. There was no way to get out of the mess we were in.

The first tear gas canister landed about twenty yards from us. The other dozen or so were fired in a circle around us. I didn't know what was happening at first. Suddenly, I heard a lot of screaming, and a large part of the crowd was stirring to my left. When I turned to look to the riot police, I realized that they had donned their gas masks and now held their billy clubs in both hands out in front of them. Then it hit us. The winds blew the gas over us, and within seconds we were completely engulfed in a cloud of burning air. Our eyes gushed with tears, and our throats suddenly felt like they were on fire. We grabbed each other's hand and fought to find a way out, but unfortunately, until the breeze blew the tear gas over the perimeter of the crowd, it wouldn't disperse enough to let the thousands of people stuck inside move out. I don't know how long it was before we were finally able to stumble our way out of the mess we were in, but it seemed like a nightmare in slow motion.

It was, without doubt, the most exciting date of my youth.

WE'LL WEATHER THE STORM

Yellow smoke hung over the panic. Our eyes were burning hot and ran with tears. Everyone was coughing and fighting the dry heaving of lungs and stomach. Pockets of rioters had slipped into the pandemonium wearing gas masks and challenging the riot police. Cops and demonstrators, backlit by the Washington Monument and the U.S. Capitol building, went after one another in a frenzy of fists and nightsticks. I looked up in time to see one young girl's head take a crack from a club and then watched her body fall in a heap.

Everything was out of control. We had to get out of there, or we would have no chance of avoiding serious injury. It was time to act. I was grateful for all the years I spent as a running back in high school. We bobbed, weaved, and dodged demonstrators and police as we made our way to the edge. And as fast as the nightmare began, it was over. We jogged to the fountain at Dupont Circle and washed our faces in its filthy water. Eventually, our breathing returned to normal, our eyes cleared up, and the muscles in our faces relaxed. Half an hour later we were sitting on the ledge of some government building watching the most spectacular fireworks display that we had ever seen.

Later, we found our car and headed home. Driving out New York Avenue and picking up Route 50 for the trip back toward Annapolis, I found myself reflecting on the evening. It struck me how the tensions and contradictions at street level seldom add up. I had been enjoying a picnic in freedom's backyard when, suddenly, I found myself in a sinkhole of anarchy. The entire nightmare had taken place in the shadows of the buildings that are supposed to symbolize a people who have figured out how to rise above that kind of conflict. It was an antinomy. It just didn't make sense.

A few miles off Route 50 and a few more miles down Route 214 my confusing reverie was interrupted by a symbol that had lit up my life since the day I was born. The cross on the front of the little church I'd attended since childhood held its watch over the night. There was a light on in a second floor of the Sunday school building. It was the room where much of my belief system had been forged by kind and patient Sunday school teachers.

In that church I learned how God raises up nations, sustains families, and rescues people from their own folly. That little church was dwarfed in size by the U.S. Capitol, the Washington Monument, and the White House. But it overshadowed them in its eternal impact. That night our famous symbols of freedom had formed a backdrop to hate, fear, and anger. Meanwhile, a little church in Edgewater waited with its running lights on for the dawn to come next Sunday so that a confused young man could slip into a pew, sing a few hymns, and then sit back and listen to a man of God make sense out of life.

VERY LITTLE POMP
BUT LOTS OF CIRCUMSTANCE

In a way, Sunday morning is a low-grade review of God's soldiers. It usually can't compare to the pomp and ceremony of a military parade. It usually lacks the color, brilliance, and pageantry of a military review. Often it is an hour or two of quiet worship, reflection, and prayer. But the power of its influence in the believer's heart is impossible to quantify. An amateur attempt at worshiping the King of kings trumps the best that Hollywood and Washington, D.C., could ever muster.

Basic training for any good man has to include an overview of the role of the church and how to bring your best to it. Church serves a lot of the same purposes that a military review serves. They're strategic. Hardly a person alive doesn't stand up straighter and step livelier when soldiers march by. The pageantry and power that come from flags waving and cannons roaring give both the participants and the spectators a sense of awe. It helps you stay focused and hold your ground when the flags coming over the hill belong to the enemy and the cannons roaring in the distance are aimed at you.

God has provided a dress parade for his army too. It usually starts about 11:00 A.M. every Sunday. But it is much more than a parade of the saints and a celebration of the victors. It's a vital link to our fellow Christians and a strategic communion with the Savior we serve.

Worship songs, special music, prayers, Bible teaching, Communion, and the giving of tithes and offerings are designed to stir our hearts and lift our spirits. The number of gifts and the level of talent that God has made available to his church are extraordinary. If you want to hear some of the most hauntingly beautiful music ever written, just slip in the side door of any church filled with God's Spirit. And God has assembled the finest army of communicators in the history of the Christian movement. I'm fortunate to get to meet and listen to many of these treasures of the church.

But a good church has so much more to offer than the obvious worship and teaching. It's designed to be a key part of the strategy you are using to prepare your family for godly living and to protect them from the dangers within their culture. Unfortunately, too many believers head to church on Sunday with an improper understanding of the purpose of the church and therefore miss much of its benefit and undermine a lot of its potential impact. In this chapter I want to discuss specific ways you can benefit from church and it can benefit from you.

RAISING THE SPIRITUAL STOCK VALUE OF YOUR CHURCH

There are several things you can do that will enhance your church's ability to serve your needs as well as enable you to be used in the lives of others. When you follow these suggestions, your church's influence in the community skyrockets.

1. DON'T GO TO CHURCH ON EMPTY; MAKE SURE YOU COME FULL

The standard way people view church is that it's a shot in the arm at the beginning of the week that usually lasts until Tuesday or Wednesday. The last half of the week is spent anticipating the next "spiritual fix." This is an improper way to view church. It puts burdens on pastors and Sunday school teachers that they are incapable of bearing.

Your pastor is not responsible for your walk with God. You are. His job is to teach, reprove, and correct. He is not supposed to do the work of the ministry; he is supposed to equip you to do the work of the ministry. Evangelism is your job; he is supposed to show you how. Meeting the physical and social needs of the people around you is your job; the pastor is just supposed to see that you get organized enough to be effective. Visiting the sick, praying with people who cannot leave their homes, providing meals, and helping chase down a stray teenager are your jobs. The pastor is there to direct you in how to do these things most effectively.

Most churches are spiritually anemic because they relegate responsibility for the things I've mentioned above to the "paid help." Ministry is our responsibility. God gave spiritual gifts to all believers, not just the hired help.

Let me suggest ways you can make sure that you, and your family, come to church on full:

- Read your Bible every day.
- Pray for your spouse and children throughout the week that God will prepare them to make a contribution to their Sunday school classes and church service the following week by showing up with a good attitude.
- Pray for your pastor, worship leaders, children's workers, and Sunday school teachers at the Saturday evening meal and breakfast on Sunday.
- Handle your money wisely throughout the week. It makes it easier to be able to give joyfully to God on Sundays.
- Get your family and yourself to bed at a decent hour on Saturday night. On Saturday night you determine the level of impact that you will have on church and that it will have on you.
- Lay out the kids' clothes, set the breakfast table, and make sure your house is picked up on Saturday night.
- Get everyone up a little earlier on Sunday. It's a lot easier to nap in the afternoon than sleep in and then operate at a panic level trying to get to church on time.
- Avoid turning on Sunday morning news or cartoons. They tend to cover you and your family with a thick coat of the world when you really need to focus on the Lord.
- Get there early. Dropping kids off at the nursery or Sunday school after the teachers are already into their lesson plan undermines the entire class.
- Keep an eye out for visitors or new faces. Your smile, handshake, and warm greeting may be the very things God uses to prepare their heart for his message.

- Make sure you are not harboring any resentment or bitterness toward anyone in the church or your family. Make peace and offer forgiveness before Sunday morning.
- Bring your Bible and follow along with the various teachers you listen to.
- Faithfully, generously, and joyfully drop your offering into the plate when it is passed.
- Bow your head and whisper a brief word of prayer for the pastor as he approaches the pulpit to deliver his message. Ask God to give him boldness, clarity, and enthusiasm for his sermon, and ask God to give you a heart that is ready to receive it.
- Pray for all soloists, musicians, or people making a special presentation.
- If an invitation is offered at the end of a message, pray that God will stir in the hearts of people who need to make decisions.
- Make it a point to say at least ten encouraging things to ten different people.
- After church is over, pick up your kids from their classes before you socialize. It honors the teachers who have worked hard on your behalf. Thank them when you pick up your kids.
- Serve in some way each Sunday: teaching, helping in the nursery, handing out bulletins, directing traffic or overseeing parking, ushering, hosting a class, making coffee, or cleaning up after everyone has left. There is always some way that you can make a contribution to the effectiveness of your church each Sunday.

2. NEVER DO ANYTHING TO SHAME THE NAME OR REPUTATION OF YOUR CHURCH

You need to make sure that your business dealings and your relationships with your neighbors speak well of your association with your local church. When you do happen to make a mistake, you need to own up to it and do what's necessary to repair any damage to your testimony.

3. MAKE SURE YOU ARE AN ALLY TO WHAT GOD IS DOING THROUGH YOUR YOUTH PASTOR AND YOUTH VOLUNTEERS

In most churches, the youth pastor is the youngest staff member and the lowest paid person in the church. Youth brings enthusiasm, energy, and idealism. It also brings inexperience and immaturity. God wants you to show grace to youth pastors. They'll make mistakes. They'll act immature at times. They'll often lack polish, tact, and insight. Your role is to encourage them and come alongside with wisdom and a helping hand.

Churches have a bad reputation of chewing up youth pastors. They pay for an amateur but expect him to perform like a pro. God often judges churches who abuse their youth workers and withholds his blessing from parents who viciously attack the staff.

Parents become frustrated when their children don't relate to the youth department. The kids don't like the Sunday school program or Wednesday night gathering. They find fault with the youth pastor and his staff and refuse to participate. The standard response of parents is to assume that their children are right and the youth ministry is all messed up. In most cases they've got it backward.

During the teenage years, most kids step away from their parents' belief system and question the church. Most of the time the reason a kid doesn't relate to the youth ministry is that he's in a state of active antagonism to God's Spirit. He might say the right things that make you think otherwise, but in most cases the problem is with the kid and not the church. This is a time for a lot of prayer and a lot of support for what God is trying to do through the youth workers at church.

One final point about youth pastors and workers. Because I travel so much around the country and see a lot of different works, I often get calls from search committees looking for a youth pastor. When I inquire about what they're looking for, I usually hear the same thing: "We're looking for someone who really relates well with the kids, has great up-front skills, and is really good with details and organization." Unfortunately, they're talking about two different people. Youth workers who relate well with the kids and have great up-front skills usually lack detail skills. You can send him to every time management course in the country, but you will still have someone who finds that the details don't come naturally. I tell people that should they happen upon a man who has extraordinary people skills and is highly organized as well, they should pay him double, because he is rare indeed.

You need two people. If you get a good people-skilled pastor or youth pastor, assign him a quality secretary whose detail skills are off the chart. They'll make an excellent team and cover all the bases well.

Occasionally, we have to let people go. When we do, we want to exercise the advice that Jesus gave us when he told us to deal with people the way we'd like to be dealt with. We don't want to send someone to his next assignment covered with scar tissue from his dismissal. God wants to use us to heal and grow his servants so that they can build on the experience they had with us and ultimately become major assets to the work of God in the world.

4. HONOR YOUR PASTORS

Here are some specific ways:

- Organize a group of men who meet in the corner of the parking lot at a specific time before church each Sunday to specifically pray for your pastor.
- Keep a picture of your pastor and his family on your refrigerator door to remind you to pray for them and treat them like part of your family.
- Never pass on gossip about your pastor, and stand up to people who do.
- Every so often get the keys to his car from his wife and have his car washed.
- Drop encouraging notes in the offering plate and the mail to him.
- Buy an old stuffed fish at a flea market and give it to him as a World's Greatest Fisher of Men award.
- Make sure he has a good computer with adequate Bible study software.

- Send him and his wife to a Family Life Marriage Conference for a weekend. Don't expect him in the pulpit that Sunday.
- See if you can arrange with a local diner to name one of the lunch specials after him.
- Give him the freedom to fail.
- Pray for his kids, and let them make mistakes. Don't sin by expecting mature behavior from his children simply because their dad happens to be a pastor. Kids are kids. They have to grow in the Christian life. Extend the grace and love to his kids that he extends to yours.

5. NEVER FORGET THAT THE CHURCH BELONGS TO THE LORD JESUS CHRIST

He bought and paid for it with his blood. He cleansed it through his suffering. It belongs solely to him. It isn't your church, your piano, your organ, your choir, your Sunday school room, your parking place, or your pew. Everything belongs to the Lord Jesus, and you want to do everything within your power to make sure that the way you use his resources brings glory and honor to him.

GOD'S GIFT TO YOU

The Lord wants you to enjoy your Sunday morning experience. It's his way of saying, "Well done," for the way you served him on the front lines throughout the week. He wants to use it to spur you on to love and good deeds. He wants it to be a set of strong arms he wraps around your family to protect them and love them.

Sometimes you'll show up Sunday beaten and battered from the skirmishes of life. You'll still be flinching from ducking the latest missile that the enemies of the Cross have thrown. You might still have the telltale smell from the cultural tear gas you've been breathing. That's okay. There's always room in the pew for you, there's a cup of coffee in a Sunday school class with your name on it, there's a lesson tailor-made for your heart, and there's a Savior who wants to pull you in close to his bosom and remind you once more just how supremely loved you are.

And he is the head of the body, the church; he is the beginning and the firstborn from among the dead, so that in everything he might have the supremacy. (Col. 1:18)

STUDY AND DISCUSSION QUESTIONS

UP FRONT AND PERSONAL

1. Do you attend church regularly? What does the Bible say about it? See 1 John 1:7.

2. What gifts from God have you passed on for the benefit of the church?

3. Name someone you know who feels he doesn't have to attend a church to "believe." Where has his thinking gone off the mark? Is there anything you can say to convince him otherwise?

FOR THE GROUP TO DISCUSS

1. Who does the work of the ministry? Who are the evangelists in your church?

2. List several things you and your family can do to prepare for worship, before and during the church service.

3. Do you become upset if church runs a bit long on Sunday morning? Do you feel the service has to be highly structured and on a strict timetable—in by 11:00 and out by noon?

4. Share with the group the enjoyment and positive things you experience by attending church.

5. How can we honor our pastors? At home? At church?

APPLYING GOD'S WORD

1. Join a men's prayer or study group in your church and attend regularly.

2. Make it a personal mission to visit some men you haven't seen at church lately and bring them back to fellowship with the brethren.

CHAPTER 13

SEMPER FI

The auditorium for the assembly was about two-thirds filled. Only junior and senior boys had been invited. All but a few had shown up. It was an excused absence from class—worth it no matter what it was about. It was also long before we had such a thing as a coed army.

Four folding chairs, a music stand, and a microphone were the only props on the otherwise bare stage. The school principal sat in the chair to the right. Next to him sat a recruiter from the army, next to him, one from the air force, and the last chair held a marine with perfectly chiseled features.

It happened about the same time each year. Uncle Sam's finest would try to convince at least a handful of the upperclassmen that their first few years after graduation would be well spent in one of the branches of the military.

It was a forty-five-minute assembly. Each recruiter was given fifteen minutes. With their discipline and canned presentations, that shouldn't have created a problem. But numbers were low and quotas were high. Each needed to land some solid prospects from the fifteen-minute time slot. Which explains what caused the first two recruiters to get carried away. The army recruiter presented first. He talked of the opportunities and bragged about the incentives. He dropped a few historical names and seasoned it all with some riveting quotes. But he went twenty minutes.

The air force recruiter went next. He led with a joke and then followed with a few war stories. He didn't hold back as he embellished his presentation with stories of exotic locations, endless adventures, and free travel. The most famous places in the world fell off his tongue as if they were standard stopovers for anyone who would throw in his lot with the U.S. Air Force. He went twenty-two minutes.

It was three minutes before the bell was to ring when the air force recruiter took his seat. The principal leaned forward and pointed to his wristwatch as he nodded to the Marine Corps recruiter who was slowly rising to his feet.

He wore his dress blue uniform. Shoes: spit shined to a mirrored deep ebony. Back: hardwood straight. Hair: shaved high and tight. Eyes: piercing. Without a word, he walked past the podium, past the microphone, and down the steps into the center aisle of the auditorium. He said nothing as he moved slowly past row after row of young men. His eyes studied them in a sober, almost menacing way. Two and a half minutes later, he turned around, marched slowly back to the microphone, and assumed the "at ease" position. His words were slow, clear, and strong.

"Having studied you, I think that there are only two or three of you who could cut it as marines. If you think you're one of those few, meet me in the cafeteria after this assembly. Dismissed." Bell.

You can probably guess what happened next. He was mobbed in the cafeteria by lines of students wanting to tell him why they felt they could be one of the "few good men" he was looking for.

I wonder what would happen if the Lord Jesus were to come to your church or mine and say, "Having studied you, I think that there are only two or three of you who could cut it as soldiers in my army. If you think you're one of those few, meet me in the narthex after the worship service." Would you be ready to sign up with him?

We live in a country that has lost its national character. The American people are adrift in a sea of indifference. We need men to take over the helm and chart a clear and deliberate course.

But the stakes are high. The risks are real. It will cost you your life, one way or another. For all of us, it will determine how we live. For some of us, it will decide how we die. Since we have to die anyway, wouldn't it be nice to choose the values for which we die?

Jamie Buckingham said, "The problem with Christians is that nobody wants to kill them anymore."[1] Our goal is not to be a bunch of obnoxious twits screaming that the sky is falling. But we are to be salt and light (Matt. 5:13–16). Salt irritates people when it is sprinkled in wounds, and light annoys those who would rather keep their evil deeds safely hidden in the shadows. As our culture moves deeper into a lifestyle of selfishness and immorality, the deeds of the decent are going to be more obvious—and more attacked. We have clear marching orders. They were issued to us by Christ via the apostle Paul: "Therefore, my beloved brethren, be steadfast, immovable, always abounding in the work of the Lord, knowing that your labor is not in vain in the Lord" (1 Cor. 15:58 NKJV).

POLITICALLY CORRECT CONVICTIONS

When they set out to make a difference, good men discover that there are lots of people crowding the path of the righteous who want to redefine the issues and water down the truth. A friend of mine was combing the World Wide Web when he found this clever piece of work from a contributor to *U.S. News & World Report*:

> And Joseph went up from Galilee to Bethlehem with Mary, his espoused wife, who was great with child. And she brought forth a son, and wrapped him in swaddling clothes and laid him in a manger because there was no room for him in the inn. And the angel of the Lord spoke to the shepherds and said, "I bring you tidings of great joy. Unto you is born a savior, which is Christ the Lord." "There's a problem with the angel," said a Pharisee who happened to be strolling by. As he explained to Joseph, angels are widely regarded as religious symbols, and the stable was on public property, where such symbols were not allowed to land, or even hover. "And I have to tell you, this whole thing looks to me very much like a Nativity scene," he said sadly. "That's a no-no, too."
>
> Joseph had a bright idea. "What if I put a couple of reindeer over there near the ox and ass?" he said, eager to avoid sectarian

strife. "That would definitely help," said the Pharisee, who knew as well as anyone that whenever a savior appeared, attorneys usually weren't far behind. That's why Judges usually liked to be on the safe side by surrounding it with deer or woodland creatures of some sort. "Just to clinch it, throw in a candy cane, a couple of elves, and snowmen, too," he said. "No court can resist that."

Mary asked: "What does my son's birth have to do with snowmen?" "Snowpersons," cried a young woman, changing the subject before it veered dangerously toward religion. Off to the side of the crowd, a Philistine was painting the Nativity scene. Mary complained that she and Joseph looked too tattered and worn in the picture. "Artistic license," he said. "I've got to show the plight of the haggard homeless in a greedy, uncaring society in winter," he quipped. "We're not haggard or homeless. The inn was just full," said Mary. "What ever," said the painter.

Rum pa pum pum. Two women began to argue fiercely. One said she objected to Jesus' birth "because it privileged motherhood." The other scoffed at virgin births but said that if they encouraged more attention to diversity in family forms and the rights of single mothers, well, then she was all for them. "I'm not a single mother," Mary started to say, but she was cut off by a third woman who insisted that swaddling clothes are a form of child abuse since they restrict the natural movements of babies.

With the arrival of 10 child advocates, all trained to spot infant abuse and manger rash, Mary and Joseph were pushed to the edge of the crowd, where arguments were breaking out over how many reindeer (or what mix of reindeer and seasonal sprites) had to be installed to compensate for the infant's unfortunate religious character.

An older man bustled up, bowling over two merchants, who had been busy debating whether an elf is the same as a fairy and whether the elf/fairy should be shaking hands with Jesus in the crib or merely standing to the side, jumping around like a sports mascot.

"I'd hold off on the reindeer," the man said, explaining that the use of asses and oxen as picturesque backdrops for Nativity scenes carries the subliminal message of human dominance. He passed out two leaflets, one denouncing manger births as invasions of animal space, the other arguing that stables are "penned environments" where animals are incarcerated against their will. He had no opinion about elves or candy canes.

Signs declaring "Free the Bethlehem 2" began to appear, referring to the obviously exploited ass and ox. Someone said the halo on Jesus' head was elitist.

Mary was exasperated. "And what about you, old woman?" she said sharply to an elderly lady. "Are you here to attack the shepherds as prison guards for excluded species, maybe to complain that singing in Latin identifies us with our Roman oppressors, or just to say that I should have skipped patriarchal religiosity and joined some dumb new-age goddess religion?"

"None of the above," said the woman. "I just wanted to tell you that the Magi are here." Sure enough, the three wise men rode up. The crowd gasped, "They're all male!" And "Not very multicultural!" "Beltshasar here is black," said one of the Magi. "Yes, but how many of you are gay or disabled?" someone shouted. A committee was quickly formed to find an impoverished, lesbian wise person among the halt and lame of Bethlehem.

A calm voice said, "Be of good cheer, Mary, you have done well and your son will change the world." At last, a sane person, Mary thought. She turned to see a radiant and confident female face. The woman spoke again: "There is one thing, though. Religious holidays are important, but can't we learn to celebrate them in ways that unite, not divide? For instance, instead of all this business about *'Gloria in excelsis Deo,'* why not just say, 'Season's Greeting'?" Mary said, "You mean my son has entered human history to deliver the message, 'Hello, it's winter'?" "That's harsh, Mary," said the woman. "Remember, your son could make it big in midwinter festivals, if he doesn't push this religion thing too far. Centuries from now, in nations yet unborn, people will give each other pricey presents and have big office parties on his birthday. That's not chopped liver." "Let me get back to you," Mary said.[2]

If you plan to take a stand, then plan on hearing from the politically correct elitists. Pastor Joe Wright from Central Christian Church in Wichita, Kansas, found that out. It was January 23, 1996. He thought he had followed instructions properly. He even thought he had done an adequate job. He had been asked to open a session of the Kansas state legislature with prayer. It was standard operating procedure. Pastors or religious leaders were invited by friends in the legislature to bring a few spiritual words to kind of get things going each morning. Joe Wright had been invited on that particular morning. But there was one thing different from what he was used to. Instead of praying extemporaneously, the visiting religious dignitary was asked to write out his prayer in advance. That way, it would be easy for the recorder to simply add it to the day's proceedings when it was time to publish it in the state's *Congressional Record*.

So Pastor Joe Wright sat down the night before, wrote out his prayer, handed a copy to the legislative recorder as he stepped up to the microphone, and then read the following from his own copy:

Heavenly Father, we come before You today to ask Your forgiveness and seek Your direction and guidance. We know Your Word says,

"Woe to those who call evil good . . ."

. . . but that is exactly what we have done.

- We have lost our spiritual equilibrium and inverted our values.
- We confess that we have ridiculed the absolute truth of Your Word and called it moral pluralism.
- We have worshipped other gods and called it multiculturalism.
- We have endorsed perversion and called it an alternative lifestyle.
- We have exploited the poor and called it the lottery.
- We have neglected the needy and called it self-preservation.
- We have rewarded laziness and called it welfare.
- We have killed our unborn and called it a choice.
- We have shot abortionists and called it justifiable.

- We have neglected to discipline our children and called it building their self-esteem.
- We have abused power and called it political savvy.
- We have coveted our neighbors' possessions and called it ambition.
- We have polluted the air with profanity and pornography and called it freedom of expression.
- We have ridiculed the time-honored values of our forefathers and called it enlightenment.

Search us, O God, and know our hearts today.
Try us and see if there be some wicked way in us.
Cleanse us from every sin and set us free.

Guide and bless these men and women who have been ordained by You to govern this great state. Grant them Your wisdom to rule and may their decisions direct us to the center of Your will. I ask it in the name of Your Son, the Living Savior, Jesus Christ. Amen.[3]

Pastor Wright slipped his copy of his prayer into his pocket, walked out a side door of the legislature, and headed to the parking lot to drive his car over to his church. When he walked into his office, the church receptionist had a troubled look like a deer caught in the headlights. When he asked her what was wrong, she said that she wasn't sure but that he needed to call his contact at the legislature.

When he did, he found out that his simple prayer of repentance had turned the floor of the legislature into a cockfight. Apparently, many of the Kansas lawmakers took umbrage at Pastor Wright's words. They vilified him. They spit out their disdain for his insensitive and ridiculous assumptions and wanted to make sure they went on record as standing solidly against this right-wing, close-minded, religious extremist.

He couldn't believe it. How could any thinking person even consider disagreeing with national problems that he thought were as obvious as the nose on your face?

As those things go, there just so happened to be someone

from the radio station who happened to have his tape recorder running when Pastor Joe prayed. And it just so happened that someone from the newspaper happened to pick up a copy of his prayer. By noon the people of Kansas heard about the lynching the pastor had received on the floor of the legislature. Within seconds of the stories going out, the switchboard at the capitol lit up. Lawmakers' beepers went nonstop, and fax machines ran out of paper processing the reaction of the people. The so-called "lawmakers who speak on behalf of their constituents" found out they didn't have a clue what really burned in the heart and soul of Kansas' grassroots population. The people responded with a resounding approval of the pastor's honest words and a clear warning to any representative who tried to stand against him.

You may have to stand alone, but you won't have to stand alone forever. We are part of a powerful army of rank-and-file people who have not surrendered their convictions. Sometimes, however, it takes a good fight to draw them out.

WHEN TODAY'S CULTURE
SLIPS IN A SIDE DOOR

I share the following story with my daughter's permission. She has taught me much about how effectively God can work in the heart of a child to help her see past the cultural traps laid for her.

Karis (my older daughter) called me at work. Her voice was filled with excitement and anticipation: "Daddy, I just got back from the mall. I found the perfect dress for the Valentine's party at school, and, Daddy, it's marked down to thirty dollars! I have fifteen dollars, and I'm baby-sitting this Saturday night where I'll be making the remainder of the money I need. If you could loan me the balance, I'll pay you back Saturday night."

My first thought was, *Since when did Karis start buying her clothes?* Then I recalled that Darcy had told her that if she didn't want to wear one of the many ideal outfits already hanging in her closet, she could get something else, but she would have to purchase it with her own funds. My second thought was, *Since when can you get a party dress for $30?* When I asked Karis that question, she explained that it was a clearance sale.

I told her that I would spot her the money and she could pay me back the following weekend. She thanked me and then told me she wanted to hang up so she could call her girlfriend and make plans to go back to the mall the next day to get the dress.

The next day Karis was arriving home from the mall at the same time I was getting home from the office. She waved good-bye to her friend and came up to greet me in the garage.

"I got it, Daddy!"

"Great. What did you get?" I hadn't a clue what she was referring to.

"My Valentine's party dress."

"Great." I still didn't have a clue what she was talking about. Then my mind reversed its memory tape to the day before and the conversation we'd had on the phone.

When we got in the house, she said, "I'll go upstairs and put it on to model it for you."

"Great." But as she ran up the stairs to her room, I noticed she was carrying a bag about the size of the one they put in the slot in front of you on the airplane. I was looking for a big box or a long, flowing dress inside a plastic sheath and on a clothes hanger. Concern started to build.

I was leaning against the kitchen counter reading the mail when she came downstairs and into the kitchen wearing the dress. She was beaming ear to ear with pride, and her eyes studied me for approval. I looked at the dress. Then I looked back to her eyes. Then I looked at the dress again and said, "I can see why you wanted that dress. You look fantastic in it. It's cute, and so are you."

She went on to tell me about looking at a lot of different stores and how she fell in love with the dress as soon as she saw it. I wasn't hearing much of what she was saying because there was a war raging in my head. It was true that the dress looked great on her, but it was also true that it wasn't much of a dress—literally.

Karis is built just like her mom—tall and statuesque. The guys who would be attending the party would have enough frustrations with their eyes and their hormones without feeding the problem. But I didn't want to break my daughter's heart, and I knew why she wanted a dress like that. It was the kind that a lot of the other girls at her school would be wearing to the party. I remembered picking up Karis at the Christmas dance and noticing many of her friends wearing dresses that were next to nothing—skimpy, tight-fitting outfits that could do nothing but complicate the hormonal battle already raging in so many of the guys in attendance. I also remembered the thought that crossed my mind when I saw each dress: *Where in the world is that girl's father? Is he sleepwalking through her teenage years?*

Our teenagers need bold leadership when it comes to making these kinds of choices. And we definitely have to be prepared to challenge the social status quo. We all have to remember that the world system doesn't have to stand in front of God someday and give an account for our children. However, we do. And as a parent, I realized a long time ago that I must challenge the world's thinking when it comes to the best interests of my kids.

I also learned a long time ago that even if everyone in the world embraced a bad idea and thought it was a good idea, it would still be a bad idea. And Karis's dress was a bad idea.

"Karis, honey, your dress is cute on you, but I have just one problem with it. You see, dresses are supposed to be high at the top and low at the bottom. Somehow yours got turned upside down." I went on to explain a little about how junior high boys, even conscientious ones, are wired.

I could see her countenance fall. She had already pictured herself wearing that dress at the party, and now her "old fossil dad" was about to ruin her plans. She defended why she thought it was okay, and I let her voice her views. Then I suggested that we think about it for twenty-four hours. (By the way, rescheduling difficult decisions often gives time a chance to bring reason and balance into both sides of the conflict.) I wanted to make sure that I was being reasonable and that Karis would also have time to consider my concerns.

The next afternoon I called her from the office. "Karis, did you get a chance to think any more about the dress?"

Her response nearly knocked me out of my chair: "Dad, I really like the dress, and I'd really like to keep it, but I decided to do whatever you want me to do and not complain about it."

The secretaries had to jump-start my heart. I couldn't believe what I was hearing, but I was grateful nonetheless. My daughter is just as capable of giving me a verbal run for my money as yours is, so I was surprised and delighted.

I told her how much I appreciated her great attitude, and that it would help a lot in the position that, after talking it over with her mother, we felt compelled to take. In spite of how much she liked the dress, we wanted her to take it back. "But," I said, "I'll go with you to the mall and help you find the perfect dress for the occasion, and if it costs more, I'll make up the difference." (She was meeting me far more than halfway, so I thought that I should be willing to do the same.)

As it turned out, Darcy took her to the mall, and they found a gorgeous dress for the party. We nicknamed it Plan B. It came all the way up to her neck and all the way down to the floor. Personally, I think it would make a great school uniform!

As I've said many times before, there is little that's convenient about being a parent, but there is a ton of reward. Our teenage children need to be able to make a lot of their own decisions, but we have to retain veto rights when they make a choice that we feel genuinely jeopardizes or endangers their well-being. We've got to be courageous, and we've got to be firm. There may be tears, and we may have to hear some unkind things said about our decisions. Don't let these things keep you from your resolve to fight the hard battles. If Jesus had caved in to popular opinion, none of us would be saved today. It takes a few good men to hold the line.

GOLIATHS IN THE MIST

One of the great benefits of history is that you can learn from the example of others. If it worked for them, there's a good chance that it will work for you. Biblical history is even better. The men and women who live and breathe within the pages of Scripture were people just like you and me. They liked their coffee as soon as they got up in the morning, they got frustrated with their waistlines, and they had bad hair days. And just like us, they committed a good amount of their mental energy to worrying about their families.

They had mouths to feed and bills to pay, and they often felt they were at the mercy of forces that they couldn't do anything about. Because back then, just like today, there were giants in the land—visible and invisible Philistines who made it their daily goal to prey on the weak and the easily intimidated.

Nothing is new. Nothing has changed. We have Philistines living among us who get a real kick out of putting us in a bowl, sprinkling on some salt and pepper, and having us for lunch. Sometimes these Philistines are organized and visible, like the examples mentioned above. Other times they're just a faceless force to be reckoned with.

They might be the gangs that graffiti our neighborhoods, plunging property values; unreasonable taxes; a gossip at church; a neighbor with a chip on his shoulder; cancer; a school board with an anti-Christian agenda; guilt or shame from past regrets. The list is endless, and so is the intimidation that can come from it. What these forces pose, more than anything else, is an ongoing reason to worry. We tend to worry about them, not so much because of what they can do to us personally, but because of what they can do to the people we love. We hate seeing our families being pushed around, and we hate it even more when we feel helpless to do anything about it.

The Philistines usually have a Goliath—some giant representative who overshadows us and turns our wills to Jell-O simply by showing up in our lives. The nation of Israel had theirs. We talked about him briefly in chapter 2 when we developed the reasons that brought David, the accidental soldier, to the battlefield. It's one of the classic stories of all time. Goliath went out into the valley that separated the two armies and challenged the Israelite soldiers individually. That was what made him so intimidating. He leveraged his size and strength against them, and they made the mistake of letting him set the ground rules for the conflict as well as convince them that none of them could defeat him. And while the Philistine army sat back in camp playing cards and having seconds on dessert, the Israelites lay in their tents trembling.

Enter David. He was barely a teenager, the runt of the family litter, and a bit moody. But he had one thing going for him that the rest of the people lacked: he had a galvanized resolve to put his total confidence in God and in the power that God placed within him. So when he showed up at camp to check on the welfare of his older brothers, he was shocked to see what was going on. He wasn't shocked that Goliath was standing out in the valley shouting obscenities toward God, but he was shocked that the Israelite soldiers were tolerating it.

And so he took off toward the nine-and-a-half-foot insult in the valley to personally and permanently shut him up. He rejected the idea of wearing Saul's armor and using Saul's weapons. They didn't fit, and he wasn't used to them. He wanted to go with his strong suit—his slingshot. It had served him well in the past; it would be his best chance in the present.

But as he approached the giant, he needed some ammo for the slingshot. The Scriptures tell us that he paused at a brook and selected five stones to put in his pouch. Why five? Lots of reasons. He might miss on the first, second, third, or fourth shot. Why take one when your pouch can hold five? And the Scriptures tell us that Goliath had a big family (1 Chron. 20:4–8). You know how some families are. You fight one; you fight them all. As it turned out, one stone was all it took to bring Goliath down. But David had the four other rocks in the bag just in case.

A POUCH PACKED WITH POWER

You want to be found faithful. You want to stand in the gap, but like it or not, you're going to face some Goliaths in the process. If you're like the rest of us, you'll probably face a couple this week. This is no time for intimidation and no place for cowards. God is with you. He will give you strength. He will work through your strong suit (your natural abilities). But you need to take at least five stones with you into the battle. As you stoop down at the edge of the brook, I'd like to direct your attention to at least five stones to slip into your pouch.

1. TRUTH

I see this wonderful stone glistening just beneath the surface of the running stream. It's called truth. Pick it up. You'll definitely need it. The most effective weapon in Satan's arsenal is doubt. He has used it since the Garden of Eden to trip up and then ultimately destroy the people who claim faith in God. He loves to get us second-guessing ourselves, questioning others, and focusing on our problems. There is only one way to combat falsehood and doubt, and that's with the uncompromised truth of God's Word.

Genesis 3:1–13 outlines the human race's first encounter with the devil:

Now the serpent was more crafty than any of the wild animals the LORD God had made. He said to the woman, "Did God really say, 'You must not eat from any tree in the garden'?" The woman said to the serpent, "We may eat fruit from the trees in the garden, but God did say, 'You must not eat fruit from the tree that is in the middle of the garden, and you must not touch it, or you will die.'" "You will not surely die," the serpent said to the woman. "For God knows that when you eat of it your eyes will be opened, and you will be like God, knowing good and evil." When the woman saw that the fruit of the tree was good for food and pleasing to the eye, and also desirable for gaining wisdom, she took some and ate it. She also gave some to her husband, who was with her, and he ate it. Then the eyes of both of them were opened, and they realized they were naked; so they sewed fig leaves together and made coverings for themselves. Then the man and his wife heard the sound of the LORD God as he was walking in the garden in the cool of the day, and they hid from the LORD God among the trees of the garden. But the LORD God called to the man, "Where are you?" He answered, "I heard you in the garden, and I was afraid because I was naked; so I hid." And he said, "Who told you that you were naked? Have you eaten from the tree that I commanded you not to eat from?" The man said, "The woman you put here with me—she gave me some fruit from the tree, and I ate it." Then the LORD God said to the woman, "What is this you have done?" The woman said, "The serpent deceived me, and I ate."

Did you notice the lies? "Did God really say . . . ," and then the devil misquoted God. After Eve corrected him, he came back with a series of lies and half-truths:

- You won't die—lie.
- Your eyes will be opened—half-truth.
- You will be like God—lie.
- You will know good and evil—half-truth.

From the beginning, Satan has operated in the realm of falsehood. The best way to counter his lies is with the truth. I shared a great verse with you in an earlier chapter, but it bears repeating here: "We demolish arguments and every pretension that sets itself up against the knowledge of God, and we take captive every thought to make it obedient to Christ" (2 Cor. 10:5).

Truth blows Satan right out of his sandals. There is no way he can stand against it. Speaking of truth, look at this one:

His divine power has given us everything we need for life and godliness through our knowledge of him who called us by his own glory and goodness. Through these he has given us his very great and precious promises, so that through them you may participate in the divine nature and escape the corruption in the world caused by evil desires. (2 Peter 1:3–4)

Through Christ's divine power, you and I have "everything we need" to stand up to Satan's lies.

You can turn to Revelation 20:1–3 and see his ultimate demise. I find it interesting that when it comes time to take Satan and throw him in the abyss, God sends one of his angels to do the job. Watch this:

And I saw an angel coming down out of heaven, having the key to the Abyss and holding in his hand a great chain. He seized the dragon, that ancient serpent, who is the devil, or Satan, and bound him for a thousand years. He threw him into the Abyss, and locked and sealed it over him, to keep him from

deceiving the nations anymore until the thousand years were ended. After that, he must be set free for a short time.

What I find so amazing about that is that "an" angel can throw Satan into prison. This isn't some mighty archangel; it's like a second lieutenant. You'd think that "an" angel wouldn't be strong enough. The point here is that Satan is not so tough—when you face off with him through the power of Christ's shed blood on the cross and armed with the truth!

2. REST

A medium-size rock near the edge of the brook is called rest. Put it in your pouch. You're going to need it more than you think. It's going to be hard to defeat the Goliaths you face this coming year if you face them physically exhausted. I feel certain that had David been trying to hold down two jobs, maintain up-to-date recall on all current events, read the latest books, see all of the first-run movies, and function on six hours of sleep a night, the biblical narrative would have had quite a different and disappointing ending.

You can't maintain a courageous front if you are constantly running on empty. Cars don't run on empty, stomachs don't run on empty, bank accounts don't run on empty, and neither do you nor I. If we want to be men of courage, we must pace ourselves and get adequate sleep at night.

When the allied forces finally invaded the borders of Iraq in the brief but crucial war called Desert Storm, they were surprised to encounter so much wholesale surrendering by the Iraqi army. Sometimes garrisons that had been fortified in the desert would surrender en masse. One Iraqi officer was being interviewed in our prisoner of war camp by an American intelligence officer and he was asked why they had given up so quickly. He responded, "For the past forty-five days your air force has flown over our fortress and dropped a bomb on us around the clock, every fifteen minutes, for forty-five days. We had lost our courage."[4]

If we want to be courageous men who are ready to stand with the Lord, we need to be men who are not neglecting our rest. One of the new commitments you may have to make is a commitment to your pillow!

Slow down. Take a nap every once in a while. Go to bed earlier. Don't try to accomplish so much. Remember, when you get to heaven, you're graded not on your accomplishments but on your faithfulness.

3. QUIET

There's a third rock I see in the brook. You probably wouldn't think it would be very effective at knocking down the Goliaths you face. Trust me, it packs a wallop. It's called quiet. Drop it in your pouch. You'll need it.

If you could go through a time warp and see David out in the wilderness keeping an eye on his father's flock, he wasn't wearing headphones and bopping to the sounds coming from his Walkman. I realize he couldn't have, even if he had wanted to. But every generation has had its noisemakers. We've got to make a deliberate choice to quiet down our lives.

Pick a few days when you drive to and from work with the radio off. Turn off the television four nights a week. Get up before the kids so that you can enjoy a few moments of quiet with the Lord. I guarantee you that you'll get a lot of strength for your efforts.

David didn't write the words found in Psalm 46, but he practiced them. Here they are: "Be still, and know that I am God" (v. 10 NKJV). God wants to convince you in the quiet of what is still true in the midst of the threatening noises of life.

4. PRAYER

A truthful heart, a rested heart, and a quiet heart naturally lead to a prayerful heart. I don't know what's waiting for you in the valley, but I know that prayer is one of the best forms of ammunition that you could take with you. Men who are always faithful are committed to prayer.

One of the best reminders of this is found in 2 Chronicles 7:14: "If my people, who are called by my name, will humble themselves and pray and seek my face and turn from their wicked ways, then will I hear from heaven and will forgive their sin and will heal their land."

Notice the condition or posture that your heart should be in when you pray—*humble.* You are to be diligent about it—*seek his face.* You have to do something else simultaneously—*turn from wicked ways.* When you do this, God promises to *hear you, forgive you,* and *heal the infection that has resulted from your sin.*

As you consider your relationship with God, is there some sin you need to confess? Is there some haughtiness you need to recognize and acknowledge to God? God loves you and longs for you to seek his face with your whole heart and soul in prayer.

When it comes to prayer, you need to organize less and agonize more. The Bible and church history are filled with examples of people who prayed and saw results:

- Abraham prayed; his ninety-year-old wife had a son.
- Moses prayed; the sea parted.
- Joshua prayed; cities fell down.
- David prayed; Goliath fell down.
- Elijah prayed; fire came down from heaven.
- Daniel prayed; the lions lost their appetite.
- Paul prayed; prison doors fell off their hinges.
- John Knox prayed; Mary, Queen of Scots trembled.
- George Mueller prayed; orphanages were maintained.

One night a fierce battle raged among the rocky crags called Heartbreak Ridge. It was one of the many battlefields in the Korean War that were bathed in gallons of tears and blood. An American GI had worked his way about fifty meters through the enemy's lines when a bullet struck him. He went down bleeding badly. His frightened voice cried out into the night, "Someone come rescue me. I've been hit!"

No one moved. Taking off through the constant spray of North Korean machine-gun fire would be suicide. Everyone just kept his head down and felt a sense of helplessness. However, every time a flare was set off in the sky above them, one soldier kept lifting his wrist up and then putting it back down. Another flare, wrist up, wrist down. Finally, another flare lit up the night sky, but when the man lifted up his wrist, he immediately jumped up and raced to the voice of his dying comrade.

He reached him, lifted him over his shoulder, and carried him safely back behind their own lines.

A few minutes later, the field commander joined the brave young rescuer in his foxhole and asked him what gave. "I saw you kept lifting up your arm and then putting it down. Then I saw you take off. Are you crazy?"

"No, sir. You see, every time a flare went off, I checked my watch. When it finally got to 11:00 P.M., I had calculated that it would be 9:00 A.M. back in Kansas where my mother is. The last thing my mother told me before I shipped out for Korea was, 'Son, I'll be praying for you every morning at 9:00.' I knew I was safe."[5]

If you want to stay faithful, you need to be a man who prays. Prayer doesn't need proof; it just needs practice because

> those who hope in the LORD
>   will renew their strength.
> They will soar on wings like eagles;
>   they will run and not grow weary,
>   they will walk and not be faint. (Isa. 40:31)

5. LAUGHTER

I want to encourage you to drop one final rock into your pouch. You wouldn't usually think to include it in your selection, but after you consider it, you realize just how vital it will be when it comes to facing the Goliaths who will step out to confront you in the future. It's called laughter.

Don't take yourself so seriously. No matter how big the challenges that face you, and no matter how many times you stumble on your way to encounter them, your life would fare better if you would just lighten up. No man's life is as good as he may think it is, but it's not as bad as he may think it is either. And a little laughter helps you keep your attitude positive and contagious.

A story is told of two little boys. One was always pessimistic. The other was always optimistic. The powers that be decided to do an experiment with them to see if they could figure out what made them tick.

They took the pessimistic boy and put him in a room filled with all kinds of things that a little boy would like. There were toys, a jumping horse, and a few puzzles. And there was candy. Lots of it.

The pessimistic boy sat down in the middle of all the fun temptations, and as they closed the door on him, they said, "We'll be back to check on you in a little while."

They took the optimistic boy by the hand and led him down the hallway and then shoved him into a room where he was waist deep in horse manure. As they closed the door on him, they said, "We'll be back to check on you in a little while."

They waited. They went to the first room to check on the pessimistic kid. He was right where they had left him, and he hadn't touched a thing.

"What's wrong with you, child? Why didn't you play with the jumping horse?"

Pessimist: "I thought I'd fall off and break my arm."

"Why didn't you play with the cool puzzles?"

Pessimist: "They looked too complicated."

"But what about the candy? Every kid loves candy. Why didn't you eat any?"

Pessimist: "I thought I'd get sick and hurl all over myself."

They left the pessimist and went down the hallway to check on the optimist. There was manure all over the walls and all over the ceiling. The boy had it all over himself, and he was throwing a chunk of it just as they opened the door. They said, "What on earth are you doing?"

Optimist: "With all this manure in here, I figure there's got to be a pony in here somewhere, *and I'm going to find him!*"

Laughter is great medicine, but it's an even better weapon. Use it against the fears within and the foes without. You'll be amazed how quickly your Goliaths will hit the ground.

One final note. David stopped by the brook and put five stones in his pouch. When he finally encountered Goliath, he reached in and pulled one out. Which one did he grab? Who knows? You may not know which of these five stones you'll need to face the Goliaths around you. That's why it's best to have them all available when you need them. By the way, when you stop by the brook to load up your pouch, take a good, long drink from the living water. You'll be amazed how much stronger you'll feel in the middle of the battle.

SEMPER FI

We've been issued a call to arms. Our weapons are truth, rest, quiet, prayer, and laughter. God wants us to be faithful in carrying out our marching orders. It's the least we can do based on all that he has done for us.

Late in King David's life, he made a major mistake. God punished him for his sin and then asked him to go to a certain man's place to offer a sacrifice at his threshing floor. The man saw David and his entourage from a distance and ran to meet him. When the man inquired about the king's visit, David informed him that he had come to purchase his threshing floor so he could offer a sacrifice to God.

"Buy it? You can have it!" He not only offered David the threshing floor, free of charge, but also begged him to use his oxen for the sacrifice and their yokes for the wood—free of charge. David responded, "No, but I will surely buy it from you for a price; nor will I offer burnt offerings to the LORD my God with that which costs me nothing" (2 Sam. 24:24 NKJV).

God calls us to stand by the truth, to guard our rest, to commune with him in the quiet, to pray, and to keep our sense of humor. And even when we blow it, God is willing to help us build a bridge back to him. Sometimes there's a price to pay, but it's worth it. As David said, "I will not offer a sacrifice to the LORD my God that costs me nothing." Of one thing we can be certain: he will always be faithful.

You're a warrior for the cause of Christ. Will you lay everything on the line for him?

ALWAYS READY, ALWAYS WILLING, ALWAYS FAITHFUL. *SEMPER FI.*

STUDY AND DISCUSSION QUESTIONS

UP FRONT AND PERSONAL

1. Are people really more indifferent today to immorality than ever before, or is immorality just more noticeable because of things such as television and the movies? What is your personal tolerance level?

2. How swayed are you by the opinions of others? Are you willing to challenge another's opinion if you know you are on moral high ground?

3. Do you really believe in the power of prayer? What should be the subject of your prayers, and should they relate to a specific goal or promise from God?

FOR THE GROUP TO DISCUSS

1. Complete this statement: "On a scale of 1 to 10 (with 1 being great and 10 being poor), I rate my prayer life at ____." If it's 5 or higher, what steps can you take to increase your personal fellowship with the Lord?

2. Cite an example of answered prayer in your life. How do you know that God was moving on your behalf and it wasn't just coincidence?

3. The author states, "We have Philistines living among us." What does he mean, and how can we recognize them?

4. The weapon of Satan is _____, and you shall overcome him with God's weapon for you, which is God's _____.

5. Describe how simple rest fortifies you to stand with the Lord.

6. Faithful men are committed to prayer. Think of a few good men of the Bible and discuss what prayer achieved for them. Were the results always immediate? Why, or why not?

7. Of the five stones of faith the author tells us to have in the Christian soldier's pouch, which one will you need today? Stay steadfast in your faithfulness and study of God's word, and your pouch will always be full.

APPLYING GOD'S WORD

Is there some sin in your life that you have not confessed to God? If so, it is hindering your Christian walk. Confess it now to him and know the meaning of 2 Timothy 2:25–26.

CHAPTER 14

TAPS

I t was a brisk autumn after-
noon. The winds slipping up the Potomac sent a nasty chill
down the back of my neck and forced me to pull the zipper up
on my jacket until it was scraping the bottom of my chin. I was
walking down the hill from the grave of President Kennedy. It
had been a day, much like this day, when I heard the news that
he had been gunned down in Dallas. Now, so many decades
later, I found myself wondering what had become of his dream.

He had challenged the flower of America's youth to lock
arms and stand toe-to-toe in the gap on behalf of a world in
need. More than fifty-eight thousand of our finest would
become the down payment on that promise. Many of them lay
beneath the white marble lines that surrounded me in Arlington Cemetery. John Kennedy was waiting for them, when they
got there, at the foot of an eternal flame.

My reverie was broken by the crisp crack of a precision
honor guard firing a salute to a fallen warrior. Just through the
trees to my left, a small group of mourners sat beside a flag-
draped casket. The white gloves of the honor guard snapped
open the breeches of their rifles and then brought them back
up to their shoulders in tight exactness. Crack! The second
shot was fired, followed in perfect cadence by the third.

I leaned against a sweet gum tree and watched as the funeral
detail lifted the flag from the casket, stretched it taut in their
hands, made two lateral folds, and then started the tumble of
the colors until it tucked nicely into a stars-on-blue triangle.
An officer handed the flag to the widow, whispered something
on behalf of the president and a grateful nation, and then stood

back to offer her a slow, tight salute. On the hill, standing between the rows of white marble markers, a bugler lifted his instrument to his lips and played the haunting notes of the final serenade known as taps.

Arlington Cemetery is a quiet metaphor honoring the might of a nation. Its grit and spirit, its passion and dreams, lie buried beneath the endless acres of grass. I try to go there every time my journey takes me through Washington, D.C. It's a reminder to me that peace comes at a price, and it usually demands from us our best.

While putting the final touches on this book, I was called to another cemetery. But this time I wasn't an innocent onlooker to someone else's grief. This time my brothers, my sister, and I were sitting in those chairs facing the casket. And my father lay inside. We buried him next to my mother in a simple graveyard outside the same town in which he was born.

When I first received the call that my father's body finally succumbed to the cancer that had seized him more than a year ago, I slipped out into the night and sat for a long time in a lawn chair looking up at the stars. It seemed that every back alley my memory ran down left me smiling at the things my father did. He loved to laugh. He loved to make people laugh. He didn't take himself too seriously, and he helped people see that life is a lot easier to process if we'd all just lighten up. They say that heaven doesn't seem so far away when someone you love and miss is living there. Heaven felt so close to me that night that I thought I could just about reach up and touch it.

My father had been a warrior. He fought in the famous Battle of the Bulge. Tenth Armored Division. The Third Army. His commanding general was the legendary and infamous General George Patton.

Dad would be the first one to downplay his role in the war, and he would be quick to get after me if he thought I was playing it up. He never viewed himself as anything more than a ground pounder doing his duty.

In the world's eyes, Dad never really rose above the rank of private. He was a simple man from a blue-collar family, who worked for other people most of his life. He sang in the church choir, bowled every Friday, tapped his feet to a lot of big band music, and loved to spend his summer weekends in his camper.

Fortunately for us, Dad figured out that his time was up early enough to use the last months of his life to tie a bow on his relationship with each person close to him. He communicated his love, his pride, and his confidence to each of his six children. He did it publicly and privately. Although we are scattered throughout the country, we were all able to gather at his home for one last reunion before he died. A little more than a week before he took his last breath, the six of us spent a few days together with him. The Sunday afternoon we all assembled at his home was a glorious day. Dad was overwhelmed with joy. We all agree that God gave us a gift that weekend that we'll cherish for the rest of our lives. And then, as soon as we left to return to our homes, Dad's body started the process of shutting down for good.

But fifty-one years earlier he had prepared himself for it. That was when, fresh from the war, he learned the story of Christ's love for him from a man named Homer McKinney. He surrendered himself completely to the carpenter's son from Nazareth. We're all the beneficiaries of his unwavering faith.

When Dad died, it was like finishing the reading of a great book. It was a story filled with adventure, surprises, and lots of laughs. And when we closed the back cover of that book and rested it in our hands for one last time, we realized that Dad finished writing his story without regrets. It's a story we'll all reread in our memories and, I hope, retell in our actions.

My father died a wealthy man because of the way he had invested himself throughout his life. He wasn't wealthy in the way most people determine bottom lines. He had little of this world's goods to his name the moment he died. Yet he was wealthy in the way that matters most when you finally come to the end of your journey. He was rich in friends, he was rich in family, and he was rich in faith.

Dad proved that you don't need a long list of academic degrees to be wise, you don't need a Fortune 500 résumé to make an impact, you don't need gold-plated friends to be admired, and you don't have to be tall to be looked up to.

FINAL REVIEW

Someday, the bugler on the hill will be playing taps for you and me. We're going to come to the end of the journey, slip through a crease in time and space, and then stand before the King of kings.

We have a choice. God has given us the final say on how that scene will play out. He has allowed us to decide whether we get to bow before him as faithful servants or as men who hang our heads in regret.

Life doesn't really last that long. Eternity does. On this side of the grave we have an opportunity to leave an impression. My father's legacy is a reminder to me of the sheer force of a life well lived. You and I have the chance to leave a similar mark.

We've gone through basic training together. We've even spent a few chapters in Officer Candidate School for the Lord Jesus Christ. Now it's time to fight the good fight. Good people are standing in our shadows—good wives, good sons, good daughters, who need you and me to follow our orders, do our duty, and stand our posts. They long for us to hold tight to our convictions and not flinch when the air is filled with adversity.

My older daughter, Karis, reminded me of the call of the Christian soldier in a poem she wrote while sitting beside me on an airplane trip:

Tireless

If you can hurt but move on,
If you can fall but get up,
If you can bleed but then heal,
If you can be wronged, and still can forgive,
If you can give without ceasing,
If you can go without stopping,
If you can love unconditionally,
If you can comfort unselfishly,
If you can worship unashamed,
If you can mourn without giving up,
If you can fight till you win,
If you can try, fail, and then keep on trying,

If you can learn how to trust,
If you can say, "No" when you must,
If you will pray till all know,
If you will preach till all see,
Then a tireless Christian Soldier you will be.

One day, the people you love so much will gather by your side to say good-bye. All that you were, and all that you stood for, will become the part of you that they'll be able to carry into the future. Because that day is a certainty, you need to live this day and the next ones with that end in mind. As the final notes of taps fade over the hill, a fresh call of reveille will sound on the other side. You will muster at the nail-scarred feet of the Savior and draw your orders for eternity. Let him find you faithful enough here that he can strategically use you there . . . a few good men in eternal service to one *awesome* God.

NOTES

Chapter 5
1. Scott O'Grady, "I Knew I'd Never Be Lost Again," *Parade* magazine, October 29, 1995.
2. W. E. B. Griffin, *Behind the Lines* (New York: Jove Books, 1995), p. 3.

Chapter 6
1. I learned of the actual location of the death of General Armistead from a conversation with Alabama State Senator Bill Armistead, a distant relative of the Confederate general. He was led to the site of his relative's death by one of the oldest and most knowledgeable historians of the Battle of Gettysburg.

Chapter 7
1. Larry Donnithorne, *The West Point Way of Leadership* (New York: Doubleday, 1994), p. 25.
2. Ibid., pp. 68–69.

Chapter 8
1. James C. Dobson, *Straight Talk to Men and Their Wives* (Waco, Tex.: Word, 1980), p. 21.
2. Etched on the wall of the old Annapolis High School, Annapolis, Maryland.
3. Tim Kimmel, *Raising Kids Who Turn Out Right* (Portland: Multnomah Press, 1989), p. 77.
4. Paul Lee Tan, *Encyclopedia of 7700 Illustrations* (Rockville, Md.: Assurance Publishers, 1980), p. 282.
5. Etched on a statue of Teddy Roosevelt, located about four blocks from the White House.

Chapter 9
1. H. Norman Schwarzkopf and Peter Petre, *It Doesn't Take a Hero* (New York: Bantam Books, 1992), pp. 110–21; quote, pp. 120–21.
2. Ibid., p. 121.
3. Tim Kimmel, *Powerful Personalities* (Colorado Springs: Focus on the Family, 1993), p. 13.
4. A. T. Robertson, *Word Pictures in the New Testament*, vol. 6 (Nashville: Broadman Press, 1933), p. 111.
5. William F. Arndt and F. Wilbur Gingrich, *A Greek-English Lexicon of the New Testament* (Chicago: Univ. of Chicago Press, 1957), p. 262.
6. Robert Lewis and William Hendricks, *Rocking the Roles: Building a Win-Win Marriage* (Colorado Springs: NavPress, 1991), lists adapted from chapter 10, pp. 75–78.

Chapter 10
1. Major General Courtney Whitney, *MacArthur: His Rendezvous with History* (Westport, Conn.: Greenwood Press, 1955), p. 100: on the occasion of MacArthur's being voted Father of the Year in 1944.
2. "What Love Means to Me," *Parade* magazine, March 8, 1992, p. 4.
3. James Webb, "A Legacy for My Daughter," *Newsweek*, November 7, 1988, p. 13.
4. Quoted by Tom Skinner in a chapel service at Dallas Seminary, spring 1978.
5. This clever observation is the brainchild of two friends of mine, Roy Fruits and Kirk Greenstreet.
6. For a more elaborate development of this subject, see Tim Kimmel, *Powerful Personalities* (Colorado Springs: Focus on the Family, 1993), pp. 153–74.

7. William F. Arndt and F. Wilbur Gingrich, *Greek-English Lexicon of the New Testament* (Chicago: Univ. of Chicago Press, 1957), p. 855.
8. This insight was gleaned from the syllabus of the class "Effective Servant Leadership," taught by Dr. John Vawter for the Doctor of Ministries program of Western Seminary, Portland, Oregon.
9. Bob DeMoss, "The Wise Watch What They Watch," *Parental Guidance, Focus on the Family*, August 1993, vol. 4, no. 2.
10. Second Vatican Ecumenical Council, Dogmatic Constitution on the Church, Lumen gentium, no. 11; Decree on the Apostolate of the Laity, Pope John Paul II, Homily for the opening of the Sixth Synod of Bishops (September 26, 1980), 3: AAS 72 (1980): 1008; Pope John Paul II, *The Role of the Christian Family in the Modern World* (Boston: St. Paul Editions, n.d.), p. 75.
11. Alan Bash, "Understanding Different Types of Students," *USA Today*, September 30, 1993, p. D1.
12. Paul Lee Tan, *Encyclopedia of 7700 Illustrations* (Rockville, Md.: Assurance Publishers, 1980), pp. 432–33.

Chapter 11
1. This story was related to me by John Politon, who heard it on John DeBrian's radio show, *Song Time*. It was a taped interview of Albie Pearson on WIBC, Indianapolis, Indiana.

Chapter 13
1. Quoted by Dennis Rainey, director of the Family Ministry of Little Rock, Arkansas.
2. John Leo, "Jesus and the Elves," *U.S. News & World Report*, Dec. 27, 1993–Jan. 3, 1994.
3. This prayer was published in numerous newspapers in both the United States and Canada. My copy came from a private source who had received it by fax from a friend.
4. Notes from a CNN interview, February 28, 1991.
5. Billy Kim, "The Power of Prayer," Amsterdam '86, sponsored by the Billy Graham Evangelistic Association.

ABOUT THE AUTHOR

Dr. Tim Kimmel hosts a daily radio talk show and speaks throughout the country on issues relating to the family.

He speaks to churches, groups, and corporations on the subjects of marriage, parenting, and men.

For information on how you might have Tim speak to your marriage conference or men's conference or how you could sponsor a Raising Kids Who Turn Out Right Seminar in your area, contact him by:

Phone: 602-948-2545
Fax: 602-948-7704
E-mail: TKINAZ@AOL.COM

or you can write him at:

10214 N. Tatum Blvd.
Suite B-300
Phoenix, AZ 85028

PUBLICATIONS BY TIM KIMMEL

Books

Little House on the Freeway
Raising Kids Who Turn Out Right
Homegrown Heroes: How to Raise Courageous Kids
How to Deal with Powerful Personalities
Basic Training for a Few Good Men

Mini-Book

Little House on the Freeway Home Maintenance Manual:
301 Ways to Bring Rest to Your Hurried Home

Video Series

The Hurried Family
Raising Kids Who Turn Out Right

Study Guides

Surviving Life in the Fast Lane

Printed in the United States
66301LVS00003B/100-381